THE ROLE OF SELF
IN
TEACHER DEVELOPMENT

SUNY series, Studying the Self
Richard P. Lipka and Thomas M. Brinthaupt, editors

THE ROLE OF SELF
IN
TEACHER DEVELOPMENT

EDITED BY

Richard P. Lipka

and

Thomas M. Brinthaupt

STATE UNIVERSITY OF NEW YORK PRESS

Published by
State University of New York Press, Albany

For information, address State University of New York Press,
State University Plaza, Albany, N.Y., 12246

Production by Marilyn P. Semerad
Marketing by Anne M. Valentine

Library of Congress Cataloging-in-Publication Data

The role of self in teacher development / edited by Richard P. Lipka
and Thomas M. Brinthaupt.
    p.   cm. — (SUNY series, studying the self)
    Includes bibliographical references and index.
    ISBN 0–7914–4015–X (alk. paper). — ISBN 0–7914–4016–8 (pbk. :
alk. paper)
    1. Teachers—United States—Psychology. 2. Teachers—Training of—
United States. 3. First year teachers—United States—Attitudes.
4. Teacher effectiveness—United States. 5. Self. I. Lipka,
Richard P. II. Brinthaupt, Thomas M., 1958– . III. Series.
LB1775.2.R65 1999
371.1´0023—dc21   98-8361
                                               CIP

10 9 8 7 6 5 4 3 2 1

CONTENTS

CONTRIBUTORS

Karen J. Agne
Department of Education
State University of New York, Plattsburgh

Gary D. Borich
Educational Psychology
University of Texas, Austin

Thomas M. Brinthaupt
Department of Psychology
Middle Tennessee State University, Murfreesboro

Don Hamachek
Counseling and Educational Psychology
Michigan State University, East Lansing

Richard P. Lipka
Special Services and Leadership Studies
Pittsburg State University, Pittsburg (Kansas)

S. Vianne McLean
Department of Education
Arizona State University West, Phoenix

Paul G. Schempp
Curriculum and Instruction Research Lab
University of Georgia, Athens

Andrew C. Sparkes
School of Education
University of Exeter, U.K.

Thomas J. Templin
Department of Health, Kinesiology, and Leisure Studies
Purdue University, West Lafayette (Indiana)

Les Tickle
School of Education and Professional Development
University of East Anglia, U.K.

Linda F. Tusin
Department of Education
Elmhurst College, Elmhurst (Illinois)

Stanley J. Zehm
Department of Instruction and Curriculum Studies
University of Nevada–Las Vegas

Balancing the Personal and Professional Development of Teachers

Richard P. Lipka and Thomas M. Brinthaupt

One of the most rewarding and demanding vocational journeys is surely the selection of teaching as a profession and living one's life as a teacher. Who are those individuals who choose to dedicate themselves in service to others, at a time when the teaching profession is under attack from seemingly every corner? Why would anyone decide to take such a journey? There are numerous ways to consider the career of teaching and the factors associated with becoming a teacher. For example, past writers have successfully examined philosophical and sociological issues in the teaching profession (e.g., Broudy, 1972; Dreeben, 1970; Lortie, 1995).

In this book, we have attempted to address the question of becoming a teacher from the perspective of the teacher's self and identity concerns, especially as it applies to teachers of preschool through grade 12. By recognizing and addressing the instrumental role of self in teacher development, our contributors have provided a set of excellent road signs and maps for the journey to becoming a teacher. Their contributions provide us with a compelling view on teacher development that has been sorely lacking and much needed.

As Jersild (1955) so aptly stated: "The teacher's understanding and acceptance of [him or her] self is the most important requirement in any effort [he or she] makes to help students to know themselves and to gain healthy attitudes of self-acceptance" (p. 3). During the past forty years or so, Jersild's message has been lost in the din of the "cult of efficiency" movement sweeping the field of education. We seem to have forgotten that the quality of life for the student is directly tied to the quality of life of the teacher. Does it matter how teachers perceive and evaluate themselves as individuals? What are the personal and social obstacles and dilemmas that teachers must face? To answer these questions, we structured this book to reflect some of the major transition points in becoming a teacher and asked our contributors to focus explicitly on how issues of self and identity bear on these different points.

The book starts with two chapters on deciding to teach. The emphasis here is on who goes into teaching and why they do so, from a self perspective. The second part addresses making the transition and becoming a teacher, focusing on preservice education and teacher training. In the third part of the book, we examine the first years of teaching, in particular issues pertaining to inservice education and developing an emerging identity as a teacher. Finally, we consider the characteristics of the master teacher and the process of reexamining and affirming one's identity as a teacher.

A common theme (or perhaps we should say "plea") that all of the contributors bring to this book is the importance of balancing the personal development of teachers with their professional development. As several contributors argue, these two aspects are not mutually exclusive. Rather they serve to complement each other. In fact, however, the major way that these two parts of a teacher's identity complement each other is unidirectional—few people would argue that training a teacher to become a competent technician is the best way to open up new avenues for personal and self-related exploration. Our contributors argue for placing personal (self-related) issues up front, from the start, and throughout one's career as a teacher. Doing so results in a recognition of one of the major (for the most part missing) pieces to the puzzle of what it means to be a teacher.

Deciding to Teach

Who decides to go into teaching and why? In chapter 1, Professor Tusin discusses the many demographic factors related to selecting teaching as a career. Included among these factors is a most disturbing finding of a decline in persons of color becoming teachers at a time when the United States continues to become more ethnically diverse. Later in the chapter the emphasis shifts to the development of the teacher's vocational self-concept with the attendant processes of self-concept formation, exploration, differentiation, self-fulfillment, and self-efficacy. As she puts it, selecting and pursuing an occupation as a teacher is essentially a process of implementing a "concept of self as teacher." The chapter ends with a discussion of student self-concept development and how a healthy sense of self for students is dependent upon interactions with teachers. Tusin illustrates the necessity for teachers' personal sense of self to be actualized to the point that they can enter into meaningful and growth-facilitating relationships with students. She ends her chapter by pointing out the need for a greater focus on the self-perceptions of beginning teachers.

In chapter 2, Professor Zehm provides an excellent overview of the kinds of self-related perspectives stressed by Tusin as needed in pre-service teacher preparation programs. Zehm forwards the proposition that a person's decision to become a teacher involves not only the acquisition of a knowledge base, but also the conscious development of a refined sense of self. Zehm makes a case for formally adding self-concept and self-esteem to the preservice teacher preparation sequence. Numerous reasons are offered, with the most compelling being the replacement of test scores and grade point average for admission to teacher education with coherent, structured experiences that ask students to seriously address the question: "Do I really want to become a teacher?" Zehm then situates the self-development perspective in a historical context and introduces the reader to a number of the seminal works in the field of teacher education.

Zehm's chapter also examines contemporary issues involved in a self-development perspective. Zehm suggests that self-development could be effectively utilized as a "gatekeeping" function. That is, critical criteria for teacher selection might include "personal" aspects such as one's level of maturity, self-esteem, personal responsibility, and overall emotional and psychological fitness. It is noteworthy that such criteria have been used for some time by graduate programs designed to train counselors and clinicians. It is also noteworthy that teachers get very little (if any) training for dealing with the behavioral and psychological problems of their pupils. This section of the chapter also offers interesting insights into the attractiveness of the teaching profession to individuals from dysfunctional families. The chapter ends with a coherent discussion of promising approaches (such as the emphasis on personal stories and critical reflection) that could be embedded into any preservice teacher education program. Other contributors to this book provide more details about some of these approaches.

MAKING THE TRANSITION

Once a person has made the decision to teach and begins teacher education, he or she enters an often amorphous transition period or marginal status. Professor McLean begins chapter 3 with a most compelling observation—while teacher educators and beginning teachers have very different knowledge bases, to conceptualize those differences as "deficits" in the beginning teacher is useless at best and at worst keeps beginning teachers powerless in the process of their own professional development. With this as the referent, McLean explores three theoretical perspectives that place emphasis on the person in the process of becoming a teacher. First, McLean discusses "Constructivism," a perspective with roots in the works of Jean Piaget, in terms of the development of knowledge and its emphasis upon the psychological changes within the individual as he or she acquires new knowledge. The individual seen as thinking and acting in complex, contextual, and emotional ways characterizes the second perspective known as the "Practical." The literature within this perspective captures how teachers acquire their personal practical knowledge and how this changes throughout their careers. Drawing more from sociology and philosophy, the third approach, the "Critical Pedagogists," suggests that teachers and teaching can only be understood in terms of the wider social and cultural context.

After extensive contrasts and comparisons of the three perspectives, McLean homes in on their strongest commonality—that of the need to develop ongoing self-reflection and self-analysis. The remainder of the chapter explores the thesis that to help beginning teachers become reflective practitioners requires teacher educators that are themselves reflective practitioners. This thesis calls for a reconstruction of contemporary teacher education. The chapter concludes with an extensive discussion of one strategy for this reconstruction process. This strategy focuses upon the telling and sharing of stories and autobiographies of teachers and teachers-to-be. It is clearly aligned with the "Self as Narrative" work of Freeman (1992), who argued that "one sensible way of studying the self is to study the changing narratives which people use to tell about who and what they have been and become" (p. 21).

Professor Borich uses chapter 4 to explore the dimensions of self-concept that have the potential to extend our current-day notions of effective teaching. As other writers (e.g., Beane & Lipka, 1986) have noted, Borich demonstrates that teachers with clear self-concept and positive self-esteem function effectively within the teaching role as significant others for students. They also create a classroom environment that fosters clear self-concept and positive self-esteem in their pupils. A theme throughout his chapter is what Borich calls the "behavioral dialogue." This refers to the modeling, feedback, and interaction dynamics present in the teacher-student interaction. Borich notes that teachers' extreme self-concerns can actually work against their establishing an effective behavioral dialogue. The idea that the self might interfere with teaching effectively or with acquiring an identity as "teacher" is an intriguing one.

Borich emphasizes the absolute necessity for teachers to have work environments and significant others in their lives (e.g., administrators, teacher educators, colleagues) providing the facilitating conditions necessary for the promotion of a healthy, functional view of self as teacher. The absence of effective and healthy social support systems for beginning teachers will undermine the efforts of the person who is trying to make the transition to "teacher" and leave behind his or her marginal status. Clearly, an emphasis on the "external" or social aspects of teacher self and identity is critical in facilitating those efforts.

THE FIRST YEARS OF TEACHING

Once the "teacher-in-training" makes the transition to "new teacher," a whole new set of issues and implications arise for those interested in a self perspective on teaching. As the teacher is inducted into a professional environment, he or she must learn to assimilate the key aspects of that environment and at the same time attempt to get that environment to accommodate to his or her needs. In chapter 5, Professor Tickle offers us the opportunity to explore the affective realms of teaching that have an impact on the educative experiences of the teacher self, the student self, and the development of individual identities in this new environment. Reflecting some of the points made by Zehm and Borich, Tickle notes that taking the self into account in teaching can be a challenging, threatening, and anxiety-provoking venture.

Focusing upon teachers early in their careers (i.e., those with 2–4 years of teaching experience), Tickle describes a "Self-Appraisal for Professional Growth" unit situated in an in-service teaching degree program. Utilizing the features of action research, teachers are asked to build a comprehensive image of self-appraisal. This includes an emphasis upon aspects of self as a professional as opposed to the more traditional approach of the appraisal of teaching practices by oneself. The emphasis upon the former rather than the latter is predicated upon the conception of teachers as those who have an understanding of self, have a sense of self-realization, and use the self as an instrument in both their own and their students' development. In competition with the necessary development of self is the international preoccupation for national curriculums and national standards / assessments. As Tickle and several other contributors point out, such preoccupation deflects time and other resources away from teachers' efforts to develop the important dimensions of self as professional.

In chapter 6, Professors Schempp, Sparkes, and Templin focus on the mutual interplay of teacher and institution as the induction and adjustment process proceeds for new teachers. A key aspect of this process is the "transition shock" that occurs as beginning teachers search for and establish their identities in schools. Oldtimers tend to attach less value to the newcomer's university experiences and training than to their own insights obtained through "real-world" experiences and trial and error. Throughout their chapter (and paralleling the other chapters of this book), Schempp, Sparkes, and Templin describe some of the major personal and institutional forces that work against establishing a sense of self or identity as teacher.

The authors describe three key elements affecting the emerging identity of the new teacher placed into this setting: biography, establishing the self in teaching, and establishing the self in schools. In the biography section of the chapter, the authors show how those work and teaching experiences one has prior to becoming a teacher (such as summer camps, Sunday school, coaching, etc.), as well as the experiences with teachers one had as a pupil, can be an important part of the teacher's rite of passage. In the self in teaching section, Schempp, Sparkes, and Templin detail some of the richness and demands of that amazing work context known as the "classroom." They emphasize classroom management as a key ingredient in the formation of "self as teacher," noting that the new teacher's concerns with managing one's class and controlling one's students is not ultimately how teachers come to define themselves. The chapter ends with a treatment of "self in school" and the code of culture we associate with interactions with administrators, peers, and students. This is the arena where a good deal of professional assimilation and accommodation takes place. Most unsettling is the observation that one of the chief ways to address the dialectic tension between self and school culture is to remain silent—for beginning teachers to literally form a society of the silent in order to fit in! As in most other groups and organizations, it seems that one must wait to assert oneself (and one's self) in school.

REEXAMINING AND AFFIRMING: THE MASTER TEACHERS

In the final part of the book, we address the selves of the "oldtimers," particularly those teachers who have emerged through the socialization and professionalization process with a well-defined and healthy sense of self. Not coincidentally, these teachers also turn out to be those we call "masters" of their trade. In chapter 7, Professor Agne explores the concept of "caring" as it relates to the self of the master teacher. Very early in her own teaching career, she realized that children learn by absorbing who you are, not by memorizing what you say, to them. For Agne, caring must be examined through the use of the principles of a caring belief system. After initiating the definition of caring as trusting, accepting, respectful, democratic, self-disciplined, and so on, she fully explores what stops or distorts the caring belief system. For Agne, the issues of fear and control in a consumer-driven society serve as the greatest barrier to caring, as teachers and students deal with such commodities as grades, promotions, and degrees.

Agne argues that it is only when we come to realize that people are perfectly imperfect and there is nothing to "fix," will the coming of age of the caring ethic be realized in our schools. Master teachers have acquired deep-caring styles because experience, careful observation, and self-awareness (coupled with a commitment to the understanding of the teaching/learning process) have taught them that caring works. As Agne notes, these are individual attributes that cannot be internalized through instructional methodology. The chapter closes with a treatment of what the caring belief system looks like in the classroom. Central to this classroom description is a set of questions that teachers must ask themselves. These questions help to frame the issues and explore potential solutions that engender personal growth, healing, productivity, and transforming environments.

In chapter 8, Professor Hamachek addresses the question: What sorts of behaviors and self-perceptions tend to distinguish expert or master teachers from the rest? To answer this question, Hamachek looks for distinguishing patterns drawn from the dimensions of personal characteristics, intellectual characteristics, interaction styles, and instructional approaches. Reading his treatment of the personal characteristics literature leads us to the humbling insight as to the tolerance and humanity possessed by students in our nation's schools. Students are desirous of teachers who are human in the fullest sense of the word, yet they fully realize that to be fully human does not mean being totally perfect! Exploring the other three dimensions leads Hamachek to the conclusion that expert/effective teachers enjoy life. As individuals they are reasonably at peace with themselves and they possess realistic yet high expectations for themselves and their students. They generally enjoy their work, possess a quality sense of humor, and tend to be viewed by their students as firm but fair.

Hamachek argues that the teacher's "self" is always present as the second, private curriculum in the classroom. The chapter ends with a comprehensive treatment of how self-understanding helps to make an individual a better teacher. Hamachek's treatment of self-understanding introduces the reader to the concepts of "intrapersonal intelligence" and "emotional intelligence." Underlying these concepts are components such as self-reflection, self-evaluation, self-awareness, unconscious processes, mood management, self-maturation, empathic skills, and relationship skills. Seeing the role of self in teaching in these terms can serve us well as teacher educators and researchers of teaching and teachers. In short, Hamachek clearly reminds us that in the absence of functional self-knowledge we lack the ability to overhaul or to fine-tune those aspects of ourselves that may be blocking our teaching effectiveness. As he puts it, one must look "in here" for answers to effective teaching rather than "out there."

In summary, this book explores the journey from selection of teaching as a career to developing the skills, attitudes, and beliefs that we associate with masterful teaching. We end as we began with the belief, supported by abundant evidence, that those teachers with the clearest and most positive sense of self are in the best position to facilitate the growth, development, and education of the millions of young people who greet us each morning at the schoolhouse doors.

REFERENCES

Beane, J. A., & Lipka, R. P. (1986). *Self-concept, self-esteem and the curriculum.* New York: Teachers College Press.

Broudy, H. S. (1972). *The real world of the public schools.* New York: Harcourt Brace Jovanovich.

Dreeben, R. (1970). *The nature of teaching: Schools and the work of teachers.* Glenview, IL: Scott, Foresman and Company.

Freeman, M. (1992). Self as narrative: The place of life history in studying the life span. In T. M. Brinthaupt & R. P. Lipka (Eds.), *The Self: Definitional and Methodological Issues.* Albany: State University of New York Press.

Jersild, A. T. (1955). *When teachers face themselves.* New York: Teachers College Press.

Lortie, D. C. (1975). *School teachers: A sociological study.* Chicago: University of Chicago Press.

PART I

Selecting Teaching as a Career

CHAPTER 1

DECIDING TO TEACH

Linda F. Tusin

Who decides to become a teacher? What influences the decision to teach? These questions have been asked and studied throughout the years. Researchers, teacher educators, and educational policymakers all have asked these questions. Preservice and inservice teachers have been surveyed and interviewed, often within individual teacher education programs, more recently in larger national samples. They have been studied as a group, as teaching specialty subgroups, and they have been compared to those selecting nonteaching careers. Several reasons for selecting a teaching career emerge from studies over time. Findings follow patterns and offer initial insights into the decision to become a teacher. The decision to teach is examined first with an overview of the research on the attractors to the teaching career, the characteristics of those who select a teaching career, and influences on this decision. Next, new issues were raised about teachers and those selecting teaching careers during the educational reform discussions and research of the 1980s. Issues of academic ability, the entry to the profession of second-career teachers, and the recruitment and retention of teachers of color are explored. The connections in research between self-development and the teaching career choice are examined. This decision to teach is linked to the growing body of literature on teacher education and teaching in the 1990s and beyond, specifically the understanding and development of self and self-reflection as a professional. Finally, the initial choice to become a teacher is presented as the starting point for understanding teacher self-development throughout the career.

The author wishes to thank Debra Meyer and Ernest T. Pascarella for their thoughtful comments on an earlier version of this manuscript.

Attractors to Teaching

Lortie's (1975) work exemplifies the research findings about attractions to teaching. Consistently, teachers' reasons for teaching have fallen into the five themes he outlined. Most frequently cited was the interpersonal theme, the desire to work with children and youth. Next in importance was the service theme, the idea of contributing in a profession of moral worth. The desire for continuation in a specific subject or in the school setting was commonly noted. Material benefits such as salary, prestige, and security, especially for women, were cited. Finally, time compatibility, especially for women who were mothers and wives, was listed as an attractor to teaching. Academic interests and abilities are often omitted or listed secondarily by teacher candidates, despite the obvious academic focus of teaching and classrooms. Those who select teaching are frequently influenced in their career choice by family members and by significant teachers in their own schooling. While some variations occur over time, these basic themes emerge even in the more current studies of the teaching career choice (Andrew, 1983; Hutchinson & Johnson, 1993–94; Jantzen, 1981; Lortie, 1975; Su, 1993; Weiner, Swearingen, Pagano, & Obi 1993; Wong, 1994; Wood, 1978; Zimpher, 1989).

Intrinsic factors such as making a difference in the lives of children, giving back to society, and a love of learning have been consistently cited as motivators. That these motivators are stated seems almost a given (Serow, 1993). What future teacher would not state these reasons publicly? Serow felt that altruism was often the stated reason, while personal needs for self-esteem and for extrinsic rewards and material benefits went unstated. Salary, status, and prestige have been cited as benefits and as disadvantages (Berg, Reno, & Coker, 1992; Su, 1993; Weiner et al., 1993). More recently they have been cited as negative aspects of the career. Murname, Singer, Willett, Kemple, and Olsen (1991) found that job opportunities, salary, and costs to enter or reenter teaching all influenced the decision to teach. For those who decide to become teachers, these extrinsic rewards are stated as secondary in importance compared to other motivations. For those students who decide not to pursue teaching as a career, the extrinsic rewards are reported as problematic and a detractor from the career (Pate, Derdeyn, & Goodnough, 1989).

Freshman interest in teaching as a career declined significantly from the 1960s through the 1980s (Opp, 1989). Multiple reasons explain this declining interest. Teaching lost recruits as career opportunities for women and people of color expanded during this time period. Teaching opportunities decreased due to declining school enrollments. Murname et al. (1991) found that students compared teaching opportunities and salaries with other career choices and that a substantial number also compared employment opportunities among various teaching specialties. Further, they found that increased licensing regulations influenced who became teachers, especially for African American graduates (existing data for other racial groups was insufficient for analysis in their study). Taking standardized exams for certification became a detractor for students of color (King, 1993a). Many factors contributed to the declining interest in teaching between 1976, when 28 percent of graduates majored in education, and 1984, when only 9 percent selected teaching as a career.

A Teacher Profile

A teacher profile emerges in the research. The majority of teachers have been and continue to be Caucasian women. A national longitudinal study, Research about Teacher Education (RATE), reported that 93 percent of teacher education students were female and 93 percent were Caucasian (Zimpher, 1989). A majority were from small town or suburban communities, not urban environments. While reporting a similar profile in another national project, The Study of the Education of Educators (SEE), Su (1993) noted that the percentages of female students and of Caucasian students enrolled in teacher education had increased since the 1970s. The number of nontraditional students also increased during this time from 25 percent to over 33 percent of the total enrollment.

Differences between Teaching Specialties

Many studies have looked at schoolteachers as a singular group. Some studies have, however, studied the unique characteristics and career paths of teacher subgroups. Bredekamp (1992) found three career entry paths taken by early childhood educators (defined as "individuals who are responsible for the care and education of children, birth through age eight, in centers, homes, and schools and others who support that delivery of service," p. 52). Some early childhood educators begin in the traditional college route with a major in education or child development and begin teaching in a preschool, kindergarten, or primary grade classroom. Others begin after becoming parents and working with their own children and other children, perhaps as volunteers in school settings or as child care providers. Finally some enter in what

Bredekamp labels the serendipitous route. They begin working with young children accidentally. Through an initial work experience they go back to school for education and certification, similar to the parent group.

Other researchers have compared students across majors or programs, noting significant differences in those selecting various specialties, for instance, elementary or secondary education (Book & Freeman, 1986; Ethington, Smart, & Pascarella, 1987; Stiegelbauer, 1992; Tusin, 1991). Book and Freeman reported that secondary teachers had stronger high school academic coursework, but fewer actual experiences with children and youth. Their reasons for teaching centered on their interests in a field of study while elementary majors centered on helping children. Secondary majors, especially males, expressed greater confidence in their ability to teach, a finding congruent with collegewide research studies showing higher ratings of self-concept for men than for women (Astin, 1977).

Stiegelbauer (1992) found different motivators for selecting a teaching career between those selecting primary, intermediate, and secondary level programs in a fifth-year teacher education program. Primary teacher candidates spoke of the helping relationship, the parental role, and helping students establish self-esteem and a foundation for learning. Intermediate candidates addressed the challenge of the age group and their ability to work effectively with them. Secondary candidates saw themselves as role models and as facilitators to help students develop their interests. Secondary candidates felt they had academic expertise and experiences to share. All three groups felt a sense of social responsibility and wanted to make a difference for their students, especially in today's complicated world. Book and Freeman (1986) found similar motivational differences between elementary and secondary teacher candidates.

Sears, Kennedy, and Kaye (1992) examined personality types as measured on the Myers-Briggs Type Indicator of freshmen who later completed teacher certification programs. They found significant differences between those students who completed elementary, secondary, and special education majors. The most common profile of an elementary major (sensing, feeling, judgment) was the antitype for secondary teachers. The common secondary profile was intuition, thinking, judgment. The most common personality profile of special education majors (intuition, feeling, perception) resembled a counselor profile more than the profiles of other teacher subgroups.

Following the earlier work of Astin (1977) and Astin and Panos (1969) on the effects of college on career choice, Ethington, Smart, and

Pascarella (1987) and Tusin (1991) developed causal models examining background characteristics and college effects of those who became elementary and secondary teachers. They found that the models explained greater variance for elementary than secondary teachers. They found differences in academic and social self-concepts between the elementary and secondary groups as well as differences in background characteristics and in the effects of college on the career choice.

College Effects on a Teaching Career Choice

While career choice at the start of college is frequently the best predictor of career at the end of college, many students also change career plans during the college years (Astin, 1977; Astin & Panos, 1969; Ethington et al., 1987; Opp, 1989; Pascarella & Terenzini, 1991; Tusin, 1991; Tusin & Pascarella, 1985). Students appear to become more mature in thinking about themselves and their career. They are influenced in vocational decisions by the competitiveness of subject fields, employment opportunities, and economic benefits as well as by their faculty interactions, work experiences related to their field of study, and the percentage of students in academic majors. Students are more likely to continue in or change to a major with a large number of students on campus (Astin; Astin & Panos). Ethington et al. found that students who felt better prepared to teach after their college experiences were most likely to become teachers. Lyson and Falk (1984), utilizing data from the National Longitudinal Study of the High School Class of 1972, found that over three fourths of those who selected a teaching career in high school were not teaching seven years later. Additionally, they found that of those actually teaching seven years after high school, nearly half had not stated plans to do so in high school.

EDUCATIONAL REFORM IN THE 1980s

The educational reform movement of the 1980s saw a pronounced interest in schools and teachers. "Nation at Risk" (National Commission on Excellence in Education, 1983), "A Nation Prepared: Teachers for the 21st Century" (Carnegie Task Force on Teaching as a Profession, 1986), and *Teachers for Tomorrow's Schools* (Holmes Group, 1986) all helped focus a new attention on those who select teaching as a career. From this reform movement, a variety of themes and interests in the study of those selecting a teaching career have emerged: the academic ability of preservice and inservice teachers, the choice of teaching as a second career, and recruitment of students of color to teacher education.

Academic Ability

Academic rigor in the schools was a foundational theme of the reform literature. Therefore, the teacher characteristic of greatest interest became academic ability. Numerous studies examined the academic ability of teachers or those who wished to become teachers, often comparing academic qualifications across careers or across time (Opp, 1989; Pate et al., 1989; Roberson, Keith, & Page, 1983; Savage, 1983; Vance & Schlechty, 1982; Weaver, 1979). Opp looked at freshman interest in teaching from 1966 to 1988 as indicated in the Cooperative Institutional Research Program (CIRP) studies. A high correlation (.827) with followup data indicated this freshman interest was an accurate predictor of a later teaching career choice. He concluded that teaching was attracting less of the academically well-prepared freshmen. Mean high school grade point average of freshmen selecting a teaching career dropped from 13th place in 1966 to 26th place in 1988 of 44 probable careers listed in the CIRP survey. Murname et al. (1991) found similar results. They found that the proportion of graduates with high standardized test scores who become teachers decreased significantly.

Pate et al. (1989) looked at career values and aspirations of academically able high school students. Only 1.1 percent of the students categorized as academically talented (SAT scores above 1000 or taking Advanced Placement courses), 6.1 percent of the students categorized as academically oriented (SAT below 1000 and not taking advanced placement courses but enrolled in academic sections of English), and 1.3 percent of the students categorized in the leadership group (involved in school activities and academically talented or academically oriented) selected public school teaching as their career choice. Students saw teaching as meeting their needs for intellectual challenge and moral fulfillment, but did not see the career as meeting their needs for economic gain or advancement. Murname et al. (1991) found that the most academically able students were the most sensitive to financial incentives in career choice decisions.

When examining grade point average, Su (1993) found that capable students were enrolled in teacher education programs. Approximately 75 percent of enrolled students had grade point averages of 3.0 on a 4 point scale and that only a small number were below 2.4. She attributed this finding to recent higher standards for entrance to teacher education programs. Ethington et al. (1987) reported that of students initially aspiring to become teachers at college entrance, those who actually became teachers had a stronger high school and college academic performance than those changing to other careers.

Ethington et al. (1987), Tusin and Pascarella (1985), and Tusin (1991) found that those who became teachers were less likely to attend highly selective colleges and universities. The percentage of students graduating in education at an institution influenced the career choice for elementary majors. These findings reflect the progressive conformity theory advanced by Astin (1977) and Astin and Panos (1969). Students are more likely to maintain or shift to a teaching career choice if a relatively high percentage of the students at the institution also have that career choice. The effects of background characteristics on career choice were mediated through the institution attended (Tusin). That is students who select teaching careers at the start of college and are of lower socioeconomic status and academic ability attend less selective institutions where they are then likely to become teachers. Tusin and Pascarella also found evidence that women who initially aspired to teaching at entry to selective and academically rigorous institutions were likely to change majors by sophomore year. These findings are consistent with those of Zimpher (1989) in which the academic rigor of an institution appeared less important than other characteristics in selecting an institution for their studies to become a teacher. Weiner et al. (1993) found more similarities than differences when comparing Harvard graduate students and students at a public northeastern college pursuing teaching careers. While demographic characteristics varied, their stated reasons for teaching were quite similar.

Many of the schools in which large numbers of students graduate with education majors began as normal schools. As Lortie (1975) noted, these normal schools were founded for the purpose of training teachers in state-funded low-cost schools, a necessity to attract students to a career in need of recruits yet without substantial financial rewards. Warren (1985) found that teaching was usually viewed as part-time, temporary employment throughout the nineteenth century. Moral qualifications often superseded academic qualifications. The best candidate frequently was the one requiring the lowest salary. Coupled with the working conditions and duties, the picture of the occupation was rarely viewed as a career option for able, career-minded individuals. Concerns about the academic ability of prospective teachers are not new (Learned & Wood, 1938), nor is the concern for professionalization (Thorndike, 1912). Thorndike envisioned that increased training (from a time of only three or four years beyond elementary school to a vision of four years of postsecondary schooling), higher admissions standards, testing requirements, and improved salaries were needed to change teaching "toward the status of a profession deliberately chosen, requiring preparation, and holding its members throughout their working lives" (pp. 245–246).

Teaching as a Second Career

Another outcome of this reform movement was the interest in enabling career changers to enter teaching. Engineers, scientists, and other subject specialists seeking teaching positions as second careers were seen as a means to recruit academically able teachers, especially in math and science. Murname et al. (1991) found that the age patterns of newly licensed teachers changed from 1975 to 1982. While the largest group of new teachers continued to be women under the age of 24, this number was declining while both the age 24–30 and over-30 age groups were increasing. The percentage of men and women over age 30 who were newly licensed to teach doubled during this time period. Su (1993) reported that over one third of teacher education majors were nontraditional students, an increase of 12 percent from the 1970s.

Who are these career changers? Why are they interested in becoming teachers? Of the nontraditional students, 56 percent already had a four-year degree, and some additionally had master's degrees or other advanced education (Su, 1993). Sixty-four percent of this group reported teaching as a second career, as did 5 percent of the traditional student group. In reporting previous careers, 31 percent worked in business, 19 percent in secretarial or clerical work, 7 percent in health care, 4 percent in social work, and 39 percent in other careers. Nontraditional students reported intrinsic motivators for entering teaching similar to traditional students. Elementary and early childhood students listed working with children, job satisfaction, and being of service to others, while secondary students listed pursuing a favorite subject as their reasons for teaching.

Serow (1993) classified twenty-three prospective second-career teachers into four categories based on their decisions to teach and their other life experiences. The largest group was labeled extenders, becoming teachers to use skills and talents discovered or developed in prior work or life experiences. Another group wished to continue in a subject area of interest. A third group stated the practical aspects of the career such as job availability, security, or time schedule. Finally, rectifiers were selecting teaching to correct an earlier career decision. The rectifiers in this sample were all women who had been persuaded away from teaching and into other careers during their undergraduate college years.

Rectifiers and extenders expressed long-term interest in the career and their natural talents as a teacher. Altruism appeared to blend with personal needs for self-esteem and self-efficacy. Candidates wanted to do something to feel good about themselves. Serow asserted that practical considerations such as benefits and working conditions influenced these second-career candidates more often than was said. Freidus (1989) found evidence that gender roles, as shaped by early home and school experiences, influenced second-career teaching candidates.

Adult college students have been defined both by age and their sense of responsibility (Post & Killian, 1992–93). They show commitment to career goals and the effort to reach those goals. Their varied life and work experiences provide a foundation for understanding and applying new concepts. They are frequently balancing numerous responsibilities and often attend college on a part-time basis. In the case of education students they reported plans to remain in teaching for more years than traditional-age students (Su, 1993).

Students of Color in Teacher Education

The research on teachers and schools in the 1980s helped focus attention on the need for a more diverse teaching force. The profile of Caucasian female teachers in schools teaching an increasingly diverse school population created a demand for the recruitment of more students of color to teacher education. Murname et al. (1991) found that the percent of African American teachers in American schools dropped from 8 percent in 1970 to 7 percent in 1983, while at the same time the percent of African American students rose from 15 percent to 16 percent. In Texas in 1991, over 50 percent of school-age children were members of ethnic minority groups (Contreras & Nicklas, 1993). In North Carolina between 1975 and 1982, the number of new teaching licenses for African Americans declined by 73 percent while new licenses for Caucasian candidates declined 49 percent.

Murname et al. (1991) found several reasons for this declining interest of students of color in teaching as a career. African American graduates found greater career opportunities and better salaries during this time in fields previously closed to them. Lack of educational opportunity and inferior high school preparation influenced college attendance and graduation rates. The percentage of low-income African American and Hispanic students enrolled in college declined between 1976 and 1988 while comparable rates for low-income Caucasian students remained stable. Of significance in their data, African American students were sensitive to new licensing requirements and opted out of or were not allowed to enter teaching due to the standardized testing requirements. Historically Black colleges and universities have a long history in teacher education, yet these schools saw many enrollment changes as college opportunities broadened for African American students. Finally, African American teachers were more likely than Caucasian teachers to begin teaching in urban schools, where the attrition rate for all teachers is relatively high. Contreras and Nicklas (1993), Garabaldi (1989), and King (1993a, 1993b) cite similar problems in the recruitment and retention of teachers of color.

Teachers of Tomorrow

The desire to see increased diversity in teacher education enrollments helped connect the research on a teaching career choice and recruitment to teacher education and teaching. Studies examined career choice and increasingly looked at younger age groups for beginning the exposure to teaching career information. Lortie (1975) described teaching as a wide decision-range career, many children first deciding on the career based on their own school experiences and the models of their own teachers. Recruitment strategies focused on school-age minority students to increase the likelihood they would view teaching as a viable career option.

Hutchinson and Johnson (1993–94) studied high school students who expressed an interest in teaching through their membership in Future Teacher Clubs or in their Upward Bound Programs. The twelve students in their sample, Mexican American, African American, and Caucasian males and females, all expressed similar reasons for their interest in teaching, mirroring the attractors delineated by Lortie (1975). Their similarities in attitudes, beliefs, and ideas about teaching provide a foundation for better recruitment of students of color. Hutchinson and Johnson suggested mentors, Future Teacher Clubs, and financial support for early deciders, such as the high school students in their sample, as well as recruiting school paraprofessionals as means to increase teaching diversity.

Mack and Jackson (1993) found that 30 percent of Hispanic high school seniors enrolled in Grand Rapids, Michigan schools stated they would become teachers if scholarships were provided. Barriers to this career were financial support, lack of career awareness, lack of positive career information, and lack of encouragement from significant others. Only 16 percent of these students had talked to someone about a possible teaching career. Sixty-one percent did want to attend college and 27 percent had high school grade point averages above 3.0. In a collaborative program involving a university, school districts, and the Educational Testing Service, high school juniors interested in teaching were supported in building academic, test-taking, and study skills, in preparation for the transition to college, and to better understand their career choice (Zapata, 1988). Role models and mentors were included for support in the process of becoming a teacher.

Wong (1994) surveyed diverse seventh- and eighth-grade students in California about their interest in teaching careers and their perceptions of schools. He found no differences between cultural groups in the desire to teach and motives for teaching. Those who wanted to teach wanted to work with children and with people. They wanted to earn a good salary, but salary was not their highest motive. They felt teachers were respected. They felt their families supported their career interests. Wong found that students with negative perceptions of their school experiences were less likely to want to become teachers. Asian students reported the most positive perceptions of school.

Contreras and Nicklas (1993) recruited students of color in community colleges for a summer bridge program. Based on a pilot program, they recommended developing collaborative alliances between community colleges and colleges of education that include programs for socialization to the teaching profession, a bridge experience that includes financial, academic, and social support to begin the teacher education program, and forgivable loans. They suggested targeting nontraditional-age community college students to teaching. Through the supportive summer bridge program, Contreras and Nicklas addressed recruitment issues by including support and preparation for academics and certification testing, addressing negative public perceptions about teaching, and countering recruitment efforts from other academic majors and careers.

King (1993b) studied a cohort of African American, Caribbean American, and African graduate students in a teacher education program. Most decided to teach while college undergraduates, yet one fourth made this decision in elementary school. The major attractors again mirrored Lortie's (1975) findings with the addition of the desire to work with diverse students cited by 56 percent of the students. Being creative and the intellectual challenge of teaching were also cited by a majority of the students. Based on these recent studies, early recruitment and support of school-age students with aspirations to teach and the recruitment of nontraditional students are promising avenues for increasing the number of students of color in teacher education.

UNDERSTANDING SELF

The issue of self-understanding has emerged in importance when viewing career choice in relation to preservice and inservice teacher development. Preparing reflective teachers for schools of tomorrow has become a primary goal in teacher education. While the knowledge base of teaching increases, becoming a teacher and understanding this knowledge base builds upon the personal foundation of recruits. Understanding the development to become a teacher begins with those who select a teaching career. Understanding of self in relation to schools and teaching becomes essential.

Selecting a Career

Selecting an occupation is an important decision in one's life. An occupation provides not only personal or family income but also satisfaction, social status, and social integration. In selecting an occupation, a person is implementing a concept of self (Super, 1963). Occupation provides a new role for the self. The vocational self-concept develops in a process: self-concept formation, exploration, differentiation, identification, role play, and reality testing. As a person explores and transforms this developing self-concept, the self-perceptions are checked against reality through experiences, tests, and the perceptions of others. Entering occupational training and entering the occupation provide opportunities for implementing this self-concept and ultimately for reaching self-actualization in the career.

Holland (1973) posited that career choice is a function primarily of personality type and preference for a certain environmental situation. He argued that most persons could be categorized within six personality types: realistic, investigative, artistic, social, enterprising, or conventional. A person's interests, experiences, and competencies create a personality pattern fitting primarily within one of these types but also across types. People select an environment congruent with their personalities. Each environment is dominated by its type of personality, thus being a reflection of the interests, competencies and outlooks of the corresponding dominant personality type. Behavior is a function of the personality in the environment. The various personality types select and process information in different ways, yet all types seek fulfillment using their skills and talents in reaching goals in their occupational environments.

Looking specifically at the career of schoolteacher, Holland (1973) found the social personality as a commonality in seventeen teaching occupations. Within his Occupational Classification, each occupation is categorized by a ranked cluster of the three personality types members of the occupation most resemble. The social personality ranked first for teachers of history, social science, home economics, foreign language, speech, elementary education, special education, and teachers not elsewhere classified. It ranked second for mathematics, natural science, English, drama, dancing, art, literature and music teachers, and third for industrial arts teachers.

College and Self-concept

Self-concept has been considered an important variable in studying the achievements and outcomes of elementary, secondary, and college students (Calsyn & Kenny, 1977; Hansford & Hattie, 1982, Kubiniec, 1970; Pascarella & Terenzini, 1991). Astin (1977) found that conceptions of self during the college years became more sharply differentiated, with more increases than decreases in the various facets of self-concept. He found that women tended to rate themselves lower than men in most areas, especially in popularity; math, mechanical, and athletic ability; and intellectual and social self-confidence. This was in spite of findings that women earn higher grades than men in high school and college. Self-ratings generally increase during the college years. While modest in effect, the college experience does contribute to a variety of measures of self-perceptions.

Tusin (1991) examined academic and social self-concepts of those selecting teaching careers, using Shavelson, Hubner, and Stanton's (1976) model of self-concept as multifaceted, hierarchical, and differentiable. She found differences in academic and social self-concepts between those selecting elementary and secondary level teaching. Institutional effects on self-concept and on the teaching career choice varied by elementary and secondary levels as well. For elementary teachers, initial academic self-concept had a negative indirect effect on the choice of a teaching career, mediated through institutional selectivity, percentage of students graduating in education, and education major. While this was a modest effect, it was an important finding. There was a tendency for those becoming elementary teachers to start college with a slightly lower academic self-concept than for female students selecting other career options. Social self-concept had a positive indirect effect on the teaching career outcome for secondary teachers nine years after the start of college, mediated through first occupation as a teacher. Women who became secondary teachers started college with a slightly greater initial social self-concept than did females selecting other career options.

For elementary teachers, the outcome of later social self-concept (nine years after the start of college) was negatively affected by the initial choice of teaching as a career. This significant negative indirect effect on later social self-concept was mediated through the percentage of students graduating in education, which itself evidenced a significant negative direct effect on later social self-concept. Elementary teachers' initial choice of a teaching career influenced their decisions to attend a school with a large percentage of students graduating in education. While a significant finding, this impact was modest compared to other variables in the model.

Whether this finding for elementary teachers was a causal effect or whether these variables were related in a way not represented in the causal model was not clear. The lower social self-confidence ratings could reflect attendance at a college with a large number of education students or a perception developed in college of their social abilities, or they could reflect the nature of teaching in elementary schools, after graduation. Elementary teachers spend their days in classrooms with young children, using social skills they may view as being quite different from their social abilities with adults. Do they lack confidence in working with adults when they state their desire for a career working with children? Tusin and Pascarella (1985) found that women selecting a teaching career had a lower academic/intellectual self-concept than women selecting other careers and also questioned the direction of influence. Do those with lower initial academic self-concepts select teaching or does the choice of a career with only semiprofessional status and limited esteem and reward affect academic self-concept?

Self-confidence in the ability to teach successfully has been reported in several studies of teacher education students (Powell & Weaver, 1993; Stiegelbauer, 1992; Weinstein, 1990). Powell compared students entering field-based and campus-based teacher education programs and found those in the field-based program to report greater confidence in their abilities to be successful. These students noted affective strengths such as motivation, organization, leadership, punctuality, and creativity. Powell and Weaver wondered if this was, in part, unrealistic optimism, as advanced by Weinstein, as these were also the qualities the students reported that their favorite teachers demonstrated. Older, nontraditional students reported greater self-confidence. Steigelbauer found students entering a fifth-year postbaccalaureate program to express strong confidence in their abilities as future teachers. Their average age was twenty-nine. Secondary candidates, especially men, expressed greater confidence in their ability to teach than did elementary candidates (Book & Freeman, 1986). In reviewing studies of entering teacher candidates, Brookhart and Freeman (1992) found entering candidates had high confidence in their abilities, with men's ratings generally higher than women's ratings. Self-ratings increased with age as well. The findings that men report higher self-ratings than women and that self-ratings increase with age are consistent with other postsecondary research (Astin, 1977; Pascarella & Terenzini, 1991). Teacher candidates also reported anxieties about how well they would perform in their careers, seemingly contradicting their high ratings of confidence.

The high confidence of entering teacher candidates may stem from their perception of selecting the correct career and how well suited they see themselves (Holland, 1973). Certainly their years of experience in schools have given them extensive information about the environment, the people, and the behaviors of people in that environment. Understanding this personal foundation of preservice teachers, while not a new issue in teacher education (Combs, 1965; Lortie, 1975), has gained in importance as contructivism has increasingly emerged in teacher education (Weinstein, 1990). Using this foundation to assist in the meaningful growth and learning of preservice teachers and to reduce the reality shock and accompanying lower self-ratings of student teachers and first-year teachers (Gaede, 1978; Walberg, 1970) builds a professional program of continuity for individuals entering a complex and changing profession.

Limitations of the Research

Most research on the decision to teach has focused on demographic characteristics and self-perceptions reported in survey research methodology. Brookhart and Freeman (1992) suggested that this methodology has been overemphasized and that research methodology must be expanded for better understanding of the beliefs and perceptions of preservice and inservice teachers. In the forty-four individual studies they reviewed, even though information generalized into a similar picture of beginning teacher education candidates, they found significant variations in demographic data, motivations to teach, confidence, and beliefs about teaching. They suggested a need for improved research designs, broader samples, and stronger theoretical foundations to enrich future research on those selecting teaching as a career. Ethington et al. (1987) and Tusin (1991) suggested separating elementary and secondary teacher groups, based on differences they found between the two groups.

Serow (1993) reinforced the idea of looking at more than descriptive statements about motivators to teach. In studying nontraditional teacher education students who were changing careers, he found that issues of self-esteem, self-efficacy, and personal satisfaction were underlying their altruistic statements about motivations for teaching. Students agreed that a reason for teaching was self-fulfillment through helping others while at the same time they did not state a sense of obligation or duty to do so. Purely altruistic statements such as helping children and providing a service to society may sound better, especially in public statements.

Variations in definition, measurement, methodology, and theoretical foundations make understanding and generalization difficult from the growing research on self-perceptions (Brinthaupt & Lipka, 1992; Brookhart & Freeman, 1992; Byrne, 1984; Hamachek, 1994; Juhasz, 1992; Marsh, Byrne, & Shavelson, 1992; Pascarella & Terenzini, 1991; Super, 1963). Common usage and understanding of terms like self-concept become confused with quite specific, narrow, and varying operational definitions. As the research base expands, theoretical foundations are revised and clarified. Research on specific limited samples often is not informed by constructs, concepts, and theory in the broader studies of self-perceptions. While a growing body of research on the self-perceptions of those deciding to teach does exist, it would be enhanced by a more thorough understanding and integration of definitional, methodological, theoretical, and developmental issues of self.

Teachers and the Self-Concept Development of Their Students

Teachers are involved with the self-concept development of their own students. Individuals develop a sense of self from a young age, strongly influenced by the environment, including significant others in that environment (Juhasz, 1992; Lipka, Hurford, & Litten, 1992). The school environment plays an important role. At the elementary level where the self-contained classroom environment is most common, the individual teacher plays an especially significant role. The evaluative atmosphere of the classroom (Jackson, 1968) and age-based norms and grouping patterns (Lipka et al.) can impact the self-esteem of children. The National Board for Professional Teaching Standards document "What Teachers Should Know and Be Able to Do" (1994) includes student self-concept as an important concern of teachers, both on its own, and essential for student intellectual development. The increased number of self-esteem programs and curriculums in the schools demonstrates the importance to educators of helping students develop positive self-perceptions (Beane, 1994). While enhancing students' self-perceptions has been of interest to educators, the various reasons, goals, methodologies and actual school practices often appear contradictory and confusing. That teachers know about self-perceptions appears essential. The role of the teacher and the school environment in the self-development of students as well as the stability and change in self over a life span are concepts for teachers to understand (Beane; Lipka et al.; Hamachek, 1994).

Humanistic psychologists, especially Combs (1965) and Combs, Avila, and Purkey (1973), included self-concept as an essential aspect of teacher education and in the preparation of all helping professionals. Understanding self was viewed as a necessary component of teacher education due to the personal nature of learning and learning to teach and for teachers to be able to help others in their career role. A teacher first is a person and teaching is an intensely personal profession. The effective teacher is "a unique human being who has learned to use himself effectively and efficiently to carry out his own and society's purposes in the education of others" (Combs, p. 9). Behavior is a function of self-concept which makes self-concept an essential aspect of teaching and learning to teach. Teachers' self-perceptions influence their effectiveness in helping students develop self-esteem. Boy and Pine (1971) discussed the importance of personhood and expanded self for teachers. From psychologically whole teachers would come self-actualized teaching and classroom environments conducive to growth of the holistic child. "To develop people with expanded selves, the schools must have teachers who are themselves in the process of becoming, and who can enter into meaningful and growth-facilitating relationships with students. This calls for teachers who are, first and foremost, persons." (p. 119). Teachers with positive self-concepts were clearly viewed as the significant factor in fostering this positive growth in students in the humanistic education popular in the 1970s.

Reflective Teachers for Schools of Today and Tomorrow

Teacher educators have become increasingly interested in preparing reflective teachers (Schon, 1983). Becoming a reflective practitioner builds upon the development of self-understanding in preservice teachers (Bullough & Stokes, 1994; Combs, 1965; Weinstein, 1990). Teacher educators want to influence thoughtful growth and change in their students, building upon existing beliefs, reinforcing and modifying as appropriate (Kagan, 1992; Lortie, 1975). Learning involves both exposure to new information and experiences and the personal discovery of what it means (Combs, 1982). Hutchinson and Johnson (1993–94) found similarities in the attitudes, beliefs, and ideas about teaching of diverse high school students interested in teaching careers. They suggested this foundation becomes a filter for processing teacher education curriculum, an essential consideration for teacher educators. Hollingsworth (1989) found that preservice teachers' prior beliefs about teaching and learning did play a critical role in learning to teach. Learning about these beliefs and using this information in teacher education programs is clearly indicated when viewing teacher education through the constructivist lens.

The degree to which students felt prepared to teach after their undergraduate teacher preparation was a significant predictor of those who went on to actually teach (Ethington et al., 1987). Powell and Weaver (1993) found few differences between beginning field-based and campus-based teacher education students in attitudes about teaching and motivators for teaching. They found that the field-based students thought the school experiences would help them in the process of becoming a teacher and they expressed greater confidence in their abilities as a teacher. Changing schools require thoughtful teachers open to and capable of new ways of knowing and learning in schools. Schubert's study of teacher lore, "the study of knowledge, ideas, perspectives and understandings of teachers" (1991, p. 207), was based on the idea of praxis, a blend of theory and practice. "Praxis assumes a continuous process of critical reflection that joins and mediates theory and practice" (p. 214). Greater understanding of the self-perceptions and professional foundation of those who select teaching careers is of importance when viewing teacher development from preservice through inservice teaching (Bullough & Stokes, 1994). Understanding the prior attitudes and beliefs of those selecting a teaching career and using that knowledge to design a teacher education program addressing and building upon that foundation seems essential.

CONCLUSIONS

Deciding to teach is a complicated process. For some, first thoughts to become a teacher begin as a child. For others, the thoughts to become a teacher begin in adulthood, after other career and life experiences. Thoughts alone are not enough to understand the career decision. Many students state the desire to teach, but do not realize this goal. Consistent attractors to teaching focus on the desire to work with children and youth and to provide a meaningful service to society. These intrinsic motivations are most frequently stated as the primary attractors. Extrinsic rewards are not always stated as attractors, but they do influence the career decision. Salary is viewed more positively when teaching is seen as social and economic upward mobility. The benefits of working in a school setting, in a subject of interest, and on the school time-schedule certainly do influence the career decision. That recruits derive satisfaction and self-esteem from their service in helping children and youth is an underlying factor, not often stated in the purely altruistic reasons teacher candidates state.

Along with self-perceptions about being well suited to teaching, students are also influenced by their college experience, including the college attended, their academic studies, interactions with other students and with faculty, teacher education programs, certification requirements, work experiences, and vocational opportunities. Students mature during the college years and grow more confident in their abilities in their career. For late entrants to teaching, the career change offers the opportunity to extend skills and talents realized in earlier career and life experiences. For other late entrants, the career change allows them to rectify earlier decisions leading initially to nonteaching career paths. The maturity of these candidates, their focus on reaching career goals, and their stated desire to remain in teaching longer than traditional age students make these nontraditional students strong candidates. Including more students of color is a goal in teacher education, yet recruitment and retention increases have not yet been realized. Building upon the early career interests of junior and senior high school students as well as looking to adult community college students offer recruitment opportunities not fully utilized. Programs providing support and information to students of color in their career decision and in their education offer promise in reaching the goal of a more diverse teaching force.

The self-perceptions of those deciding to teach have become more important in the recent literature on teaching careers. Recognizing the personal and professional foundation of teacher candidates informs teacher educators about their students and about future teachers. The personal nature of learning and of teacher development must blend with the ever growing knowledge base of learning to teach. While Combs (1965) suggested that theoretically it is possible to prepare any candidate to become a teacher, the reality of constraints urges a selection process allowing for candidates to enter programs who with reasonable resources and time will be able to become teachers. The best candidates bring with them a foundation upon which teacher educators can build, producing candidates able to face the challenges of their career. Current literature on the self-perceptions of teacher candidates would benefit from a broader perspective inclusive of both higher education and self-development research. Understanding the complexity of becoming a teacher, the multiple factors influencing this process, and the variations between teaching subgroups such as elementary and secondary teachers are important considerations.

A climate of change exists in the schools of today. Are those who select teaching as a career prepared for the teacher's role in schools today and in the future? Knowing who selects teaching as a career is valuable information for teacher educators, for school practitioners, and for educational policymakers. The links between research on choice of teaching and recruitment to teaching, preservice teacher development, and the growth and development of teachers in schools provide meaningful connections and the opportunity for greater understanding of teachers and teaching. Helping teachers understand their own personal development begins with the first thoughts to become a teacher and continues throughout professional life.

REFERENCES

Andrew, M. (1983). The characteristics of students in a five-year teacher education program. *Journal of Teacher Education 34*, 20–23.

Astin, A. W. (1977). *Four critical years: Effects of college on beliefs, attitudes, and knowledge.* San Francisco: Jossey-Bass.

Astin, A. W., & Panos, R. J. (1969). *The education and vocational development of college students.* Washington, DC: American Council on Education.

Beane, J. A. (1994). Cluttered terrain: The schools' interest in the self. In T. Brinthaupt & R. Lipka (Eds.), *Changing the self: Philosophies, techniques, and experiences* (pp. 69–88). Albany: State University of New York Press.

Berg, J. O., Reno, T. R., & Coker, W. (1992). Motivation factors for careers in teaching. *North Central Association Quarterly, 66*, 541–545.

Book, C. L., & Freeman, D. J. (1986). Differences in entry characteristics of elementary and secondary teacher candidates. *Journal of Teacher Education 37*, 47–51.

Boy, A. V., & Pine, G. J. (1971). *Expanding the self: Personal growth for teachers.* Dubuque, IA: W. C. Brown.

Bredekamp, S. (1992). Composing a profession. *Young Children, 47*, 52–54.

Brinthaupt, T. M., & Lipka, R. P. (1992). Introduction. In T. M. Brinthaupt & R. P. Lipka (Eds.), *The self: Definitional and methodological issues* (1–11). Albany: State University of New York Press.

Brookhart, S. M., & Freeman, D. J. (1992). Characteristics of entering teacher candidates. *Review of Educational Research, 62,* 37–60.

Bullough, R. V., & Stokes, D. K. (1994). Analyzing personal teaching metaphors in preservice teacher education as a means for encouraging professional development. *American Educational Research Journal 31,* 197–224.

Byrne, B. M. (1984). The general/academic self-concept nomological network; A review of construct validation research. *Review of Educational Research, 54,* 427–456.

Calsyn, R. J., & Kenny, D. A. (1977). Self-concept of ability and perceived evaluation of others; Cause or effect or academic achievement? *Journal of Educational Psychology, 69,* 136–145.

Carnegie Task Force on Teaching as a Profession. (1986). *A nation prepared: Teachers for the 21st century.* New York: Carnegie Forum on Education and the Economy.

Combs, A. W. (1965). *The professional education of teachers: A perceptual view of teacher preparation.* Boston; Allyn & Bacon.

Combs, A. W. (1982). Affective education or none at all. *Educational Leadership, 39,* 495–497.

Combs, A. W., Avila, D. L., & Purkey, W. W. (1973). *Helping relationships: Basic concepts for the helping professions.* Boston: Allyn & Bacon.

Contreras. G., & Nicklas, W. L. (1993). Attracting minority community/junior college students to teaching. *Action in Teacher Education, 15,* 1–7.

Ethington, C. A., Smart, J. C., & Pascarella, E. T. (1987). Entry into the teaching profession: Test of a causal model. *Journal of Educational Research, 80,* 156–163.

Freidus, H. (1989, March). *Gender and the choice of teaching as a second career.* Paper presented at the Annual Meeting of the American Educational Research Association, San Francisco.

Gaede, O. F. (1978). Reality shock: A problem among first-year teachers. *The Clearing House, 51,* 405–409.

Garabaldi, A. M. (1989). The impact of school and college reforms on the recruitment of more minority teachers. In A. Garabaldi (Ed.), *Teacher recruitment and retention with a special focus on minority teachers.* Washington, DC: NEA.

Hamachek, D. (1994). Changes in the self from a developmental/psychosocial perspective. In T. Brinthaupt & R. Lipka (Ed.), *Changing the self: Philosophies, techniques, and experiences* (pp. 21–68). Albany: State University of New York Press.

Hansford, B. C., & Hattie, J. A. (1982). The relationship between self and achievement/performance measures. *Review of Educational Research, 52*, 123–142.

Holland, J. I. (1973). *Making vocational choices: A theory of careers.* Englewood Cliffs, NJ: Prentice Hall.

Hollingsworth, S. (1989). Prior beliefs and cognitive change in learning to teach. *American Educational Research Journal, 26*, 160–189.

Holmes Group. (1986). *Tomorrow's teachers: A report of the Holmes Group.* East Lansing, MI: Author.

Hutchinson, G. E., & Johnson, B. (1993–94). Teaching as a career: Examining high school students' perspectives. *Action in Teacher Education, 15*, 61–67.

Jackson, P. W. (1968). *Life in classrooms.* New York: Holt, Rinehart, Winston.

Jantzen, J. M. (1981). Why college students choose to teach: A longitudinal study. *Journal of Teacher Education, 51*, 45–48.

Juhasz, A. M. (1992). Significant others in self-esteem development: Methods and problems in measurement. In T. Brinthaupt & R. Lipka (Eds.), *The self: Definitional and methodological issues* (pp. 204–235). Albany: State University of New York Press.

Kagan, D. M. (1992). Professional growth among preservice and beginning teachers. *Review of Educational Research, 62*, 129–169.

King, S. H. (1993a). The limited presence of African-American teachers. *Review of Educational Research, 63*, 115–149.

King, S. H. (1993b). Why did we choose teaching careers and what will enable us to stay? Insights from one cohort of the African American teaching pool. *Journal of Negro Education, 62*, 475–92.

Kubiniec, C. M. (1970). The relative efficacy of various dimensions of the self-concept in predicting academic achievement. *American Educational Research Journal, 7*, 321–335.

Learned, W. S., & Wood, B. D. (1938). *The student and his knowledge: Bulletin number 29.* New York: The Carnegie Foundation for the Advancement of Teaching.

Lipka, R. P., Hurford, D. P., & Litten, M. J. (1992). Self in school: Age and school experience effects. In R. Lipka & T. Brinthaupt (Eds.), *Self-perspectives: Across the life span* (pp. 93–115). Albany: State University of New York Press.

Lortie, D. C. (1975). *Schoolteacher: A sociological study.* Chicago: University of Chicago Press.

Lyson, T. A., & Falk, W. W. (1984). Recruitment to school teaching: The relationship between high school plans and early adult attainments. *American Educational Research Journal, 21,* 181–193.

Mack, F. R. P., & Jackson, T. E. (1993). *Teacher education as a career choice of Hispanic high school seniors.* Grand Rapids Public Schools, Grand Rapids, MI. (ERIC Document Reproduction Service No. ED 358 087)

Marsh, H. W., Byrne, B. M., & Shavelson, R. J. (1992). A multidimensional, hierarchical self-concept. In T. Brinthaupt & R. Lipka (Eds.), *The self: Definitional and methodological issues* (pp. 44–95). Albany: State University of New York Press.

Murname, R. J., Singer, J. D., Willett, J. B., Kemple, J. J., & Olsen, R. J. (1991). *Who will teach? Policies that matter.* Cambridge, MA: Harvard University Press.

National Board for Professional Teaching Standards. (1994). *What teachers should know and be able to do.* Detroit, MI: Author.

National Commission on Excellence in Education. (1983). *A nation at risk.* Washington, DC: U.S. Government Printing Office.

Opp, R. D. (1989). Freshmen interest in teaching: Recent trends. *Journal of Teacher Education, 40,* 43–48.

Pascarella, E. T., & Terenzini, P. T. (1991). *How college affects students.* San Francisco: Jossey-Bass.

Pate, K. H., Jr., Derdeyn, M., Goodnough, G. E. (1989). Perceptions held by academically talented high school students of teaching as a career. *The School Counselor, 36,* 352–358.

Post, D., & Killian, J. E. (1992–93) Accommodating adult students in undergraduate teacher education programs. *Action in Teacher Education, 14,* 9–15.

Powell, K., & Weaver, E. (1993). *Perceptions of characteristics of candidates in two teacher education programs.* Bibb County School District GA & Georgia College. (ERIC Document Reproduction Service No. ED 355 223)

Roberson, S. D., Keith, T. Z., & Page, E. B. (1983). Now who aspires to teach? *Educational Researcher, 12,* 13–21.

Savage, T. V. (1983). The academic qualifications of women choosing education as a major. *Journal of Teacher Education, 34,* 14–19.

Schon, D. (1983). *The reflective practitioner: How professionals think in action.* New York: Basic Books.

Schubert, W. H. (1991). Teacher lore: A basis for understanding praxis. In C. Witherell & N. Noddings, Eds.), *Stories lives tell: Narrative and dialogue in education* (pp. 207–233). New York: Teachers College Press.

Sears, S., Kennedy, J. J., & Kaye, G. L. (1992, October). *Personality types of prospective educators who complete and who do not complete their preparation to become teachers.* Paper presented at the annual meeting of the Midwestern Educational Research Association, Chicago.

Serow, R. C. (1993). Why teach? Altruism and career choice among nontraditional recruits to teaching. *Journal of Research and Development in Education, 26,* 197–204.

Shavelson, R. J., Hubner, J. J., & Stanton, G. C. (1976). Self-concept: Validation of construct interpretations. *Review of Educational Research, 46,* 407–441.

Stiegelbauer, S. (1992, April). *Why we want to be teachers: New teachers talk about their reasons for entering the profession.* Paper presented at the Annual Meeting of the American Educational Research Association, San Francisco.

Su, J. Z. X. (1993). The study of the education of educators: A profile of teacher education students. *Journal of Research and Development in Education,* 125–132.

Super, D. E. (1963). Self-concepts in vocational development. In *Career development: Self-concept theory: Essays in vocational development* (Research Monograph, No. 4). New York: College Entrance Examination Board.

Thorndike, E. L. (1912). *Education: A first book.* New York: Macmillan.

Tusin, L. F. (1991). The relationship of academic and social self-concepts with women's choice of teaching as a career: A longitudinal model. *Journal of Research and Development in Education, 24,* 16–27.

Tusin, L. F., & Pascarella, E. T. (1985). The influence of college on women's choice of teaching as a career. *Research in Higher Education, 22,* 115–134.

Vance, V. S., & Schlechty, P. C. (1982). The distribution of academic ability in the teaching force: Policy implications. *Phi Delta Kappan, 64,* 22–27.

Walberg, H. J. (1970). Professional role discontinuities in educational careers. *Review of Education Research, 40,* 409–420.

Warren, D. (1985). Learning from experience: History and teacher education. *Educational Researcher, 14,* 5–12.

Weaver, W. T. (1979). In search of quality: The need for talent in teaching. *Phi Delta Kappan, 61,* 29–32, 46.

Weiner, L., Swearingen, J., Pagano, A., & Obi, R. (1993, February). *Choosing teaching as a career: Comparing motivations of Harvard and Urban College stu-*

dents. Paper presented at the Conference of the Eastern Educational Research Association, Clearwater, FL.

Weinstein, C. S. (1990). Prospective elementary teachers' beliefs about teaching: Implications for teacher education. *Teaching and Teacher Education, 6,* 279–290.

Wong, R. E. (1994, April). *The relationship between interest in teaching as a career choice and perceptions of school-classroom environment of 7th and 8th grade students*. Paper presented at the Annual Meeting of the American Educational Research Association, New Orleans, LA.

Wood, K. E. (1978). What motivates students to teach? *Journal of Teacher Education, 29,* 48–50.

Zapata, J. T. (1988). Early identification and recruitment of Hispanic teacher candidates. *Journal of Teacher Education, 39,* 19–23.

Zimpher, N. (1989). The RATE project: A profile of teacher education students. *Journal of Teacher Education, 40,* 27–30.

CHAPTER 2

DECIDING TO TEACH: IMPLICATIONS OF A SELF-DEVELOPMENT PERSPECTIVE

Stanley J. Zehm

INTRODUCTION

The decision to become a teacher in a postmodern world riddled with political uncertainties, culture wars, economic instability, and the erosion of traditional moral values is fraught with much anxiety and complexity. Faced with the staggering intellectual, emotional, social, cultural, linguistic, and class differences they observe among public school students in their field experience, many would-be teachers doubt whether they have the "right stuff" to be effective teachers.

In order to assist prospective teachers to deal with the anxiety and complexity associated with the decision to enter the teaching profession, teacher educators are revising traditional programs and courses to assist their students to consider and assess whether they have the qualifications to be effective teachers in today's troubled schools. In addition to the traditional focus on the acquisition of professional knowledge and skills, many teacher educators are urgently addressing topics associated with self, self-esteem, and self-understanding (Wilson, 1990; Pagano, 1991; Schubert & Ayers, 1992; Zehm & Kottler, 1993; Beattie, 1995).

The purpose of this chapter is to frame and support a proposition that a continuing focus on the development of the self, the human dimension of teaching and learning, should be given a place of prominence in preservice teacher preparation programs. This proposition is based on the premise that a person's decision to become a teacher must

I wish to thank my colleague Dr. Rosemarie Deering and Teresa Delgadillo-Harrison, my graduate assistant, for the assistance they provided me in the preparation of this chapter.

not only be based on the successful acquisition of technical skills and professional knowledge, but also on the conscious development of a refined sense of self.

The chapter is divided into the following four sections:

1. A rationale focused on the importance of this topic to programs of preservice teacher preparation and to decisions about entrance to the teaching profession
2. An examination of the historical origins of a self-development perspective in teacher preparation
3. An analysis of contemporary issues regarding self-development that influence decisions about who become teachers
4. A brief discussion of promising approaches within the field of teacher education and potential applications from the social sciences for use by teacher educators in assisting preservice teachers with decisions about entering the profession.

To avoid confusion over the meaning of terms related to self-development, let me define the three terms I will be using most frequently, *self-esteem*, *mutual esteem*, and *self-concept*. *Self-esteem* refers to an individual's ability to assess his/her understanding and appreciation of personal worth (Demo & Savin-Williams, 1992). *Mutual esteem* refers to an individual's ability to provide honest and supportive feedback regarding the worth of peers (Zehm & Kottler, 1993). *Self-concept* refers to the descriptive information about an individual's cognitive and affective dimensions that he or she collects, interprets, and can use to make predictions about future experiences (Wells, 1992).

RATIONALE

Teacher educators, interested in establishing a focus on the development of the self-esteem and self-understanding of preservice teachers, must articulate a clear and compelling rationale for adding this focus to the preservice teacher preparation sequence. The curriculum of preservice program, already under siege from a variety of contemporary needs competing for the limited credit-hour allocations, will resist the inclusion of additional foci and content without convincing arguments of substance and benefit.

In August of 1985, during that frenzied time when teachers are trying to get ready for the annual student invasion, I was asked to conduct the traditional, mandatory inservice workshop for the entire faculty of a middle school in the Pacific Northwest on the topic, "Helping Middle School Students to Construct Self and Mutual Esteem." After the workshop was concluded, I was approached by five veteran teachers. They politely thanked me for sharing my ideas and strategies for helping them encourage the development of their student's self-esteem. Then they confronted me with the following need and challenge that I have maintained as one of the primary foci of my work with both preservice and inservice teachers during the past decade: "When are you people in teacher education ever going to provide teachers with instruction and support in developing their own self-esteem, self-understanding, and personal growth?"

This story highlights the central importance of the need for a self-development perspective in teacher preparation programs. If teachers do not possess optimal levels of personal self-esteem, they are not likely to be effective in modeling and supporting their students' development of self-esteem. If teachers do not invest time and energy in processing the feedback they receive from self and others regarding their individual self-concepts, they are less likely to be effective providers of feedback to support the development and maintenance of the self-concepts of their students. The ancient axiom "No one gives what he/she does not possess" is as applicable to supporting student growth in self-esteem as it is to supporting student growth in mathematics. Teachers with optimal levels of self-esteem have been demonstrated to be more flexible in their thinking, more enthusiastic about their own learning, and more effective in applying what they learn to improving the learning of their students (Bellon, Bellon, & Blank, 1992; Zehm & Kottler, 1993).

Another critical aspect of the importance of a self-development perspective for teachers follows from the first. The esteem our nation once accorded the teaching profession has been seriously eroded during the past two decades. It used to be that extended families identified with pride the one or two family members, aunts or cousins, who honored the entire family by choosing to serve in the profession of teaching. Today, when the idealism of teachers is often mocked, the authority and respect for teachers diminished, and the financial compensation of teachers declining, teachers are questioning their self-efficacy as persons and professionals. For those who are in the process of deciding to become teachers, it is imperative that they understand the contemporary challenges to the professional esteem of teachers prior to their own entry into teaching.

A third factor that highlights the importance of a focus on self relates more directly to the critical question students in preservice teacher education programs regularly ask themselves: "Do I really want to become a teacher?" Traditional teacher education programs, structured around a prescriptive view of teaching that emphasizes acquisition of a complex maze of technical knowledge and directive rules and procedures (Zehm & Kottler, 1990; Rubin, 1989), give teachers little time or support in examining this critical question. The technical complexity of the prescribed knowledge-base required of preservice teachers frequently obscures the importance of their personal knowledge, that is, their feelings, self-understanding, self-esteem, and personal ways of knowing (Colton & Sparks-Langer, 1993). In many such programs, methods courses and field experiences are so concentrated on assisting preservice teachers to understand pedagogical theories and put them into practice, that little attention is given to constructing a knowledge base grounded on their own personal ways of knowing.

Clandinin and Connelly emphasize the importance of the personal-practical knowledge of teachers. "What we mean by teachers' knowledge is that body of convictions and meanings, conscious and unconscious, that have arisen from experience . . . and that are expressed in a person's practices . . . practice, broadly conceived to include intellectual acts and self-exploration, is all we have to go on," (Clandinin & Connelly, 1995, p. 7). If teacher educators gave more attention to self-exploration and the development of the personal practical knowledge of prospective teachers, it is likely these preservice teachers would have more substantive information with which to make decisions about becoming teachers.

Finally, if we agree in whole or part with the preceding arguments for including a continuing focus on self-development in preservice teacher education programs, it follows that the place to begin this emphasis is in programs of preservice teacher preparation. This emphasis on self-development should begin with introductory classes and be given attention in the educational psychology and methods courses. Finally, preservice students should be given assistance from classroom teacher-mentors to find and use the understandings they derive about themselves during their field experiences to help them make more informed decisions to become teachers.

ORIGINS OF THE SELF-DEVELOPMENT PERSPECTIVE

In addition to the development of clear and compelling rationale for supporting the inclusion of a self-development perspective in preservice teacher preparation programs, teacher educators should be aware of the historical roots that support this perspective. Knowledge that the self-development perspective is not a new or radical feature to teacher preparation programs, but has been a valued part of the educational tradition both in Europe and North America, may help add weight to the support for a perspective on self-development in preservice programs.

The historical roots of a perspective on self-development for students and teachers in American public schools can be traced to the movement that began in the late 1880s for a "progressive society where each individual could develop his or her fullest potential" (Williams & Fromberg, 1992, p. 56). Educational progressivism, philosophically linked to the pedagogical principles of European educational reformers Pestalozzi and Herbart, was given its initial thrust in the United States and Canada by the field research of Joseph Mayer Rice. Rice, a pediatrician, studied pedagogy in Germany at the universities of Leipzig and Jena in the late 1880s. He was influenced by the educational ideas of Friedrich Froebel, the inventor of the kindergarten, who maintained that only a "growing consciousness of self makes human freedom possible" . . . and consequently a prime objective of education must be to help human beings . . . "to become fully conscious of their powers" (Deighton 1971, p. 101). Rice shocked the nation with his accounts of the sterile, rigid, and mechanical forms of instruction in the American public schools (Cremin, 1964). "The school," Rice wrote, "has been converted into the most dehumanizing institution that I have ever laid eyes upon, each child being treated as if he possessed a memory and the faculty of speech, but no individuality, no sensibilities, no soul" (Rice 1893a, 31). He urged educators to recognize a new primary purpose for the public schools "to develop the child in all his faculties, intellectual, moral and physical" (Rice, 1893b, p. 507).

Before Rice passed the progressive torch to John Dewey, G. Stanley Hall, and a phalanx of educational reformers ready to train teachers to focus on the whole child and to observe, study, and address the interests, esteem needs, and self-concepts of their students (Power, 1991), he articulated another need frequently associated with the progressive movement. He wanted to validate educational knowledge and practice with scientific inquiry. More specifically, he wanted to make sure that novices, who had decided to become teachers, would receive training grounded on scientific principles derived from psychology and the social sciences (Good & Teller, 1973). Many educators and psychologists of the early 1900s were eager to join Rice and Hall in the construction of a "science of education" that would provide objective data to support progressive reforms. Two notable exceptions to this movement to build a more progressive pedagogical theory and practice primarily on scientific inquiry were the educator John Dewey and the psychologist William James. Dewey warned educators that a science of education could not be constructed by employing techniques from the physical sciences (Good & Teller, 1973). James likewise cautioned educators to be slow in trying to apply findings of psychology to education (Kliebard, 1993). These powerful warnings from Dewey and James were meant to alert teachers and teacher educators that no objective science could ever replace teachers' ways of knowing, which begin with intuition and subjective judgments.

It would not be until mid-century that the first text would be written to help teachers examine their own self-knowledge and esteem needs. In 1955, Arthur Jersild published the classic text *When Teachers Face Themselves*. The text clearly delineated the powerful personal and professional implications of teachers attending to self-development. Jersild maintained that "self-understanding is the most important requirement in any effort (for teachers) to know themselves and to gain healthy attitudes of self-acceptance" (Jersild 1995, p. 3). The influence of this text, however, was short-lived. In October 1957, when the Russians launched Sputnik, the United States began a frenzied focus, not on teachers' needs, but on the perceived national security need to train teachers of scientists and technicians.

In the following decade, Jersild's humanistic perspectives were again reintroduced by American educators. Arthur Combs linked student achievement directly to the perceived self-concept of the learner (Combs, 1962). Teacher educators utilized the work of psychologists Carl Rogers and Abraham Maslow in preparing teachers-to-be to understand the affective dimensions of their own self-development.

During the final moments of the "Great Society," Natalicio and Hereford (1969) edited a significant text, *The Teacher as a Person*. Three chapters of this text were excerpted from the works of Carl Rogers. They focused on the need for those who want to be teachers to become more process-oriented in their personal lives and to build personal relationships with students that would help them become self-directed learners. Rogers urged teachers to act as a vital human beings, "not a faceless embodiment of a curricular requirement, or a sterile pipe through which knowledge is passed from one generation to the next" (Natalicio & Hereford, 1969, p. 107).

This interesting book ends with a prophetic chapter written by B. F. Skinner. In this chapter, "Why Teachers Fail," Skinner asserts that teachers fail, not because of any human limitation or failure to attend to the self-esteem needs of their students, but because they are not prepared to utilize the pedagogy of technology to manage student behaviors. This end-of-the-sixties foreshadowing would become a major movement when it was translated into the "teacher as competent technician" model, the preferred model that dominated much of education in the 1970s and '80s. The teacher as technician was ruled by curriculum management systems. Management by objectives led to reductionistic, "parts-catalog" approaches to teaching and learning. Considerations of self-development were not taken into account in decisions about who became teachers; checklists of technical competencies indicating mastery became the primary means of gatekeeping.

One brief exception to the neglect of the need for an emphasis on the self-development of teachers was a small, single-edition book by Angelo Boy and Gerald Pine (1971), *Expanding the Self: Personal Growth for Teachers*. In this little known text, the counselor-authors presented a program of self-development for preservice and inservice teachers. Built on a model of involvement in four sets of experiences—(1) human, (2) vocational, (3) spiritual, and (4) recreational—Boy and Pine identified a series of principles and conditions aimed at promoting systematic opportunities for the self-development of teachers. They were convinced that continuous and balanced personal growth experiences were essential for all teachers. "We are concerned about the personal growth of teachers because we do not believe that, in themselves, good lesson plans, teaching approaches, curriculum, media, or materials produce happy, fully functioning people. Although these things can help, we are convinced it is the teacher's personhood which makes the difference in the development of productive and positive human beings" (Boy & Pine, 1971, p. 4).

The 1980s were filled with a variety of political and pedagogical issues that kept the focus away from spotlighting a need for the self-development of teachers. The conservative religious reaction to anything associated with humanism, the materialistic and narcissistic distractions of the yuppie "me generation," the strict imposition of accountability measures, and a plethora of dire reports about the declining academic performance of students in public schools were among the many issues that led to a decline in confidence in public schools and created stress for teachers.

In place of a focus on self-development for teachers during the 1980s, the focus centered on acquiring coping skills, and helping teachers to survive stress and burnout (Swick, 1985; Humphery & Humphery, 1986). A research and development focus on teacher reflection, potentially supportive of the self-development of teachers, began in the late 1980s (Brandt, 1986; Cruickshank, 1985; Pollard, 1987; Tom, 1985; and Zeichner & Liston, 1987). This focus, however, was largely directed at technical reflection aimed at improving teaching methods, learning environments, and pedagogical decisions. The use of what Sparks-Langer and Colton (1991) have called "critical reflection" aimed at consideration of the personal beliefs and moral implications of teaching was largely ignored as a means for supporting the self-development of teachers.

The last half of the 1980s and advent of the 1990s did find a renewed emphasis in the need to provide students with more self-development activities supportive of their self-esteem. This renewal of a key element of progressive pedagogy, however, was and remains mired in controversy. There is major disagreement today among educators regarding the pedagogical purposes, instructional strategies, and place in the curricular framework of a self-esteem emphasis (Beane, 1991).

The second half of the 1990s may yet provide a more fertile field for a focus on the self-development of teachers. Two related movements—(1) the empowerment of teachers, a significant dimension of current school reform and restructuring efforts, and (2) the growing interest in the professionalization of teachers—may combine to provide the vision needed to demonstrate the importance of a self-development perspective in preservice and inservice teacher development programs (Eisner, 1991; Sergiovanni, 1992).

CONTEMPORARY ISSUES

In addition to understanding the history of a self-development perspective in preservice teacher preparation programs, a number of significant contemporary issues will require serious attention prior to the development and implementation of an emphasis on self-development. This section attempts to identify some of the major issues that would likely inhibit or prevent the development of a program emphasis on self-development.

Location of a Self-Development Perspective

An issue central to the addition of a self-development perspective likely to be raised by teacher educators is the location of the self-development component. Teacher preparation programs in North American colleges and universities are, for the most part, course driven and cannot easily support the addition of courses in an already cluttered sequence. Even if it were possible to place an additional course requirement with a self-development emphasis in the preservice teacher preparation sequence, would this be the best way to address this perceived need? Some teacher educators would support this addition as the only sure way of getting the self-development emphasis placed in the curriculum.

Others would likely object to this practice as a token gesture and would advocate an inclusionary model with self-development topics emphasized throughout the preservice program.

Common Understandings of Self

Another set of issues must be addressed before the addition of a self-development perspective can be seriously considered as a component of teacher preparation programs. These issues revolve around the need of teacher educators for a common understanding about the definition of self, about the development of self, and about ways to measure a variety of dimensions of self. These tasks, obviously complex in themselves, are made even more complex given the wide disagreement among social scientists about these same critical issues (Brinthaupt & Lipka, 1992).

Gatekeeping Functions

One of the major implications of a self-development component in a teacher preparation program is the potential such a perspective might have for providing information useful for screening candidates for the teaching profession. At the present time, the gatekeeping function in teacher education programs is largely determined by GPA. If students do not possess at least a 3.0 GPA (the exact GPA will vary), the gate to the teacher preparation program will not open. Moreover, if preservice students do not maintain a stipulated GPA while in the program, they will go on probation and may not find the gate open for them to student teaching. Considerations of a candidate's self-development, that is, his or her maturity, self-esteem, sense of personal responsibility, and overall emotional-psychological fitness for the teaching profession, are seldom addressed in a substantive manner.

Teacher educators do need authority to screen prospective teachers they know are unfit from the teacher ranks. It is their moral responsibility to make decisions based on solid evidence about who gets into and out of teacher education programs. With the "gates to entry . . . ill defined and casually watched" (Goodlad, 1992, p. 91), many students with major self-development needs are successful in meeting the minimal academic requirements for graduation and certification. Faced with the complexity of establishing and maintaining a comprehensive gatekeeping system for screening out unfit candidates, many teacher educators pass the problem on to the schools, saying, "We can't play God; it's the school's responsibility to hire teachers they think are fit to teach." Other teacher educators, lacking the authority provided by a gatekeeping system, screen unfit candidates from the ranks by giving students grades of "C" for their student teaching, a sure sign of "don't hire" to personnel directors in school districts.

Dysfunctional Family Origins

Another issue that must be considered when building a rationale for a self-development perspective for preservice teacher education is the attractiveness of the teaching profession to individuals from dysfunctional families. There are a variety of factors that will determine the degree to which dysfunctional family living will affect the adult behaviors of classroom teachers. Cultural variances, assigned family roles, and interventions by strong family members may significantly mitigate the negative effects of being raised in an alcoholic, substance abusing, or abusive family.

We do know, however, that many individuals who were raised in dysfunctional families frequently develop characteristics of rigidity, denial, silence, and isolation. Fischer found that both sons and daughters who were raised in dysfunctional family settings were more likely to develop these characteristics of dependency when their fathers' parenting style was highly authoritarian (Fischer & Crawford, 1992).

When these individuals become teachers, they may find considerable difficulty in building cohesive, trusting relationships with students, parents, supervisors, and other teachers. Moreover, these teachers may find it difficult to maintain open, authentic forms of classroom communication with their students. Adapting to new and demanding changes in curriculum, student behaviors, and familiar school routines may also be difficult for teachers raised in dysfunctional families (Reviczky, 1992; Morrow, 1995).

We have written about this critical issue in other articles and books (Powell & Zehm 1991; Powell, Gabe & Zehm, 1994; Powell, Zehm, Kottler, 1995), and we refer our readers to those sources. For the purposes of this chapter, it is important to recognize the self-development needs of teachers whose families of origin were dominated by the abuse of alcohol or drugs, or by physical abuse by one or both parents.

People from such dysfunctional families, who have not had the opportunity and assistance to work on self-development needs, may be unknowingly attracted to the teaching profession for the wrong reasons. Teaching may give them the sense of control they never experienced in their own out-of-control lives.

The unfortunate results of opening the gates to the teaching profession for individuals from dysfunctional backgrounds, who have not worked on their personal self-development needs, may later be seen in negative influences on students. These negative influences may include some of the following: lowering of academic and behavioral standards, treating students as victims, fostering student dependency on teachers and peers, promoting achievement-driven behaviors, and establishing classroom climates of blaming and shaming. These teachers may also be unknowing models of lowered self-esteem. They may also fail to recognize and reward students for risk-taking, individual initiative, and authentic self-discoveries.

Other Critical Issues

In addition to these four issues we have highlighted, teacher educators working in a variety of preservice contexts will need to identify other issues that will require consideration prior to the implementation of effective self-development strategies. Among these needs may be the following:

1. The need for agreement about the aims of a self-esteem pedagogy for K–12 students and their future teachers
2. The need for a conceptual framework to assist teacher educators in understanding self-development issues
3. The need for understanding of the complexity of a self-development perspective
4. The need for an understanding of the influences of a variety of social and cultural contexts on self-development
5. The need to identify barriers to establishing a program supportive of the self-development of future teachers.

PROMISING TRENDS AND APPROACHES

In this, the final section of the chapter, we will review a few of the current trends and promising practices supportive of the development and implementation of preservice teacher education programs that balance the need for personal and professional development.

Personal-Professional Reflection

The focus on assisting preservice and inservice teachers to think reflectively about their teaching is a trend that supports a self-development emphasis (Alder, 1991; Bullough, 1989; Calderhead, 1989; Colton

& Sparks-Langer, 1993; Cruickshank, 1985; Gore, 1987; Korthagen, 1905; Zeichner & Liston, 1987). Although much of the emphasis on reflection has been directed toward the development of professional expertise of teachers, we believe that reflection on the human dimensions of teaching will make reflection a useful tool for self-exploration as well (Zehm & Kottler, 1993).

The benefits of developing habits of reflective thinking have significant implications for self-development. Hunt (1987) suggests that reflective thinking over a period of time about one's teaching enhances self-understanding and improves communications with others. Reflection can assist the preservice teacher in developing self-awareness of both effective and ineffective patterns of communication. Hunt describes this form of awareness as the inside-out approach where teachers begin with self-examination, then explore how their environment impacts them, and finally examine their reactions to these influences.

A variety of tools are being used by teacher educators to promote the reflective thinking of preservice and inservice teachers. Connelly and Clandinin (1988) have divided the reflective tools into two groups. The first group of tools are those that preservice and inservice teachers can use when they are alone, enjoying a few moments of solitude. The tools in this group include personal journals, self-assessments, personal narratives, metaphors, and picturing. The second group of tools include those a preservice teacher might use with a mentor, a trusted peer, or a learning community of future teachers who are working together to become more reflective thinkers. Action research, peer observation, and group debriefing are tools included in the second group.

Learning Communities

Another promising practice that may lend itself to the support of a self-development perspective in preservice teacher education is the use of learning communities or cohorts. This practice aims at locating a preservice teacher in a community of individuals who begin and end their preservice preparation together. Their journey to become teachers begins and ends with personal professional reflection both in their coursework and in their field experiences. They are encouraged to share their stories of self-development with each other. They become sources of mutual esteem and support for each other.

In establishing close relationships with their peers, preservice teachers help one another in making the critical decisions connected to becoming teachers. They assist one another in clarifying thoughts and values, in analyzing their motivations for considering teaching as a profession, in examining their assumptions and biases, in sharing self-disclosures, in personal exploration and discovery in learning, and in determining whether their attraction to teaching will likely result in a passionate commitment (Wilson, 1990; Zehm & Kottler, 1993).

Personal Narratives

Personal stories are another device teacher educators are using to help preservice teachers identify issues of self-development (Pagano, 1991; Schubert & Ayers, 1992). Preservice students, encouraged to write autobiographical accounts, are most likely to shape these snapshots of their lives into what Pagano describes as self-fictionalizing accounts designed to please their professor rather than to reveal or discover dimensions of self-understanding (Pagano, 1991, p. 259). Story telling and writing, however, is an alternative form of life history that can be used to assist prospective teachers in examining their own learning, beliefs, and understandings of self.

In telling and writing stories about their own learning and relationships with teachers, preservice teachers can examine settings, the environments of learning. They can explore the motivations of characters who participate in their stories. They can examine relationships of students with teachers, parents, and other students and discover those personal elements that support positive relationships. They can examine conflicts and understand more about the self in times of adversity. Moreover, preservice teachers' stories can help them learn self-understanding through the cultivation of their powers of imagination. "Selfhood," Pagano maintains, "begins in imagination, through processes of identification encouraged by stories that we tell one another" (Pagano, 1991, p. 266).

Social Science Applications

There are an increasing number of applications of theories from the social sciences that may provide assistance to teacher educators interested in including a perspective on self in preservice teacher preparation programs. The multiple intelligences theory of Howard Gardner has focused attention on the intrapersonal intelligence of individuals. According to Gardner, an individual's intrapersonal intelligence gives him/her the capacity to know him or herself, to reflect upon feelings, to observe self metacognitively, to intuit spiritual realities, and to cultivate a transpersonal sense of self (Gardner, 1982).

Inventories of personality type, such as the Myers-Briggs Type Indicator (Myers-McCauley, 1988), have been used by teacher educators to help prospective teachers understand their perceptions and judgments of self and others. Instruments such as the Communicating Styles Survey (Mok, 1985) are being used by other teacher educators to help preservice teachers understand how they interact with others in times of agreement and in times of conflict. Finally, a number of learning-styles instruments, such as the Max Inventory of Learning Styles (Ferman, 1991), are helping teacher educators to provide preservice teachers with understanding of the different ways they learn through their multiple intelligences.

CONCLUSION

Approximately 20 percent of beginning teachers leave the teaching profession after their first two years of teaching. Some are weeded out during their probationary status as beginning teachers. We do not know how many of these beginning teachers, who have voluntarily or involuntarily left their classrooms, have done so because they lacked the personal-professional esteem and understanding of self necessary to build effective relationships with students, parents, and teachers. We are convinced, however, that this loss of young, idealistic teachers will continue until teacher educators begin to reeducate themselves regarding the importance of focusing on the human dimensions of teaching and learning and find the time, places, and resources to focus on a self-development perspective for preservice teachers.

REFERENCES

Alder, S. (1991). The reflective practitioner and the curriculum of teacher education. *Journal of Education for Teaching, 17,* 139–150.

Beane, J. A. (1991). Sorting out the self-esteem controversy. *Educational Leadership, 49,* 25–30.

Beattie, M. (1995). *Constructing professional knowledge in teaching: A narrative of change and development.* New York: Teachers College Press.

Bellon, J., Bellon, E., & Blank, M. (1992). *Teaching from a research knowledge base.* New York: Merrill.

Boy, A. V., & Pine, G. J. (1971). *Expanding the self: Personal growth for teachers.* Dubuque, IA: Wm. C. Brown.

Brandt, R. (1986). On the expert teacher: A conversation with David Berliner. *Educational Leadership, 44,* 4–9.

Brinthaupt, T. M., & Lipka, R. P. (1992). *The self: Definitional and methodological issues*. Albany: State University of New York Press.

Bullough, R. V. (1989). Teacher education and teacher reflectivity. *Journal of Teacher Education, 40*, 15–21.

Calderhead, J. (1989). Reflective teaching and teacher education. *Teaching and Teacher Education, 5*, 43–51.

Clandinin, D. J., & Connelly, F. M. (1995). *Teacher's professional knowledge landscapes*. New York: Teachers College Press.

Colton, A. B., & Sparks-Langer, G. M. (1993). A conceptual framework to guide the development of teacher reflection and decision making. *Journal of Teacher Education, 44*, 45–54.

Combs, A. W. (1982). Affective education or none at all. *Educational Leadership, 39*, 495–497.

Connelly, F. M., & Clandinin, D. J. (1988). *Teachers as curriculum planners: Narratives of experience*. New York: Teachers College Press.

Cremin, A. A. (1964). *The transformation of the school: Progressivism in American education, 1876–1957*. New York: Vintage Books.

Cruickshank, D. (1985). Uses and benefits of reflective teaching. *Phi Delta Kappan, 66*, 704–706.

Deighton, L. C. (Ed.). (1971). *The encyclopedia of education*. Vol. 4. New York: Macmillan & The Free Press.

Demo, D. H., & Savin-Williams, R. C. (1992). Self-concept stability and change during adolescence. In T. Brinthaupt & R. Lipka (Eds.), *Self-Perspectives across the life span*. Albany: State University of New York Press.

Eisner, E. W. (1991). Should America have a national curriculum? *Educational Leadership, 49*, 76–81.

Ferman, M. C. (1991). *The Max inventory of learning styles*. Santa Barbara, CA: Intellimation.

Fischer, J. L., & Crawford, D. W. (1992). Codependency and parenting style. *Journal of Adolescent Research, 7*, 352–363.

Gardner, H. (1982). *Frames of mind: The theory of multiple intelligences*. New York: Harper & Row.

Good, H. G., & Teller, J. D. (1973). *A history of American education* (3rd. ed.). New York: Macmillan.

Goodlad, J. I. (1992). The moral dimensions of schooling and teacher education. *Journal of Moral Education, 21*, 87–97.

Goodman, J. (1986). Making early field experience meaningful: A critical approach. *Journal of Education for Teaching, 12*, 109–125.

Gore, J. (1987). Reflecting on reflective teaching. *Journal of Teacher Education, 38*, 33–39.

Humphrey, J. N., & Humphery, J. H. (1986). *Coping with stress in teaching*. New York: AMS Press.

Hunt, D. (1987). *Beginning with ourselves*. Cambridge, MA: Brookline Books.

Jersild, A. T. (1955). *When teachers face themselves*. New York: Teachers College Press.

Kliebard, H. M. (1993, Fall). What is a knowledge base, and who would use it if we had one? *Review of Educational Research, 63*, 295–303.

Korthagen, F. A. (1985). Reflective teaching and preservice teacher education in the Netherlands. *Journal of Teacher Education, 36*, 11–15.

Mok, P. P. (1985). *Communicating styles survey*. Plano, TX: Training Associates Press.

Morrow, M. (1995). The influence of dysfunctional family behaviors on adolescent career exploration. *School Counselor, 42*, 311–316.

Myers, I. B., & McCaulley, M. H. (1988). *Manual: A guide to the development and use of the Myers-Briggs Type Indicator*. Palo Alto, CA: Consulting Psychologists Press.

Natalicio, L. F., & Hereford, C. F. (1969). *The teacher as a person*. Dubuque, IA: Wm. C. Brown.

Pagano, J. A. (1991). Relating to one's students: Identity, morality, stories, and questions. *Journal of Moral Education, 20*, 257–266.

Pollard, A. (1987). Reflective teaching—the sociological contribution. In P. Woods & A. Pollard (Eds.) *Sociology and teaching: A new challenge for the sociology of education*. London: Croom Helm.

Powell, R., & Zehm, S. (1991). Classrooms under the influence. *Schools in the Middle, 6*, 6–11.

Powell, R., Gabe, J., & Zehm, S. (1994). *Classrooms under the influence: Reaching early adolescent children of alcoholics*. Reston, VA: National Association of Secondary School Principals.

Powell, R., Zehm, S., & Kottler, J. (1995). *Classrooms under the influence: Addicted families/addicted students*. Newbury Park, CA: Corvin Press.

Power, E. (1991). *A legacy of learning: A history of Western education*. Albany: State University of New York Press.

Rice, J. M. (1893a). *The public school system of the United States*. New York: The Century Company.

Rice, J. M. (1893b). Our public school system: A summary. *The Forum, 15,* 507–518.

Reviczky, J. (1992). A *handbook for dysfunctional teachers*. Plymouth, NH: Plymouth State College.

Rubin, L. (1989). The thinking teacher: Cultivating pedagogical intelligence. *Journal of Teacher Education, 40,* 22–30.

Tom, A. (1985). Inquiring into inquiry-oriented teacher education. *Journal of Teacher Education, 36,* 35–44.

Sergiovanni, T. (1992). *Moral leadership: Getting to the heart of school improvement*. San Francisco: Jossey-Bass.

Schubert, W. H., & Ayers, W. C. (Eds.). (1992) *Teacher lore: Learning from our own experience*. New York: Longman.

Swick, K. (1985). *Stress and the classroom teacher*. Washington, DC: National Education Association.

Wells, A. J. (1992). Variations in self-esteem in daily life: Methodological and developmental issues. In R. Lipka & T. Brinthaupt (Eds.), *Self-Perspectives across the Life Span*. Albany: State University of New York Press.

Williams, L. R., & Fromberg, D. P. (1992). *Encyclopedia of early childhood education*. New York: Garland.

Wilson, S. M. (1990). The secret garden of teacher education. *Phi Delta Kappan, 72,* 204–209.

Zehm, S. J., & Kottler, J. A. (1993). *On being a teacher: The human dimension*. Newbury Park, CA: Corwin Press.

Zeichner, K., & Liston, D. (1987). Teaching student teachers to reflect. *Harvard Educational Review, 57,* 23–48.

PART II

Becoming a Teacher: Preservice Education

Chapter 3

Becoming a Teacher: The Person in the Process

S. Vianne McLean

After several decades in which "the person" has been largely absent from thinking and writing about teacher education, over the last five years, there has been a surge of interest in the people who enter preservice professional education programs and their experiences within them. Those who teach beginning teachers[1] increasingly are interested in how they think about themselves as they master professional practice and undergo the substantial personal transformations associated with this period of their lives.

Though based in very diverse ideological positions, attention is converging on the experience of *becoming* a teacher, that complex and often conflicted intrapersonal and social process. This chapter outlines some of the agreements and disagreements in ways of thinking about the person in the process, and ways of balancing the micro view of individual experience with the macro sociocultural dimensions of the phenomenon of teaching. The final sections describe selected perspectives on teacher education programs and strategies that aim to facilitate novice teachers' personal and professional development.

Focusing on the Learner

Teacher education writers from a wide range of ideological positions are now suggesting that much greater attention needs to be paid to the individual ways of knowing that beginning teachers bring to and develop within the preservice years. They describe a reciprocal and holistic connection between these teachers and learners. Striving to understand beginning teachers as whole people, who are undergoing personal transformations as their professional personas are developed, is important, but it is not sufficient. To understand the process of becoming a teacher, one also must strive to understand teacher educators, the intricacies of their interrelationships with learners, and the contexts within which these interrelationships are constructed.

Preservice teacher education involves a process in which those taught could be construed (at least in professional development terms) as being a considerable distance from those who are their teachers (Tamir, 1991, p. 266). Undoubtedly, teacher educators and beginning teachers have very different knowledge bases about teaching, and often have different perspectives on what is valuable or necessary in teacher education programs, but conceptualizing those differences as deficits in the beginning teacher is now considered useless at best, and at worst, as perpetuating the powerlessness of beginning teachers in the process of their own professional development. Many contemporary writers (Brunner, 1994; Calderhead, 1993; Clandinin, 1992) emphasize the continuities between beginning teacher and teacher educator: Both parties are engaged in work characterized by conflicts between personal commitments and public demands; trying to enact change within the problematic entrenchment of institutional culture, both are experiencing personal uncertainties and professional dilemmas. Just as beginning teachers struggle with the ambiguities and conflicting realities of their work in becoming a teacher, so do teacher educators struggle in their work of trying to facilitate development in others, even as they continue their own personal and professional development.

To better understand the process of becoming a teacher, one needs to be cognizant of *all* of the participants in the process, and to understand more about what each brings to these encounters. Further, one needs to understand something of the multiple contexts in which such encounters occur; contexts that are reflexively both shaped by and shaping the nature of the encounter.

THE ARRIVAL IN PRESERVICE TEACHER EDUCATION: DESIRES, HOPES, AND LONG-HAUL BAGGAGE

Only in the last decade has the critical relationship between beginning teachers' lived experience and their professional development begun to be formally recognized. Previously, teacher education was seen as a matter of largely anonymous students being exposed to a body of clearly delineated professional knowledge and given opportunities to master given technical skills. For teacher educators, the major concerns were program structure and organization, and how best to "deliver instruction." Life for students within the program was thought of as a similar experience for all. Questions about what personal or sociocultural baggage students brought into the program with them and how this background influenced their individual experience of becoming teachers simply did not arise. Such questions were not part of the discourse of teacher education.

But beyond the impact of an individual's lived experience on her[2] personal experience of learning to teach, the common patterns across teachers' lived experiences have exerted a massive influence on education in general, and on the way teacher education has been conceptualized and practiced. The shared nature of these deeply rooted sociocultural understandings have formed the unacknowledged foundation the taken-for-granteds both of becoming a teacher and of teaching teachers.

Across many Western nations, up until the last decade or two, the people who entered the field of education (particularly early education) were a homogenous group—almost entirely female, White, and middle-class. In early childhood education this homogeneity in class background has been linked to the field's long-standing commitment to child-centered pedagogy. But as recent critics (O'Loughlin, 1991) suggest, child-centered approaches are both less valued by families on the margins of society (Delpit, 1988) and less utilized with children from this sector (Gomez, 1992, pp. 166–167). Though early childhood teachers as a group are now much more diverse in terms of ethnicity and class, the field is yet to come to terms with its own cultural and class origins (O'Loughlin, 1991). Contemporary early childhood teachers and teacher educators face vexing questions as they try to bring to the surface their class- and culture-related ways of viewing education, and to develop a personal pedagogy that is responsive to diverse families' needs and wishes.

Another collection of understandings that students bring with them to the process of learning to teach centered around gender. In Western societies, teaching long has been seen as "women's work," an extension of the traditional nurturing role of the mother, and nowhere is this more evident than in early childhood education, where small children clearly are in need of nurturance, and where women have formed the great unquestioned majority of teachers for generations.

Writers such as Grumet (1983) and Britzman (1991) have articulated some of the ways in which gender-based conceptualizations have shaped our understandings of educators and their work. Hidden within the discourse of teaching as "natural work for women" are a host of positions about power relationships that have helped maintain the status quo in education—often perpetuating low status and poor reward systems for women educators. Within the field of early childhood education, for example, there have been some remarkable women educational leaders and social activists, such as Patty Smith Hill, Maria Montessori, and Margaret MacMillan. But there also have been silent armies of women teachers who have toiled, in the service of children and families, without a clear sense of their own gender-boundaried identity, or any imagination of a different and better world for themselves or those they have served.

Despite the high profile gender-equity issues have assumed in Western nations over the last decade, it seems that for many women educators, the discourse of gender still is not their own language. They find it extremely difficult to give voice to their personal gendered history, and perceive that the gendered history of their field has little to do with their ways of making sense of what they think and do as teachers.

Persons entering teacher education bring with them a portmanteau of gender-based understandings that, in many cases, are invisible to them. Such understandings are crucial to the images they hold of themselves, their hopes and desires for a professional future, and the ways in which they make sense of their experiences as beginning teachers. Teacher educators too, bring a lifetime of gender-based ways of making sense of their professional world, and if they are to develop better ways of facilitating personal and professional development in others, it is essential that they unpack some of their own gender-based ways of knowing. Only then can they help beginning teachers to do the same.

Images of self-as-person and self-as-teacher are critical to the process of becoming a teacher because they constitute the personal context within which new information will be interpreted, and are the stuff of which a teaching persona is created. But not all self-images are of equal worth in terms of imagining the possible or creating pathways to attain it. The "child redeemer" (Grumet, 1983) or "Lady Bountiful" (Stonehouse, 1988) image occasionally may bring a warm glow of satisfaction that one is "doing good works," but such images do not help a beginning teacher imagine herself coping with ambiguities, negotiating conflicting demands, managing the inevitable dilemmas, and picking a path through the minefield of power relationships that together constitute the working environment for teachers. But self-images are important not only in terms of visions for the future, they also guide one's experience of the present. For example, Britzman (1991, p. 6) claims that for beginning teachers, the most powerful self-image is one that captures self as "the author of the teacher she is becoming."

Those entering teacher education programs do not have empty "How-to-Teach" compartments in their minds, waiting for teacher educators to fill. These adults already have lived full lives, and bring with them a lifetime of personal experiences, including a substantial body of personal knowledge about the work of teachers. As Lortie (1975) points out, by the time they enter college, students have spent thousands of hours living with teachers in classrooms, observing them, discussing them, criticizing them. Though they have not been privy to many of the complex deliberations and troublesome dilemmas that are the behind-the-scenes realities of teaching, students' minds are filled with their knowledge about teaching. From the teacher educators' perspective, this knowledge may be considered incomplete, and representative of the cultural myths and stereotypes of teaching, but for the student, it is what it is. It is *their* knowledge base, the means by which they make sense of their past experiences and the new ideas they encounter.

On the basis of their knowledge, beginning teachers typically conceptualize the process of learning to teach as a cumulative acquisition of concrete technical and organizational skills. For example, Angela Barritt (Barritt & Black, 1993, p. 73), a mature-age student teacher in Canada, wrote about her expectations as follows:

> When I finally did decide to go to university to become a teacher, I had a very clear vision of what it would be like. . . . I packed everything I knew about schools, about teachers, about learning, and about children. . . . I put my mothering experience with the rest and surveyed my inventory. . . . In my first two years at university I packed away more useful information. I was convinced that the more I accumulated on this journey, the better prepared I would be on arrival.
>
> [She later substantially modified her views on the process of becoming a teacher, after participating in an innovative student teaching program.]

This common conception of teacher education as a process of adding on, to a lay person, certain technical skills and desirable items of professional knowledge has been shared by many teacher educators as well as students. But increasingly, this conceptualization is being recognized as a very poor basis for making sense of the complex personal and interpersonal dynamics that characterize the whole process of becoming a teacher. As Britzman (1991, p. 10) suggests: "It is not a mere matter of applying decontextualized skills or mirroring predetermined images; it is a time when one's past, present, and future are set in dynamic tension."

Maxine Greene (1981) writes of becoming a teacher as a process of choosing yourself—making deeply personal choices about who you will be as a teacher. But this is not a solitary or self-contained process—it occurs in a time and place where others, some much more powerful than yourself, also are bent on "constructing" you, in an image they value (Britzman, 1991). Thus the whole process is heavily contextualized, not only in terms of the student's past and present, but also in terms of the past and present of the institutional context in which the program is located, and the past and present realities of the wider sociocultural and political context.

THE CONTEXT OF TEACHER EDUCATION: PAST AND PRESENT

Just as beginning teachers are largely future-oriented, so too is teacher education. Though the preservice years are neither the beginning nor the end of a teacher's story, they are an integral chapter, and teacher educators feel considerable responsibility for the futures of their students and the children they will teach. But teacher education programs also are being buffeted by forces in the present, some of which have little regard for long-term outcomes.

As we approach the closing years of this century, teacher education stakeholders are being guided by differing notions about what teachers will need in the years ahead, and different ideas about how best to prepare teachers to reach those goals. This is an exciting time for teacher education because there are a wealth of new insights emerging about the process of becoming a teacher, but it is also a frightening time, because so many of the routine practices of teacher education have been called into question. Those who work in preservice teacher education increasingly feel a tension between the need to explore uncertain innovations in their own practices, and the need to preserve their safety by relying on well-established practices.

Thus, for teacher educators as for beginning teachers, the process of teacher education is characterized by personal doubts as well as very public conflicts and questions. Teacher educators also are engaged in a process of becoming—of reconstructing ourselves as educators. As Miller (1992) suggests, this work can: "move us, I believe, from mechanistic, developmental, skill-oriented, end-product emphases in education, into reciprocal yet constantly shifting relationships with our students, with contents, and with ourselves as teachers" (p. 113).

Until the mid-1980s, the fundamental conceptualizations and practices of teacher education remained relatively stable. There were some substantive changes in content (for example, as paradigms shifted, new theories and research were presented) and in method (more technology was utilized, and new forms of assessment emerged), but the basic transmission pedagogy endured. The power relationships between teacher and taught, hierarchies of what (and whose) knowledge was most valued, and the overall practice of teacher education remained as it had been for decades—solidly entrenched in the history and practice of higher education.

This traditional "essentialist" (Delandshere & Petrosky, 1994, p. 11) model of teacher training had several strengths. Most notably, it reduced a complex and often ambiguous body of personal and professional knowledge to a relatively straightforward organizational chart, with separate items of knowledge or skills allocated to particular courses or semesters of the program. This gave both faculty and students a reassuring sense of where they were heading and what was to be achieved in a given time. It also made accountability appear much more solid, as each separate item literally could be checked off as the student proceeded through the program. And of course, it was always assumed that in the mind of the beginning teacher, this collection of fragments would somehow be recombined into the totality of "teaching" (McWilliam, 1994, p. 4). This traditional skills-based approach reached a peak of technical manifestation in the competency-based approaches to teacher training that were developed in most Western nations during the 1980s (Ruddick, 1992; McWilliam, 1994, p. 11).

The term "teacher *training*" is used to describe this approach because it is rooted in a set of minimalist assumptions about the competence and agency of the learners. In such a perspective, there is no place for a vision of unique and whole persons who are actively engaged in constructing their own idiosyncratic understandings of what it means to teach, using the totality of personal understandings, through a set of complex and dynamic interactions with others. As Ruddick (1992, p. 65) suggests, this narrow approach teaches beginning teachers to think about themselves as "deliverers of other people's policies, purveyors of other people's values, puppets moving to strings that are always manipulated by others."

Though this approach may be quite effective in helping beginning teachers acquire a set of basic technical skills, it offers little to help them understand their actions within the complex world of work, or to cope with the contradictions, dilemmas and ambiguities that characterize contemporary teachers' lives. Teaching is an "ill-structured" task, beset with problems for which there are multiple approaches and solutions (Delandshere & Petrosky, 1994, p. 11), and essentialist models of teacher education are unlikely to assist beginning teachers to decipher or address those problems. Narrowly technical self-images could well hinder their ability to imagine other possibilities for themselves and those they teach, other ways of being and doing that might help overcome some of the inequities and pain of life in contemporary society.

But though writers in teacher education may offer strong criticism of this traditional reproductive approach, there is much in contemporary university contexts and the wider society that acts to maintain and even extend it (Pratt, 1994). As the prevailing approach, it feels very comfortable and "safe" to many faculty and administrators. And though not always enjoyable for students, it is at least expected, and thus provides a degree of comfort and sense of safety for them also.

A strongly skills-based approach appeals to many outside the academy walls. This is a time when across many Western nations, university faculty are skeptically viewed as irrelevant and overvalued by some powerful members of society, and business analogies increasingly are being applied to sharpen criticisms of traditional scholarly work (Pratt, 1994). In such a climate, a focus on beginning teachers' acquisition of concrete technical skills appears to make a close connection between the world of higher education and the "real world" of employment. The approach does not involve a lot of esoteric language or obscure philosophical considerations. It is solid vocational education and to many within the field and society as a whole, this emphasis is seen as highly appropriate. As Pratt points out, though the faculty may continue to value a liberal education, "in the public at large, there is a growing consensus for a different kind of education, one that is skills-based and performance-tested" (p. 48).

The hierarchical power structures within the university also act to support the status quo. For the most part, students hold the low-power position—their knowledge has the lowest status in this community, and typically they feel at the mercy of the professors' grades, judgments they believe will determine their future employment prospects. But in many institutions, at the end of each semester, student power is dramatically increased, as students complete formal evaluations of professors. These grades are an important component of the data on which decisions are made about a professor's promotion or continuing employment. In the current climate of fierce competition for jobs, many students and professors share similar anxieties about their grades and their futures, and often, a similar nervousness about exploring innovative teaching and learning practices. Some failure is a necessary part of any creative endeavor, and support for innovation means the provision of a working environment where it is safe to take some risks. However, as the protection of tenure is weakened in universities in many Western nations, many faculty would argue that contemporary higher education institutions constitute an unsafe environment for exploring new visions and practices in teacher education.

Further, economic pressures on universities are leading to ever more parsimonious organizational structures in undergraduate education. Given current limitations on credit hours, it is indeed a challenge to provide the breadth of content deemed necessary and support for the in-depth personal exploration and gradual deepening of insight that we know is needed in the process of becoming a teacher. Of necessity rather than of professional judgment, often what is emerging in practice is a hurried, minimalist program, that may provide essential skills, but fails to do justice to the personal development of the participants (Ruddick, 1992).

New Views on Teachers and the Process of Becoming a Teacher

Emerging from this past and present context of teacher education is an extensive new literature that places much greater emphasis on the person in the process of becoming a teacher. It is drawn from a wide range of theoretical bases however, and the writers have little in common. Even within shared theoretical perspectives, there is ongoing debate over fine points of ideology, making it difficult to organize or summarize this body of literature.

Though many categorization schemes are possible, in this instance, the perspectives have been clustered in three broad groups: The first is readily self-identified as "constructivist" in orientation and these writers would claim some connection to the classic theories of Jean Piaget on the development of knowledge. Fosnot (1989) is one of the best known of the contemporary writers on applications of this theory to teacher education. The second cluster includes those who are concerned with the "Practical" perspectives on professional knowledge. These writers would claim connection to the classic works of Joseph Schwab (1969, 1971), and the large body of literature on reflective professional practice, within which Donald Schon (1983, 1987) is the acknowledged leader. The third cluster is the most wide-ranging one, and includes those who utilize understandings and concerns drawn more from the disciplines of sociology and philosophy, than from psychology. Included within this cluster are those who would describe themselves as critical pedagogists, poststructuralists, or feminists. They include Britzman (1991, 1994), Lather (1991), and Smyth (1987).

Across these diverse ideological positions, all writers are concerned with improving the quality of teacher education, and all advocate the power of their particular perspective in helping us better understand and support the process of becoming a teacher. (For example, Wildeen, Mayer-Smith, and Moon [1993, p. 7] call constructivism the "New Enlightenment" for teacher education.) Separately, they offer a number of significant insights about the person in the process, but it is not yet clear whether or how these insights might come together in a comprehensive understanding of those who are becoming teachers, or be coherently blended into new forms of practice.

CONSTRUCTIVIST VIEWS ON TEACHERS AND TEACHING

All of the approaches construe the person in the process as an active participant, not an empty receptacle for needed professional knowledge, but this is perhaps best captured by the constructivists, who "place the learner's mental activity at the center of any instructional exchange" (Noori, 1994, p. 3). Noori summarizes this position on the active learner as follows: "the learner poses problems as well as solves problems, makes inferences and investigates, resolves contradictions, and engages in reflection" (p. 4).

Constructivist teacher education shows a strong continuity between the teacher's work with children, and the teacher educator's work with beginning teachers. Constructivist approaches to teaching children have been developed over the last three decades, particularly in early childhood education (De Vries & Kohlberg, 1987; Donaldson, 1978; Kamii, 1982) and more recently have gained greater credence in math and science education (Cobb, 1994; Yager, 1993). In work with young learners, constructivists have emphasized the need to support children as they construct their own knowledge, providing environments and stimuli that will cause them to pose questions and create hypotheses to test (Brooks & Brooks, 1993). For the constructivists, the child is an inquirer, actively investigating the world around him/her, and building personal knowledge through the mental activity prompted by these encounters.

Increasingly, those who advocate constructivist approaches to teaching children also are advocating constructivist teacher education programs. They emphasize the continuity of human learning and development across all ages, and have very similar ways of viewing the child as constructor of knowledge and the beginning teacher. For example, beginning teachers too, are seen as inquirers—"scientists" or "researchers"—who need to develop skills in observing children, and methodically investigating and resolving problems in child learning. And like children, beginning teachers also are conceptualized as being theory builders; competent persons who have the intellectual power to create increasingly sophisticated understandings through their own cognitive work. The constructivist teacher is seen as an empowered thinker (Fosnot, 1989, p. 7), and teacher education as the process by which to support the learner's own mental activity.

Constructivist teacher education is highly integrated, and devises learning opportunities in which both content knowledge and pedagogy are explored in laboratory-like situations. Fosnot (1989) explains that beginning teachers "need to be part of a community that works with them *as learners* and then allows the experience to be dissected, evaluated, and reflected upon in order for principles of pedagogy and action to be constructed" (p. 21).

Field research also is highly valued in constructivist teacher education (Fosnot, 1989). Beginning teachers are placed in real-life classrooms, in which they investigate aspects of learning using an action research approach, and reflect on their own thinking about what they are observing. Such integrations of campus-based study and fieldwork are powerful in terms of the development of professional knowledge, and they also appeal to beginning teachers, because they are seen to have direct relevance to their personal development as teachers.

But constructivist teacher education has attracted the same criticisms as constructivist teaching at other levels, and reflects present-day concerns about the sufficiency of Piaget's theory as the basis for pedagogy. Piaget focused on developmental changes in people's intellectual abilities, and conceived of these changes basically as an individual psychological process—stimulated by contact with the external world, but occurring solely within the individual's mind. Piaget's theorizing was deeply rooted in the rationalism of mathematics and science, to the exclusion of other ways of knowing, other ways of thinking about the nature of the human condition. He made a massive contribution to our understandings about logico-mathematical thinking, but gave little attention to the learner as an interactive member of social groups, or a feeling, emotional creature, or an aesthetic being.

While the beginning teacher is conceptualized by the constructivists as being highly active in the process of knowledge acquisition,

interacting with the environment in order to construct new understandings, this learner also is seen as an individual intellectual mind,
developing as a result of contact with the external world, but not a creature of that world, embedded in a larger sociocultural and historical
context (O'Loughlin, 1991, p. 4).

In constructivist education, value is placed on increasingly objectified views of the world, and one of the tasks for the teacher educator
is prompting the learner to distance herself from the existing personal
theories held, so as to induce cognitive conflict, and ultimately, to allow
the emergence of new and better theories (O'Loughlin, 1991, p. 3). This
learner is not a multidimensional student engaged in a holistic process
of becoming a teacher, but a unidimensional learner engaged in a
process of constructing increasingly objectified personal knowledge of
a singular external reality.

But no perspective is free from criticism, and the constructivists'
view does have some powerful insights to offer, particularly for beginning teachers in early childhood teacher education, where the continuity of perspective between children's learning and their own experience
may help sensitize them to children's needs as learners, and cause them
to tailor their teaching decisions accordingly.

There are some similarities between the constructivists' views on
teachers and the process of learning to teach, and those in the Practical
cluster of perspectives, but there are also some noteworthy differences.

THE "PRACTICAL" VIEW ON TEACHERS AND TEACHING

Those writing from the Practical perspectives come to their understandings about the nature of teaching not via a theoretical base in
children's development of knowledge, but from collaborative investi-
gations in which practitioners examine their personal knowledge of
professional practice and the complexities of their working lives.

Despite the lay meaning of the term *practical*, these writers are not
concerned with narrow technicist concerns about what to do next,
"handy hints for teachers," or the acquisition of foolproof classroom
management skills. Rather, they see professional educational practice as
highly complex work that requires fine-grained interpretations, mastery of immense quantities of detail, and management of multiple concerns. These writers are concerned with philosophical issues about
what it means to teach, and pose probing questions about how it is that
practitioners manage the complexities and dilemmas of their practice.
As Maggie Lampert (1985) put it: "How *do* teachers manage to teach?"

For this group also, teachers are conceptualized as highly intellectual beings, but unlike the constructivist approach, the teacher is seen
much more holistically, with many interconnections among personal and
professional understandings, self-images, and lived experience. Like
Dewey, these writers emphasize the importance of personal experience in
the creation of individual understandings. For example, Butt, Raymond,
and Yamagishi (1988) say that "we need to understand how teachers
evolve, develop and change their practical knowledge [and] in the way
that they perceive their experience of it. These arguments bring with
them a regard for and an interest in the teacher as a unique *person*, and
the teacher as a *learner* who possesses a special type of knowledge" (p. 7).

Michael Connelly and D. Jean Clandinin (Clandinin, 1992; Connelly & Clandinin, 1987, 1988, 1990) have written extensively about
"personal practical knowledge," and this term has gained widespread
use among those who are interested in both the person and the practice
of teaching. For this group of writers, making a distinction between personal and professional knowledge, or knowledge and action, is not
meaningful. They believe that as the person who is the professional
makes decisions about practical action, she is drawing on the totality of
her knowledge, which is neither "personal" nor "professional," but a
unique blend of all sources of knowledge, held in idiosyncratic and
holistic images. As Kelchtermans and Vandenberghe (1994, p. 46) state,
teaching inevitably involves the teacher as person, and they quote Jen-
nifer Nias: "it matters to teachers themselves, as well as to their pupils,
who and what they are. Their self-image is more important to them as
practitioners than is the case in occupations where the person can easily
be separated from the craft" (Nias, 1989, quoted in Kelchtermans &
Vandenberghe, 1994, p. 46).

In the Practical perspectives, teachers are not seen as narrowly scientific in their work, they are seen as thinking and acting in complex,
contextual, and emotional ways. Kelchtermans and Vandenberghe
(1994) describe the ways teachers spontaneously think and talk about
their practice as: "narrative, embedded in concrete contexts, evocative,
suggestive and metaphorical" and claim their particular approach
avoids "too cognitivistic, rationalistic an approach, which would make
us lose . . . sight [of] the emotional, irrational and unconscious elements
in teachers' thinking and action" (p. 57).

This cluster of writers and thinkers is very interested in the
teacher's acquisition of personal practical knowledge, and how this
changes during the course of a career. This leads directly to concerns
about the nature of teacher education. For instance, Lampert and Clark
(1990, p. 21) write: "The ways in which teachers acquire and use knowl-

edge is contextual, interactive, and speculative." Given such understandings, the traditional transmission model of teacher education is
both inadequate and inappropriate. It gives scant attention to personal
knowledge, and its assumption that theoretical knowledge is acquired
in college courses, then later applied in practice, bears little resemblance
to the ways teachers talk about knowing and acting in their world of
work. Butt et al. (1988) describe this discrepancy as a "crisis in professional knowledge" and say the search for the "surefire" model of teaching has led to "the formation of bodies of professional knowledge
which have been largely ignored by professionals-in-action since they
have found little of this prescriptive technology is appropriate to specific situations whose nature is uniquely personal, instinctive, intuitive,
reflective, and practical" (p. 91).

Within this cluster of approaches, there is a seamless connection
between professional development for beginners and more experienced
teachers. Teachers at every point in their careers are seen as builders of
personal theories about professional matters, and great emphasis is
placed on the person coming to understand her own ways of thinking
about self and work. Professional development is conceptualized as a
process of ongoing self-scrutiny—considered thought about one's ways
of making sense of practical situations, the worth of one's actions
within those situations, and the imagining of other ways of acting.

A commitment to reflection is a common thread through all of the
contemporary views of teachers and professional practice, and Donald
Schon's (1983, 1987) writings on reflective practice have brought about
a major shift in the ways we think about teachers and teaching. Schon
saw the professional practitioner as concurrently engaged in both
thought and action, and helped us understand that the usual form of
expression for teacher knowledge may not be verbal description, but
practical action. To practice well, teachers need to be consciously thinking about the practical problems they face, their interpretations of those
situations, and the decisions they make. So educating reflective practitioners becomes largely a matter of developing the disposition to reflect, and ultimately finding the words to express those reflections to
others—through collaboration, building a shared language and a
shared knowledge of practice (Yinger, 1987).

One of the most contentious issues in the Practical cluster of perspectives centers on the extent to which the view of the teacher and
teaching is contextualized. Though those within claim they are concerned with the person in context, particularly the immediate working
environment (Kelchtermans & Vandenberghe, 1994, p. 49), external critics argue that this area is undertheorized and largely unattended. Crit-

ics suggest that writers from this cluster of perspectives still are drawing largely on cognitive psychology for their understandings (even though this connection is rarely surfaced by the Practical writers themselves), and that the focus remains on the individual teacher, rather than teachers in the historical or social context.

One approach that brings greater historical contextualization to the personal practical perspective is "autobiographical praxis" (Butt et al., 1988). Another that blends the personal with a wider social perspective is the action-research approach, which originated in the work of Chris Argyris and was later developed by Stephen Kemmis. This approach emphasizes the individual teacher not only as a researcher of personal professional practice, but also as a social change agent. For these writers, a better understanding of self is not sufficient; they are committed to taking action to right social injustices through educational change, and in this orientation, come closer to the Critical cluster (Day, 1993, pp. 84–85).

CRITICAL VIEWS ON TEACHERS AND TEACHING

The diverse cluster of theoretical perspectives here labeled as "Critical" is becoming the new mainstream of writings on teacher education. These writers are serving education well, by providing both macro- and microlevel analyses of the language and multiple realities of education in contemporary society, utilizing theoretical perspectives that previously were largely neglected in the study of education. They are motivated by strong moral convictions about social justice, and want to use their understandings to enhance schooling, a phenomenon they see as often silencing and failing large groups of children who are not members of the White middle class (Gomez, 1992, p. 170).

This group does not claim to provide concrete practical answers to the complex problems of schooling. Their contribution is in providing ways to think about, perhaps make fuller sense of teaching and education, so the injustices can be better identified and dealt with. Their discourse of teaching and learning is characterized by complexity, conflict, inherent ambiguities, and contradictions. For example, Britzman (1991), who describes herself as a poststructuralist, writes about the complex contradictory reality of education as follows: "teaching and learning have multiple and conflicting meanings that shift with other lived lives, with the theories produced and encountered, with the deep convictions and desires brought to and created in education, with the practices we negotiate, and with the ideas we construct" (p. 10).

Writers in these perspectives, while not totally negating the usefulness of thinking about teachers as individuals, argue that other approaches overemphasize the individual perspective, and fail to make clear the social construction of the phenomenon of teaching (Britzman, 1991, p. 8). They suggest that teachers and teaching can only be understood in terms of the wider social and cultural context. For example, Valerie Walkerdine (in O'Loughlin, 1991, p. 21) writes that we must: "theorize pedagogy in ways that take account of human subjectivity embedded in the social and historical contexts of people's lives."

Within these perspectives, the teacher once again is seen as a thinking being (O'Loughlin, 1991, p. 30) engaged in very demanding and often heavily conflicted work. They write of teaching as "grappling with contradictions," "working out compromises," "struggling with dilemmas," "working through conflicts" (O'Loughlin, 1991; Britzman, 1991, 1994). But through all of the demands of the working environment, the teacher does not remain a "stable humanistic self" (Britzman, 1994). Rather, the teacher has an identity that can "embrace displacement," that shifts as she encounters new challenges, new work environments, new social contexts, new questions, and new ideas (Britzman, 1994, p. 63).

This body of writing offers rich new insights on the process of becoming a teacher. It provides a framework by which to explore the dilemmas and conflicts that are inherent in the process, and it helps identify some of the tensions that arise as multiple realities are encountered and constructed, both in the interpersonal and intrapersonal spheres. But like all of the perspectives discussed, these Critical views are not easily enacted in the practices of teacher education. Even with this greater depth of understanding, many of the practical and organizational dilemmas and conflicts remain. And other dimensions of the process that previously went unnoticed, are surfaced and problematized by these new understandings.

When we have dismantled the whole process of learning to teach—at least as far as our current thinking allows—we may be better able to identify and understand the components, but some areas of unknown complexity and murky ambiguity still remain. As teacher educators, we face many questions about how to reshape and reassemble these parts, to create models of teacher education that are sensitive to and more supportive of the person in the process. Bringing theoretical or ideological positions into concrete practical reality is always a messy business. Even when one is committed to honoring the diverse knowledge constructions of diverse beginning teachers, dogma has a sneaky way of replacing dogma (Wildeen et al., 1993, p. 7).

NEW VISIONS FOR OLD: ONGOING DILEMMAS IN PRACTICAL ENACTMENT OF TEACHER EDUCATION

Given the diversity of their theoretical origins, it is somewhat surprising that the new forms of practice emerging in teacher education have anything in common, but despite their very different origins and pathways, the practical destinations do share some commonalities. One of the strongest commonalities is the commitment to developing reflection. In all three clusters of perspectives, writers agree the professional educator should be living an examined life, engaged on a never-ending search for self-knowledge, seeking deeper understandings, and ongoing reflection on elements of personal interpretations and actions. Without it, Carr (in Ruddick, 1992, p. 163) suggests, teachers will be either "inherently conservative or dangerously doctrinaire." But across the range of perspectives, quite different types of reflection are valued.

REFLECTION IN THE PRESERVICE YEARS

A number of different categorization schemes have been proposed to describe various types of reflection by teachers (Handal, 1990, in Day, 1993; Van Manen, 1977; Zeichner & Liston, 1987), and though the labels may vary, the categorization schemes all assume multiple levels. The most basic level of reflection is seen to be focused on one's concrete actions (Handal), or the formal subject matter of instruction, which Zeichner and Liston label "academic." But such a shallow level of reflection would satisfy none of the contemporary writers in teacher education.

At a little higher level comes what Zeichner and Liston (1987) call "social efficiency" and Handal (in Day, 1993) calls "practical-theoretical." This can best be captured in the phrase "What works?" and it encompasses much of the pragmatic decision-making that teachers do—consciously considering various practical strategies and making choices between them. This type of reflection makes good sense to many beginning teachers. It fits their conception of successful teaching as the application of "the right" or "the best" technical skill. As they accumulate more concrete strategies from which to select, their confidence in their progress in becoming a teacher is likely to increase (at least as long as the strategies appear to work when they try them out). So beginning teachers see immediate practical worth in methods courses that provide a lot of practical ideas, and give them the opportunity to try out the strategies and evaluate them. This pragmatic level of

reflection fits the traditional skills-based approaches to teacher education, and can sit comfortably alongside foundational courses that simply aim to transmit public domain theoretical knowledge.

But this level of reflection offers the beginning teacher little help in
understanding what it means to say something "does or doesn't work,"
or understanding situations where powerful people hold differing opinions on whether the strategy is a worthwhile one. Beginning teachers
feel at the mercy of differing opinions both within the university and beyond it in schools. They feel the need for certainty in their uncertain
lives, and formal evaluations of their progress, as well as their sense of
well-being, are threatened when they encounter powerful people who
think differently. As student teachers encounter the conflicted multiple
realities of real-life classrooms, and have to tussle with the ambiguities
and uncertainties of professional practice, this pragmatic type of reflection is a poor mental tool to help them make sense of what is going on.

Just as children's early aesthetic development is a matter of clear-
cut likes and dislikes (Parsons, 1987), beginning teachers utilizing this
type of reflection form strongly held opinions about whether they will
be "this type of teacher" or whether they will "never teach that way."
While this dichotomous thinking may be a necessary step along the
way to creating a persona as a teacher, it is not an acceptable end point
in terms of understanding the complexities of personal professional actions within given contexts, so this pragmatic reflection also would be
considered grossly inadequate by virtually all of the writers represented here.

Zeichner and Liston (1987) suggest a specific type of teacher reflection they call "developmentalist," which focuses on the child's
needs, interests, and abilities, and not surprisingly, this aligns well with
the constructivist approach in teacher education. This approach places
students in environments where they can observe real phenomena,
pose questions about them, and then investigate those questions, all the
time reflecting about the changes that are occurring in their own knowledge base. They are encouraged to be active participants, and to be di-
aloging with others about what they are finding. However, in many
cases, the object of study is not the phenomenon of teaching itself, but
the substantive content matter. In constructivist courses devoted to
early childhood science pedagogy, for example, beginning teachers are
sometimes asked to observe the world of nature (Duckworth, 1987),
and to make hypotheses about the changes that are occurring in what is
observed and why (Noori, 1994).

But the approach also can be applied to the study of teaching itself. For example, in a small but interesting pilot program at Northeast

Missouri State University (Novinger & Conner, 1995), five undergraduate students formed teams to complete an action research project of their own design, while teaching part-time in the on-campus child development center for preschoolers. This gave them a highly meaningful opportunity to investigate both children's learning and their own teaching, and through weekly seminars with faculty members, a dialogue about personal practice and issues of teaching was established that would have been impossible to emulate in a traditional university classroom.

Even with the relatively modest scope of developmentalist reflection, however, it is difficult to be sure about the extent or authenticity of the beginning teacher's reflections. For example, in the program described by Noori (1994, p. 31) much of the reflection and dialogue between faculty and beginning teachers in journals appeared limited to technical matters. Beginning teachers were described as videotaping themselves teaching, then "reflecting on their actions." When a student wrote a journal entry including some criticism of her level of preparation for the problems of real classrooms, the deeper underlying issues were not acknowledged in the faculty member's response, which was basically an admonition to "keep trying." But elsewhere, Noori does write of students' more penetrating reflections, which examine critical social issues arising from their personal experiences as African American children in White-majority schools. So it appears this program does support the disposition to reflect on one's life experiences, even if the constructivist theoretical framework is not particularly powerful in helping beginning teachers understand their own experiences in the sociocultural and professional world.

The depth and range of reflection valued in the Practical cluster of perspectives could be placed somewhere in the middle region of the categorization schemes. Both experienced and beginning teachers are asked to think not only about their practical actions, but to probe the deeper personal meanings and origins of their ideas and actions. In this perspective, the person needs to know, and to be very comfortable with, her personal theories and beliefs.

Day (1993, p. 87) believes that teachers constantly switch back and forth between public and personal theories, and suggests they need to understand and try to articulate the links between the public and personal knowledge that exist within themselves. As Tripp (1994, p. 74) suggests, the teacher needs to be problematizing her own history, constantly reworking it, thinking about its meanings, and coming to terms with it. This scope of reflection also includes thinking about self in terms of the current context, particularly examining one's place in the immediate community of the school. The target of reflection is not only the professional self, but also the personal emotional self (Kelchtermans & Vandenberghe, 1994, p. 57). As Clandinin (1986) suggests, feelings are the "glue" that holds the image of self together, and one's sense of being alienated or belonging, or feeling safe or under threat, will have a major impact on one's interpretations of events and one's practical responses. So these teacher educators try to help beginning teachers surface and talk about their feelings, as they work through the challenges of learning to teach.

Teacher educators imbued with this set of ideas about the importance of personal practical knowledge try to create environments for learning that assist beginning teachers to look deep inside their own experiences, to understand where they have come from and are going to as teachers. In the term favored by Pinar (in Butt et al., 1988, 105), they have to understand their "personal architecture" if they are to understand who they are as teachers.

In these approaches, beginning teachers are taught that answers to the problems of teaching do not lie in other people's theories, but within themselves, so considerable attention is given to learning about self, as well as about children and schooling (Barritt & Black, 1993, p. 81). Facilitating this level of reflection poses many difficulties and dilemmas for the teacher educator (Day, 1993, p. 86). To promote in beginning teachers, a trust in self as a knower, teacher educators have to reconstruct themselves as teachers. They have to learn *not* to be the expert (Barritt & Black, 1993, p. 82) and find ways to minimize the interpretive distance that separates beginning teachers, university faculty, and professionals in the field.

In their routine interactions with beginning teachers, these teacher educators need to be cognizant of and comfortable with multiple realities, and learn to delay the urge to correct or authorize a single position. With considerable skill, the teacher educator can create situations that gradually cause the beginning teacher to question her own interpretations and to seek ever-deeper insights.

Recognizing the worth of others' constructed knowledge, accepting their inherent responsibility for the creation of their own understandings, yet at the same time acknowledging the worth of one's own position, and wanting others to appreciate its value, is the paradox that lies at the heart of many practical dilemmas faced by teacher educators within the Practical perspective. The question "Whose knowledge counts?" is indeed a vexing one for these educators. They would like to answer "Everyone's," but in practice, the answer is not always as clear-cut as one would wish.

Though deeper and more wide-ranging than the constructivist approach, the level of reflection favored by the Practical writers still is seen by those in the Critical cluster as insufficient. They argue that in the Practical approach, the beginning teacher is not forced to confront the degree of adequacy of her beliefs or ideas. A phrase that occurs frequently in the writings on personal practical knowledge is the need to "feel comfortable" with your beliefs, learning to trust yourself and your ways of understanding the world. But "feeling comfortable" is not a desirable state for those in the Critical cluster. There needs to be a rupture of old ways of thinking; the person needs to "break with habitual ways of recognizing and dealing with situations" (MacKinnon & Erickson, 1992, p. 199). As Day (1993, p. 88) concludes: "reflection is a necessary but not sufficient condition for learning. Confrontation either by self or others must occur."

In the practice of preservice teacher education, confrontation is a delicate business. With a great deal of sensitivity and skill, teacher educators can nudge (Brunner, 1994, p. 52) or steer beginning teachers toward questioning their own beliefs. But if the path is too direct, or the steering too heavy-handed, the beginning teacher's fragile confidence in self as a knower can shatter, and the teacher educator is once again recast as "the authority" in the university classroom. For example, as the feminist teacher educator Brunner (1994, p. 53) discloses, even as she tries to break with authoritarian traditions, she sometimes finds herself replacing lecturing with equally directive practices that are steeped in domination. These traditional practices typically have become a part of who we are as teacher educators, and even with a high level of consciousness, and a strong desire to change, it can be extraordinarily difficult to rid ourselves of them. For a long time, the new practices still feel strange to us; we are not yet familiar with our new selves and this still-emerging knowledge of our practice.

The second criticism of reflection in the Practical cluster relates to the largely individualized nature of these reflections. To most writers in the Critical cluster, reflection is seen not as an individual process but as a social one—a form of "political action" that is embedded in a given history and is shaped by (as well as shaping) ideology (Kemmis, in Day, 1993, p. 85). Contrary to the claim of personal practical knowledge writers that many answers to teaching problems lie within oneself, the British writer Christopher Day argues that the solutions to the problems facing education will not lie within the minds of individual teachers, but will require much more public, collaborative reflective efforts: "the notion of the professional as someone who should be licensed to define his/her own needs, to find her/his own ways of meeting these in the interests of the children at school, to plan, teach, evaluate largely in private, is being examined and challenged" (p. 87).

He may well be correct, particularly given the level of scrutiny and control that characterizes contemporary British education systems (Ruddick, 1992, p. 157), but the notion of personal agency and responsibility is central to the whole concept of "professional." Some level of "collaborative" reflections to build a shared knowledge base of practice is valued by all writers in contemporary teacher education, but one wonders what is left if the individual educator doesn't have some sense of personal ownership of the collective reflections that supposedly are to guide her future actions. Such a distanced entity would seem to come closer to "organizational policy" or "system requirement," than to "reflection."

The form of reflection most valued by the Critical writers is at the highest point on the hierarchies, what Zeichner and Liston (1987) term "social reconstructivist" and Handal (in Day, 1993) describes as "ethical." This form of reflection is both social and confrontive. It problematizes every dimension of educational practice, and examines the realities of schooling as products of the social and political context. It asks practitioners to probe their own class, race, and gender experiences and to examine the ways these experiences have shaped their construction as teachers and their practices (Gomez, 1992, p. 171). Diane Brunner (1994) describes this type of reflection as a "moment of radical praxis, when the interlocking wires of constraint and possibility are loosened and we act, even if tentatively, to meld struggle with potential" (p. 47).

In this type of reflection, the work is never done—no one can provide final answers, and no one ever comes to "feel comfortable" with her identity, because that identity is not a stable, fixed phenomenon, but something that shifts as the context changes. This is a view of teaching that is indefinitely uncertain, never fully knowable, so that the teacher can only be engaged in an ever more critical reading of what Maxine Greene calls "the texts of action" (in Britzman, 1991, p. x). The complexity is well captured in Deborah Britzman's (1991) conceptualization of the process of learning to teach as dialogic. She says the process is "situated in relationship to one's biography, present circumstances, deep commitments, affective investments, social context and conflicting discourses about what it means to learn to become a teacher" (p. 8).

In many ways, this type of reflection specifically asks beginning teachers *not* to trust themselves, but to continue to question everything they think they believe in; to deconstruct what they know. For example, Diane Brunner (1994) writes of the positive value of uncertainty: "The self who critiques against the self may be uncertain, but that uncertainty does not suggest lack of awareness or lack of concern or even lack of ability to act; uncertainty in this instance may reveal instead the organic nature of critical constructive thought that is embedded in controversy, and that shifts and sorts and emerges forever containing seeds of what is past and what is possible" (p. 60).

Even for a mature, well-educated person, with a disposition for scholarly inquiry, such probing self-analysis is a difficult habit to acquire and to hold to, especially through the challenging moments of one's own professional practice. Paradoxically, it requires a level of personal confidence and tolerance for multiplicity that is often elusive, even for the most competent teachers and teacher educators. For beginning teachers, whose lives already are filled with uncertainty, and whose confidence is often fragile at best, acquiring and maintaining this level of reflection is especially difficult. Their preexisting understandings of teaching and the process of learning to teach rarely provide them with a strong personal sense of "needing to know" about these complex ideas, and descriptions of the Critical perspectives often are written in a language that is virtually incomprehensible to beginning teachers (McWilliam, 1994, p. 2). Even as it is urging practitioners to give voice to the inherent contradictions in their lives, the language of the Critical perspectives sometimes creates greater distance between the practitioner and the ideas. Though these insights may be extremely valuable to beginning teachers, the esoteric nature of the communication all too often conveys a subliminal message of personal inadequacy.

Thus it falls to the teacher educator, in this mode, to try to create, for beginning teachers, situations in which the "need to know" about these complexities of professional practice will become self-evident, and to find ways of communicating these insights that will connect with the person and not unintentionally pose a threat to her self-efficacy. It is paradoxical that the teacher educator should have to play the role of translator for these perspectives, because the Critical writers have much to say about the need for greater egalitarianism—more equal power relationships between the knowledge of the teacher and the taught. Yet as translator, the teacher educator is reenacting her authority over knowledge. So even as the substance of that knowledge is advocating empowerment of learners, it is the ideology of the teacher educator that continues to hold the dominant position in the university classroom.

To help beginning teachers become reflective practitioners, teacher educators also need to be reflective practitioners, but one has to wonder how well the institutional context of contemporary teacher education can support this reconstruction of teacher educators and their practices. For example, Day (1993) suggests that in order to promote greater reflection, the educational institution needs to be characterized by power relationships that are collegial rather than adversarial, and have a shared commitment to building a culture of enquiry (Day, 1993, p. 90). These are worthy goals for all schools of teacher education, but in many cases, the goal is not yet the reality. As Calderhead (1993, p. 99) suggests, there are "enormous difficulties" to be resolved in developing more reflective practice in the preservice years, and undoubtedly some difficulties we have not even identified as yet. But this is work that needs to be done. As Ruddick (1992, p. 164) states, if teachers are to learn from critical study of their own practice throughout their careers, this activity needs to be legitimized during the preservice years. Finding ways to promote beginning teachers' development as reflective practitioners is not a matter of adopting a few new strategies for course requirements or class formats. It goes to the very heart of our existence as a community of scholars, located within a constellation of contexts, and requires fundamental changes in how we think about ourselves and enact our own work.

STORIES IN TEACHER EDUCATION

A strategy that long has been a part of teacher education, but seldom has been acknowledged until recent years, is that of story sharing (Clandinin, 1992, p. 125). Indeed, some would argue that teacher education, as a set of practices, is itself a "discursive production" (McWilliam, 1994, p. 3). For generations, teacher educators have shared personal stories of their own or others' practice as a way to help beginners understand some practical or theoretical point, and untold numbers of beginning teachers have told each other tales of their own experiences in the field—tales of heroics, hilarity, and horror (McLean, 1991). But with the emergence of new ways of thinking about the process of becoming a teacher, work with stories has gained new credibility, and the role of story in professional development is now the subject of serious educational research (Carter, 1993).

People lead "storied lives" (Bruner, 1986; Rosenwald & Ochberg, 1992). It is not our concrete experiences that shape our sense of identity, but the stories we tell ourselves (and exchange with other people) about those experiences. Our stories become the means by which we make sense of our past, our present, and our future, even as the stories themselves gradually "fuse" with new stories, as new experiences occur (Widdershoven, 1993, p. 7).

Work with stories is favored by writers in all three clusters described here, but the Practical writers believe that stories of practice have particular relevance for teachers (Carter, 1993; Connelly & Clandinin, 1988; Witherell & Noddings, 1991). Given that so much of what teachers know is held tacitly, personal particularistic stories provide teachers with a way to communicate their practical knowledge, and build shared understandings of practice (Kelchtermans & Vandenberghe, 1994). Thus, for the Practical writers, narrative features strongly both in the methodology of knowledge generation about teaching and in the substance of what is known. As Clandinin (1992, p. 124) writes: "[We need to] highlight the importance of making sense of teachers' and students' lives as narratives of experience, a living-out of the stories we tell ourselves in order to make meaning of our experience."

Across teachers' careers, story sharing is linked to professional development, and in the preservice years, stories connect to, and build connections within the person who is becoming a teacher. Through stories, abstract ideas can be concretized in ways that enhance the construction of personal meaning, but they are much more than effective communicative devices. They also are integrative ones. As Brunner (1994, p. 58) says, "In narrative, we weave the fabric of our lives (and others), connecting information with experience to construct knowledge.'"

In the emerging practices of contemporary teacher education, two very different uses of stories are being developed. The first is autobiographical in nature, and is closely related to developing reflective practice. The second involves the use of richly detailed written stories of teachers' lives, careers, and daily work.

Autobiographical work with stories is based in the same set of assumptions as reflective practice—that the teacher needs to know herself well, and that an important component of that self-knowledge will involve investigation of one's personal history. Butt et al. (1988) have explicated the interconnection between teacher knowledge and personal experience and suggest that "knowledge and predispositions to act in certain ways in the present moment is grounded as much, if not more so, in life history than just current contexts and action; it is autobiographic in character" (p. 151).

As beginning teachers recover their own stories, they are reflecting on who they are, how they have come to be, and who they are becoming. The autobiographical approach seeks understanding of the self (or of multiple selves) by examining one's past; considering the interactions between the person and the context that have helped shape the "complex, multidimensional and dynamic system of representations and meanings" (Kelchtermans & Vandenberghe, 1994, p. 47) that we know as "self." But this does not lead only to a better understanding of a given self, it also is a way to "recover their own possibilities" (Miller, 1992, p. 114) and to forge new, more powerful selves.

This is not an exercise in solo reflection. Indeed, it is argued that stories about the self are inherently social. They are always "communal" or "participatory" in nature (Kelchtermans & Vandenberghe, 1994, p. 47), so in preservice teacher education, the sharing of one's stories with others is essential. This sharing needs to be a process in which both students and professors are engaged as participants. The teacher educator as much as the beginning teacher is involved in restorying her life and work, in this narrative inquiry approach to teacher education. As Clandinin (1992, p. 131) suggests, shared stories are both "given and given back in the context of relationships," and the responses from all participants reflect the contexts within which the stories are told. From the discussion around shared stories, in contexts where mutual trust is high, the original teller begins to see new interpretations, new possibilities for self.

With experienced teachers, story sharing as a form of collaborative professional development often is focused on specific incidents of one's past practice, the "critical incidents" of one's career (Tripp, 1994), but in preservice teacher education, where teaching experience usually is limited, many stories are drawn from childhood experience—from a time when one was on the other side of the educational fence.

Accessing the more deeply rooted dimensions of your own story, such as the influences of class background, or ethnicity, is much more difficult, but this is the type of work with stories that is most valued by the Critical writers. As O'Loughlin (1991) says: "By providing opportunities for students to speak and write about their own autobiographical experiences, teachers affirm students' social and cultural identities, and they also enable students to externalize the socially and historically constituted nature of their selves, and thus make this available for critical reflection and possible transformation" (p. 28).

Though these deeply rooted dimensions are present in every story we tell, drawing them into consciousness and finding words to express them takes determination, time, and a lot of support from others. But for those in the Critical cluster, these are essential requirements if beginning teachers are to attain the level of socially and personally critical consciousness that is needed.

The second major use of stories in preservice teacher education is centered on the exploration of other people's stories as teachers. Over the last five years, the literature on teaching has burgeoned with teacher stories, including case studies of particular teachers, personal accounts of teaching, and stories collaboratively written with narrative researchers. This literature is a very rich resource, not only because it extends the repertoire of the teacher educator's stories of practice (Tamir, 1991), but also the story form draws in the readers to become participants in the story. Beginning teachers are able to think themselves into the story, imagine how it feels to be that teacher, and to identify possible alternative images for the self (Clandinin, 1992, p. 136). Such explorations carry a high level of personal meaning and can be a springboard to further examination of one's image of self as a teacher. As the focus shifts from another's story to one's own, it is as if the frame around a portrait of a teacher gradually is transformed into the frame of a mirror. The reader begins by focusing externally on the teacher within the frame, but as she looks deeper, the image and focus of attention gradually becomes the self.

At first glance, this type of work with stories seems relatively straightforward, but it too conceals many hidden complexities and dilemmas for the teacher educator. Firstly, it calls for a high level of trust in the learners. One has to have faith that beginning teachers *will* gain valuable insights from the story, because when one introduces a story for exploration, one is never quite sure what the story is about. These are not simple "stories with a moral," but accounts that try to capture the complexity and ambiguities of teaching, so hermeneutically, it may be a different story for each individual or group of readers. If the teacher educator is to honor the multiple realities of teaching and becoming a teacher, all interpretations need to be accepted. And therein lie many dilemmas.

To illustrate, *"Bobbie's Story,"* and *"Bobbie's Story of Jake"* (McLean, McGraw, Reese, Danzig, & Aleman, unpublished manuscript) were collaboratively written narratives of a first-grade teacher that were utilized with several different groups of undergraduates.

Bobbie was teaching a regular first-grade class for only the second time, after several years as a special education teacher. She was worrying about Jake, a six-year-old, because of his lack of progress in learning to read. Bobbie suspected that "Jake's problem" might be attributed to a learning disability, but she also thought his very poor attendance, "poor home life," and low social skills also might be involved.

Originally the story had been crafted as part of a narrative research project exploring multiple perspectives on parent-professional encounters, but because the story also addressed difficult issues of early literacy—particularly the question: "When does a literacy delay become a major problem?"—it was used as the basis of a workshop in an undergraduate early childhood language arts class.

Despite a careful introduction about the need to understand the complexities of teachers' work, and to try to suspend judgment about this individual teacher, from the first comments in the discussions that followed, this became a story about "poor teaching." These beginning early childhood teachers agreed there was only one possible interpretation of the story: Bobbie had no understanding of emergent literacy and was doing a poor job of meeting Jake's needs. Similarly, when the story was used with beginning special educators, they agreed that Bobbie was at fault, not for the inadequacies of her understanding of emergent literacy (this was outside of their professional knowledge base), or the narrowness of her definition of the problem, but because she had failed to follow legislative guidelines in fully including parents in decision making about diagnostic actions. (These students felt confident in their knowledge of legislative requirements in special education.)

Just like any person, these readers were able to make sense of Bobbie's story only in terms of their existing knowledge. They drew support from peers who shared that knowledge, to narrow and harden their interpretations to the point of certainty. Given the nature of their understandings at the time, they had no language to explore the conflicted realities and practical dilemmas that teachers like Bobbie face in their daily lives. But though the speed and rigidity of their interpretations were alarming to the professors involved, the story at least provided a way to begin a dialogue that ultimately would help them see more of the multiple perspectives that were possible in this complex real-life situation.

Stories provide a vehicle by which to problematize beginning teachers' interpretations, and gradually help them question the adequacy of their views, but this is not something that can be achieved in one story, or one class period. These changes occur slowly, and the teacher educator must learn to live with a lack of closure, to have faith that over time, and with careful support, beginning teachers will move toward personal interpretations that are more cognizant of conflicts and complexities. But to facilitate this process, the teacher educator needs to resist the temptation to reoccupy the classic authority position of the university teacher, saying in effect: "Okay, now I'll tell you what the story *really* means." She needs to see the value of trusting the beginning teachers' interpretation and striving to understand it, even if personally she disagrees with it (Clandinin, 1992, p. 130).

This is one of the fundamental discomforts of the teacher educator working with stories—one has to overcome the desire to tell the learners what you think they should know, authorizing only one interpretation of the story. As O'Loughlin (1991, p. 28) emphasizes, what needs to occur is an intersection of the teacher's and student's ways of knowing. And, in this social process, all members of the class community need to be involved in retelling and responding to each other's stories in ways that deepen the insights of all participants. For the teacher educator, this type of practice calls for understandings, personal dispositions and skills that only now are being named and described. The pedagogy of stories in teacher education still is in its infancy.

Stories of teaching provide more than raw data on professional practice. They can help cross barriers between personal and public knowledge. As Brunner (1994, p. 57) states: "The only way to construct knowledge is to first make sense of the new by seeing how it fits into our lives—making the public personal, the political private." In a reversal of the traditional sequence of teacher education practice, where a generalized principle is introduced first, then a particularistic anecdote is used to illustrate that principle, stories can provide a powerful personal means of anchoring public knowledge. When a richly detailed, real-life story is provided first, the reader is drawn in to the situation, involved in the process of assigning meaning, and often takes on some personal identification with the story. If the teacher educator has the desire and the skill to "prolong the uncertainty" (Brunner, 1994, p. 47) and encourage beginning teachers not to lock into one interpretation prematurely, public domain theories then acquire real meaning and relevance, as new ways to expand, perhaps enhance thinking about the events in the story. The story becomes part of the context by which to make sense of the theory, and vice versa.

NEW MODELS OF TEACHER EDUCATION

This ongoing reexamination of personally meaningful material, weaving together exploration of others' stories with recreations of one's own, reflection on public domain and personal theories, and shared reflections on one's first-hand experiences, all suggests a very different teacher education. In this process, there could not be a host of discrete courses, each with a formal syllabus that, in advance, assigned a new topic to each week. There would need to be time to explore ideas together, and time to talk. Dialogue would be indispensable (O'Loughlin, 1991, p. 28). There would need to be flexibility to examine the urgent issues that emerged, and opportunities to address concerns of the beginning teachers, rather than only the concerns of the professor. There would need to be opportunities to recycle through ideas and dilemmas, repeatedly coming back to old discussions and creating new stories around them.

These new approaches to facilitating the development of the persons who are enrolled in preservice programs are not easily integrated on a small scale within existing models of teacher education. They call for more than changes in an individual teacher educator's personal professional practice. They require substantial shifts in collective thinking, in program organization, and in the relationships between the university and the professional field.

Across several nations, alternative programs are attempting to build new models of teacher education that are more person-centered and more attuned to the sociocultural context. Although based on different theoretical frameworks, these programs have a good deal in common. Most notably, they are built around notions of collaboration and ongoing personal relationships. In these programs, professional knowledge is not conceived as something distant and esoteric, that is the intellectual property of university faculty. It is seen as personal; something that is developed through close ongoing contacts among all participants. The source of knowledge in these programs is not limited to empirical research on child development, learning or teaching, but also is seen as originating in personal experience, shared understandings, and the wisdom of practice. Such programs strive to make everyone's knowledge count, and involve university faculty, school personnel, and beginning teachers in a collaborative experience in which all are respected as both teachers and learners.

Traditionally, preservice education of teachers has involved a substantial component of field-experience, that has made school personnel partners in the business of teacher preparation, but over the long term, this often has been an uneasy relationship. The world of university-based teacher education and the world of schools have spoken different languages, been characterized by different issues, different perspectives on what teaching is about, and very uneven power relationships in preservice education. All of these factors have created a very conflicted practicum context in which beginning teachers must survive, perform, and, hopefully, learn.

In many ways, the practicum experience at the end of traditional preservice programs encapsulates all of the conflicts inherent in becoming a teacher—being a student, yet at the same time, needing to act like a teacher; being both learner and performer concurrently. As Brunner (1994, p. 49) suggests: "We ask them to perform, to model, to have their acts together, to preserve the dignity of their teacher education programs, at the same time that they are trying to survive as strangers in a strange land."

The practicum also is the most paradoxical element in the preservice years. It can be the best of times or the worst of times for beginning teachers, the time when they perceive they have learned the most, or an experience so harrowing, they feel lucky to survive. The constructivists Wildeen et al. (1993), in reviewing data from fifteen empirical studies of practicum experiences, found both ends of this spectrum. They suggest that differences in beginning teachers' experiences during the practicum can best be accounted for in terms of perceived control. When students felt powerless—at the mercy of their evaluators or the children they were trying to teach—they retreated to a passive stance, and hoped only for survival. Wildeen et al. state: "Where students were struggling for control, we heard frustration, anger, and bewilderment" (p. 8). When students were involved in programs that encouraged them to problem-find and problem-solve their own practice, and where exploration and reflection were encouraged without the threat of negative evaluations, students were extremely positive about their practicum experiences.

The traditional approach of a practicum at the very end of the pre-service program has been enhanced by the myth that this was when what was learned in the previous years would "all come together." This was supposed to be the "authentic moment" (Britzman, 1991, p. 7) in becoming a teacher. For some lucky individuals, the myth may also have been the reality, but it is grounded in a technical rationalist set of assumptions about learning theories and skills in the "pure" isolation of the university, then unproblematically "putting them into practice in the real world" of classrooms (MacKinnon & Erickson, 1992, p. 195). This view has little responsiveness to either the learning processes of the beginning teacher, or the complexities of professional practice in the field.

Many of the alternative programs (Barritt & Black, 1993; Clandinin, 1992; Nagel & Driscoll, 1991; Gomez, 1992; Noori, 1994; Ruddick, 1992; Novinger & Conner, 1995) have dealt with the dilemmas of a final (high-stakes) practicum by replacing it with more integrated, longer-term blends of on-campus work and fieldwork. During these integrated blocks of time—up to nine months in some cases—beginning teachers spend most of their time in schools. The campus-based classes are transformed into weekly seminars, in which supervising teachers, beginning teachers, and faculty members all play a role in sharing ideas, raising questions, and introducing topics for further investigation. In such teacher education programs, the curriculum is indeed a matter of negotiation among all the participants.

These innovative programs claim noteworthy success, but typically they operate on a small scale, with carefully selected students, university faculty, and school personnel who share similar personal and professional commitments. These innovative programs are of great interest, and serve as a beacon of hope for a future of teacher education that will be sensitive to the persons in the process, but there are many practical, ideological, and organizational dilemmas still to be resolved, before these approaches can go to scale and become the mainstream of teacher education.

CONCLUSION

Across the literature and practices of teacher education, there is a wealth of new insights about the person in the process of becoming a teacher. The simple unidimensional image of the hollow student, compliantly waiting to be filled with professional knowledge and skills, has been replaced by a complex multifaceted person—people with a lifetime of personal and social experiences behind them, embedded in a present in which they are totally engaged as meaning makers, constructors of knowledge, and authors of the teachers they are becoming.

To understand this process of becoming, we cannot focus on the beginning teacher alone. We also must consider the contexts in which this process is located, and out of which it is constructed. Intra-individual understandings can never tell the whole story, for the individuals, the interactive process of becoming a teacher, and our ways of perceiving the whole process are all heavily context-dependent. To understand the phenomenon of becoming a teacher, we also need to extend the focus to include all of the traveling companions, because as so many contemporary writers have described, teacher educators, no less than the students they teach, also are engaged in a process of becoming.

The struggle to develop new pedagogies of teacher education that are sensitive to our new understandings of the persons in the process never will be concluded. Whether we describe it as "restorying," "unlearning," "reconceptualizing," or "searching for new plots," what is clear is that the certainty of knowing "which is best," is now an artifact of a bygone era; certainly a simpler time, but also a more ignorant, unjust time. For teacher educators, as for beginning teachers, this personal journey of becoming will last our entire careers.

NOTES

1. The phrase "beginning teachers" is utilized to describe those persons enrolled in preservice teacher education programs. Though formal entry to

the profession of teaching occurs only at the point of graduation, the process of becoming a teacher begins on entry to the program. This is when the person is asked to think like a teacher, and enters classrooms wearing the mantle of teacher.

2. To maintain a personal focus in this writing and avoid the rhetorical awkwardness of the more inclusive male/female personal pronouns, singular female pronouns are used throughout. This is not meant to exclude male participants in the process.

REFERENCES

Barritt, A. N., & Black, K. E. (1993). Becoming. In D. J. Clandinin, A. Davies, P. Hogan, & B. Kennard (Eds.), *Learning to teach, teaching to learn* (pp. 72–83). New York: Teachers College Press.

Britzman, D. P. (1991). *Practice makes practice: A critical study of learning to teach.* Albany: State University of New York Press.

Britzman, D. P. (1994). Is there a problem with knowing thyself? Toward a poststructuralist view of teacher identity. In T. Shanahan (Ed.), *Teachers thinking, teachers knowing* (pp. 55–75). Urbana, Illinois: National Council of Teachers of English.

Brooks, J. G., & Brooks, M. G. (1993). *In search of understanding: The case for constructivist classrooms.* Alexandria, VA: Association for Supervision and Curriculum Development.

Bruner, J. (1986). *Actual minds, possible worlds.* Cambridge, MA: Harvard University Press.

Brunner, D. D. (1994). *Inquiry and reflection: Framing narrative practice in education.* Albany: State University of New York Press.

Butt, R., Raymond, D., & Yamagishi, L. (1988). Autobiographical praxis: Studying the formation of teachers' knowledge. *Journal of Curriculum Theorizing, 7,* 87–164.

Calderhead, J. (1993). Dilemmas in developing reflective teaching. *Teacher Education Quarterly, 20,* 93–100.

Carter, K. (1993). The place of story in the study of teaching and teacher education. *Educational Researcher, 22,* 5–12.

Clandinin, D. J. (1986). *Classroom practice: Teacher images in action.* New York: Teachers College Press.

Clandinin, D. J. (1992). Narrative and story in teacher education. In T. Russell & H. Munby (Eds.), *Teachers and teaching: From classroom to reflection* (pp. 124–137). London: Falmer Press.

Cobb, P. (1994). Constructivism in mathematics and science education. *Educational Researcher, 23,* 4.

Connelly, F. M., & Clandinin, D. J. (1987). On narrative method, biography, and narrative unities. *Journal of Educational Thought, 21,* 130–139.

Connelly, F. M., & Clandinin, D. J. (1988). *Teachers as curriculum planners. Narratives of experience.* New York: Teachers College Press.

Connelly, F. M., & Clandinin, D. J. (1990). Stories of experience and narrative inquiry. *Educational Researcher, 19*(5), 2–14

Day, C. (1993). Reflection: A necessary but not sufficient condition for professional development. *British Educational Research Journal, 19,* 83–93.

De Vries, R., & Kohlberg, L. (1987). *Constructivist early education: Overview and comparison with other programs.* Washington, DC: National Association for the Education of Young Children.

Delandshere, G., & Petrosky, A. (1994). Capturing teachers' knowledge: Performance assessment a) and post-structuralist epistemology, b) from a post-structuralist perspective, c) and post-structuralism, d) none of the above. *Educational Researcher, 23,* 11–18.

Delpit, L. (1988). The silenced dialogue: Power and pedagogy in educating other people's children. *Harvard Educational Review, 58,* 280–298.

Donaldson, M. (1978). *Children's minds.* New York: Norton.

Duckworth, E. (1987). *The having of wonderful ideas and other essays on teaching and learning.* New York: Teachers College Press.

Fosnot, C. T. (1989). *Enquiring teachers, enquiring learners.* New York: Teachers College Press.

Gomez, M. L. (1992). Breaking silences: Building new stories of classroom life through teacher transformation. In S. Kessler & B. B. Swadener (Eds.), *Reconceptualizing the early childhood curriculum: Beginning the dialogue* (pp. 165–188). New York: Teachers College Press.

Greene, M. (1981). Contexts, connections, and consequences: The matter of philosophical and psychological foundations. *Journal of Teacher Education, 32,* 31–37.

Grumet, M. R. (1983). The line is drawn. *Educational Leadership, 40,* 28–38.

Grumet, M. R. (1987). Women and teaching: Homeless at home. *Teacher Education Quarterly, 14*, 39–46.

Kamii, C. (1982). *Number in preschool and kindergarten.* Washington, DC: National Association for the Education of Young Children.

Kelchtermans, G., & Vandenberghe, R. (1994). Teachers' professional development: A biographical perspective. *Journal of Curriculum Studies, 26*, 45–62.

Lampert, M. (1985). How do teachers manage to teach? Perspectives on problems in practice. *Harvard Educational Review, 55*, 178–194.

Lampert, M., & Clark, C. M. (1990). Expert knowledge and expert thinking in teaching: A response to Floden and Klinzing. *Educational Researcher, 19*, 21–24.

Lather, P. A. (1991). *Getting smart: Feminist research and pedagogy within the postmodern.* New York: Routledge.

Lortie, D. C. (1975). *Schoolteacher: A sociological study.* Chicago: University of Chicago Press.

MacKinnon, A., & Erickson, G. (1992). The roles of reflective practice and foundational disciplines in teacher education. In T. Russell & H. Munby (Eds.), *Teachers and teaching: From classroom to reflection* (pp. 192–210). London: Falmer Press.

McLean, S. V. (1991). *Teachers' work: The use of stories of practice in two preservice teacher education programs.* Paper presented at the Australian Early Childhood Association Conference, Adelaide.

McLean, S. V., McGraw, L., Reese, R., Danzig, A., & Aleman, S. (n.d.) *Stories of stories: Using narratives in professional education.* Unpublished manuscript.

McWilliam, E. (1994). *In broken images: Feminist tales for a different teacher education.* New York: Teachers College Press.

Miller, J. L. (1992). Teachers, autobiography, and curriculum. In S. Kessler & B. B. Swadener (Eds.), *Reconceptualizing the early childhood curriculum* (pp. 103–122). New York: Teachers College Press.

Nagel, N., & Driscoll, A. (1991). Influences on development of a personal model of teaching. *Teacher Education Quarterly, 18*, 5–13.

Noori, K. K. (1994). *A constructivist/reflective paradigm: A model for the early childhood program at Tuskegee University.* Tuskagee: Tuskegee University.

Novinger, S., & Conner, D. B. (1995). *Undergraduate students' development as constructed knowers.* Paper presented at the Association for Childhood Educational International, Washington, DC.

O'Loughlin, M. (1991). *Beyond constructivism: Toward a dialectical model of the problematics of teacher socialization.* Paper presented at the American Educational Research Association Annual Meeting, Chicago.

Parsons, M. J. (1987). *How we understand art.* Cambridge, MA: Harvard University Press.

Pratt, L. R. (1994). Liberal education and the idea of the postmodern university. *Academe 80,* 46–51.

Rosenwald, G. C., & Ochberg, R. L. (Eds.). (1992). *Storied lives: The cultural politics of self understanding.* New Haven, CT: Yale University Press.

Ruddick, J. (1992). Practitioner research and programs of initial teacher education. In T. Russell & H. Munby (Eds.), *Teachers and teaching: From classroom to reflection* (pp. 156–170). London: Falmer Press.

Schon, D. A. (1983). *The reflective practitioner.* New York: Basic Books.

Schon, D. A. (1987). *Educating the reflective practitioner: Toward a new design for teaching and learning in the professions.* San Francisco: Jossey-Bass.

Schwab, J. T., (1969). The practical: A language for curriculum. *School Review, 79,* 1–23.

Schwab, J. T. (1971). The practical: The arts of the eclectic. *School Review, 79,* 492–542.

Smyth, J. (1987). Teachers as intellectuals in a critical pedagogy of teaching. *Education and Society, 5,* 11–28.

Stonehouse, A. (1988). *Nice ladies who love children: The status of the early childhood professional in society.* Paper presented at the Australian Early Childhood Association National Conference, Canberra.

Tamir, P. (1991). Professional and personal knowledge of teachers and teacher educators. *Teaching and Teacher Education, 7,* 163–168.

Tripp, D. (1994). Teachers' lives, critical incidents, and professional practice. *Qualitative Studies in Education, 7,* 65–76.

Van Manen, M. (1977). Linking ways of knowing with ways of being practical. *Curriculum Inquiry, 6,* 205–228.

Widdershoven, Guy A. M. (1993). The story of life: Hermaneutic perspectives on the relationship between narrative and life history. In R. Josselson and A. Lieblich (Eds.), *The narrative study of lives* (pp. 1–20). Newberry Park, CA: Sage.

Wildeen, M. F., Mayer-Smith, J. A., & Moon, B. J. (1993). *The research on learning to teach: Prospects and problems.* Paper presented at the American Educational Research Association, Atlanta.

Witherell, C., & Noddings, N. (Eds.). (1991). *Stories lives tell: Narrative and dialogue in education.* New York: Teachers College Press.

Yager, R. E. (1993). Constructivism and science education reform. *Science Education International, 4,* 13–14.

Yinger, R. J. (1987). Learning the language of practice. *Curriculum Inquiry, 17,* 299–318.

Zeichner, K. M., & Liston, D. P. (1987). Teaching student teachers to reflect. *Harvard Educational Review, 57,* 23–48.

CHAPTER 4

DIMENSIONS OF SELF THAT INFLUENCE EFFECTIVE TEACHING

Gary D. Borich

Research efforts to discriminate between more and less effective teachers have been well chronicled (Brophy & Good, 1986; Gage, 1985; Fisher, Filby, Marliave, et al., 1979; Brophy & Evertson, 1976). However, attempts to study the contribution of personality to teaching effectiveness have met only limited access. Few personality traits have been found that generalize across classrooms and grades other than those that characterize the teacher as a nice, helpful, socially acceptable individual who is appreciated by most people everywhere. If an equally global concept were applied to the definition of a master marksman, and performance criteria ignored, the definition might be "a person with a gun and good vision," two essential but not distinguishing characteristics of the marksman.

What may be needed to better discriminate more effective from less effective teachers is the identification of specific and distinctive dimensions of personality that can inform our definitions of effective teaching. This chapter describes several dimensions of personality—specifically dimensions of self-concept—that may extend our current day notions of effective teaching and provide a framework for the study of teacher affect.

THEORETICAL FRAMEWORK

Every person who will ever occupy a bed in a mental hospital, every parent, every professional, every criminal, every priest, was once in some teacher's first grade. Somewhere, sometime, everyone in our society has known a teacher who might have influenced him or her. The teacher's opportunity for impact is thus both broad and deep.

—F. Fuller, O. Bown, and R. Peck,
Creating Climates for Growth

The hypothesis that teachers are influential in the lives of pupils assumes that teacher behavior affects pupil self-concept. This hypothesis also assumes that "self-concept" is acquired through social interaction and is subject to change through experience. Both assumptions imply that there is a psychological event occurring with the interaction of teacher and pupil that is specifically related to the formation of a psychological concept of the "self." The words "teacher" and "pupil" imply a communication structure characterizing the relationship between these two roles and influencing the psychological events occurring in teacher/pupil interaction.

Inherent in the hypothesis that teacher behavior affects pupil self-concept, are the "self" theories of social interactionists and social psychologists, particularly that advanced by G. H. Mead (1934). Mead theorized that the "self" is a social product formed through the processes of internalizing and organizing psychological experiences. These psychological experiences are the result of the individual's exploration of his or her physical environment and the reflections of "self" he or she receives from those persons considered significant or salient others, shown in figure 4.1.

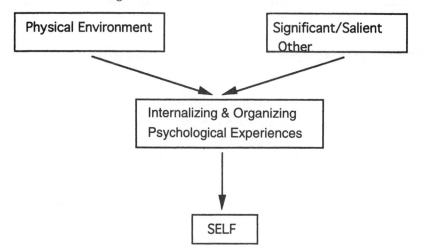

FIGURE 4.1. Self as a Social Product Formed through the Process of Internalizing and Organizing Psychological Experiences.

Applying Mead's theory to the classroom, the beginning teacher may be viewed as the "developing self," gradually forming a concept of one's professional self through interaction with significant and salient others (principals, supervising teachers, teacher educators) and the environment (the classroom and school). Within this interaction, or "behavioral dialogue," are psychological experiences in which the classroom, school, and teacher-training institution reflect to the teacher an image of his or her professional "self." If the teacher values this image, that is, does indeed consider the principal, supervising teacher, and teacher educator a significant or salient other, the teacher will internalize the psychological experience to influence the development of his or her self-concept.

The application of Mead's theory to the relationship between teacher and significant/salient others summarizes a model of self-concept that can be used to interpret and categorize teacher as well as pupil self-concept. The key components of this framework can be defined as:

- *The Developing Self.* The developing self conveys a dynamic concept of "self," a concept always subject to change through the impact of experience.
- *The Performing Self.* The performing self is the concept of "self-as-doer," the self exhibiting behaviors and producing products.
- *The Significant Other.* The significant other is an individual selected and unconditionally valued by the developing self as a source of self-reflection and an interpreter of the behavioral dialogue.
- *The Salient Other.* The salient other is an individual, selected or accepted by the developing self and conditionally valued for a specific reflection of the "self" and for interpretation of specific events in the behavioral dialogue.
- *The Environment.* The environment consists of the physical milieu of the classroom, school, and professional environment in which the developing self exists and in which the behavioral dialogue occurs. This physical milieu includes the developing self and all those who function as significant or salient others.
- *Psychological Experience.* A psychological experience occurs when the developing self receives, responds to, values, and internalizes the reflective, interpretive, or informative stimuli offered by significant/salient others in the environment, incorporating these stimuli as aspects of self-concept that influence behavior, beliefs, and attitudes.
- *The Behavioral Dialogue.* The behavioral dialogue is a psychosocial concept of dyadic interaction encompassing the phenomenal field, or subjective reality (Rogers, 1959), of both the developing self and significant/salient others. It also contains the observable, objective real-

ity that can be perceived and described as the behavior of teacher and significant/salient others in the professional environment—the participants in the dialogue.

The extent to which teachers accept themselves, their role, and their pupils determines the extent to which they can, if nominated, function positively in the role of significant/salient other to their pupils. Teachers who can express unconditional acceptance of pupils have acquired both self-knowledge and awareness. Through self-knowledge they recognize their own values and the biases that might color their perception of others; and through self-awareness they can assess the effects of their behavior on pupils. Teachers who are comfortable and nondefensive in their role can acknowledge their own limitations while accepting those of their pupils. They do not perceive pupils as an extension of themselves or as a reflection of their personal and professional adequacy. Instead, they see pupils as individuals engaged in a learning process and understand that pupil performances and products reflect the nature of their previous experiences. Teachers' unconditional acceptance of themselves and their students allows them to be sympathetic toward and supportive of pupils and at the same time constructively critical of their performances and products. In other words, they are able to use their own power as a significant other to produce positive change in their classrooms.

The concept of "self" as acquired by teachers through relationships with significant/salient others in their professional environment include the concepts of self-as-process, self-as-doer, and self-as-object. *Self-as-process* refers to the psychological processes of thinking, remembering, and perceiving, while *self-as-doer* describes the physical acts or performances that are observed, reflected and evaluated by the "self" and others. The *self-as-object* is defined as the attitudes, feelings, and thoughts about one's self. The self-as-doer *participates* in the significant/salient other relationship; the self-as-process *experiences* the relationship; and the self-as-object *feels* the impact of this relationship.

Most of us employ the concepts of self-as-process, self-as-doer, and self-as-object in everyday conversation. And most of us demonstrate that our current self-concept is an active participant in the formation of our future self-concept. The phrases, "I think," "I feel," "I am," "I can," "I'm a person who," all reflect the concepts of self-as-process, self-as-doer, and self-as-object, and demonstrate that our present concept of self actively guides and directs our future behavior.

The General Self-Concept

Cassius: Tell me, good Brutus, can you see your face?
Brutus: No, Cassius; for the eye sees not itself,
But by reflection, by some other things.
Cassius: Tis just.
And it is very much lamented, Brutus,
That you have no such mirrors as will turn
Your hidden worthiness into your eye,
That you might see your shadow.

Therefore, good Brutus, be prepar'd to hear;
And since you know you cannot see yourself
So well as by reflection, I, your glass,
Will modestly discover to yourself
That of yourself which you yet know not of.
—William Shakespeare, *Julius Caesar* I.ii

From Allport's (1961) concept of the evolving senses of self and the theories of affective development of Erikson (1974, 1964), the general self-concept can be divided into five senses of self: the sense of *bodily self*, the sense of *self-identity*, the sense of *self-extension*, the sense of *self-esteem*, and the sense of *self-image* (Kash & Borich, 1978). Using this framework we can identify beliefs about the self that may distinguish effective teachers from the general population, differentiate novice from experienced teachers, and that influence pupil behavior. Just as the biological form of the human body allows us to describe each human being as like all others in some respects, like some others in some respects, and unlike any other in other respects, the model of the general self-concept, with its five senses of self, allows us to describe the similarities between, differences among, and idiosyncrasies of both teacher and pupil self-concept.

It is difficult to visually represent the general self-concept without losing the interactive, interrelated, and interdependent nature of the component senses. The sense of bodily self can be described as the dominant sense of self that emerges first in an individual's life, and should be viewed as the primary or central core of the conceptualized self. The senses of self are acquired in a developmental sequence, shown in figure 4.2 by incomplete circles, suggesting that in a normal, healthy individual, no sense of self is ever "finished" or entirely separated from the other senses. Although these five senses of self are divisible only as psychological concepts, we can find examples of them in

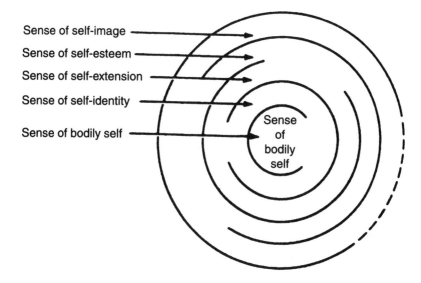

Sense of self-image
Sense of self-esteem
Sense of self-extension
Sense of self-identity
Sense of bodily self

Sense of bodily self

FIGURE 4.2. The General Self-Concept as Five Senses of Self.

our own behavior and those of pupils and teachers of all ages. Consider, for example, some excerpts from the professional diaries of these student teachers:

> My first thoughts before arriving to my first class were "What would the kids think of me?" Would I be attractive to them, would they like me, what would they think of what I was wearing, and would they notice that I was actually shorter then most of them? Silly as it may seem, these thoughts consumed many of my thoughts during my first days in the classroom. [Sense of bodily self]

> I've spent a lot of time wondering these first weeks if I really fit in. What I mean to say is that I'm having trouble thinking of myself as a teacher. Last month I was a student and, in some respects, a lot like the kids I'm teaching. But, now I'm the authority, the "know it all," someone who can give advice to others—and I don't feel comfortable with that. I guess I'm having trouble learning to be someone else in front of my class. [Sense of self-identity]

> Today I did the impossible. I got everyone to quiet down at the bell and actually begin their work on time. I finally figured out how to do it without getting everyone mad at me. I can't believe it,

but I'm finally starting to get the hang of it. [Sense of self-extension]

Yesterday I peeked at the student evaluations of my teaching and was I surprised. I thought most of my students didn't really care if I lived or died, but they wrote the nicest things about me. I decided to save them, if ever I have second thoughts about becoming a teacher. [Sense of self-esteem]

I think student teaching in this school has been good for me, even though I didn't want to be here. It brought out the best and the worst in me as a teacher—and I think I needed to see both sides. I'm a lot more realistic about myself from having to cope with so many problems. I know what I have to improve on but also what I'm good at—like relating to the personal problems of the kids. I'm beginning to discover who I really am. [Sense of self-image]

These five dimensions of self may be summarized as follows:

The Teacher's Sense of Bodily Self

The sense of bodily self is the awareness of self as a physical entity. It begins in early childhood, develops in adolescence, and continues with the teacher's experiences in the classroom. In the process of the teacher's experiencing himself or herself in the context of the classroom, the bodily self performs the function of significant other and provides feedback to the self for further exploration and limitation. As the process of differentiating self from others in the classroom continues, the teacher begins to interact with others in more meaningful, professional ways, thus acquiring additional sources of reflection. This sense of self includes the sense of a physical self and the sense of self differentiated from others. It is acquired when the teacher acknowledges, accepts, or celebrates those physical properties that distinguish him or her from others.

The Teacher's Sense of Self-Identity

The sense of self-identity represents the teacher's sense of self in relation to significant/salient others (e.g., school administrators, peers, supervising teachers, and teacher educators)—a sense of self built upon the reflections and responses supplied by these external sources. From the outset, the beginning teacher's sense of self-identity initiates a dialogue that prompts others to assume their interpreting and responding roles. This sense of self includes the sense of self in affiliation with others in the professional environment, and the sense of self as related to others by communication. It is acquired by willingly accepting a professional role together with its responsibilities, privileges, and obligations.

The Teacher's Sense of Self-Extension (The Performing Self)

The teacher's outward behavior—his or her performing self—and the cognitive concepts that produce these visible behaviors together comprise the sense of self-extension. Through the sense of self-extension, the concepts of self are not only coordinated, but also arranged and orchestrated to produce behavioral performances that feature the self's most highly valued attributes. Consequently, the performing self exhibits repeated, characteristic patterns of valued behavior. This sense of self includes the sense of self as doer, learner, and knower through performance. This sense of self is acquired when the teacher feels he or she can exhibit behaviors that will be acknowledged and rewarded by significant or salient others in the professional environment.

The Teacher's Sense of Self-Esteem

The teacher's sense of self-esteem, sometimes called the sense of self-worth, is the sum of all valued affirmation experienced in the behavioral dialogue of the school and classroom. Through this behavioral dialogue the teacher receives confirmation of his or her impact, to which the experiences of affirmation add a positive quality. If the teacher experiences little affirmation, he or she is more likely to develop a negative sense of self-esteem. This sense of self includes the sense of affirmation, recognition, and confirmation of impact that is acquired when the teacher is accorded acknowledgment or reward from the school or classroom that the behaviors exhibited are valued.

The Teacher's Sense of Self-Image

The teacher's sense of self-image represents perceptions of self formed from the dominant values pertaining to standards, beliefs, and goals set by and for the self. All self-images, past, present, or future, reflect the value system of the professional environment and the circumstances and conditions he or she has experienced. The sense of self-image can be likened to an album of self-portraits, sometimes candid, sometimes posed. Those that are candid are more objective and insightful; those that are posed are more suggestive and ideal. This sense of self includes the sense of past and present images of self and the sense of an ideal self. It is acquired when the teacher integrates both strengths and weaknesses into a unified picture of self and matches that picture to the dominant values set by and for the self.

THE TEACHER AS SIGNIFICANT OTHER
AND MANAGER OF THE ENVIRONMENT

> I have come to a frightening conclusion. I am the decisive element in the classroom. It is my personal approach that creates the climate. It is my daily mood that makes the weather. As a teacher I possess tremendous power to make a child's life miserable or joyous. I can be a tool of torture or an instrument of inspiration. I can humiliate or humor, hurt or heal. In all situations it is my response that decides whether a crises will be escalated or de-escalated, a child humanized or de-humanized.
>
> —H. Ginott, *Teacher and Child*

What can weigh more heavily on the dedicated and caring teacher than the implications of the statement above? Almost every adult can tell a story beginning "I had a teacher who . . ." and go on to recite the remembered vices or virtues—the impact—of an individual whose name he or she cannot recall or "will never forget." This impact is not only assumed by society and recalled by former pupils, it is also held by teachers themselves. While most teachers may not consciously consider the long-term consequences of a child's classroom experience, many have, like Ginott, sensed at least an immediate, day-to-day power over pupils.

The professional functions of the role of teacher that reflect this power range from surrogate parent, to instructor, to authority figure. They can include:

> *Negative roles:* Scapegoat, detective, and disciplinarian
> *Authoritarian roles:* Parental surrogate, dispenser of knowledge, group leader, model citizen
> *Supporting roles:* Therapist, friend, and confidant

Superimposed on these "professional" duties are the roles of salient/significant other and controller of the classroom environment. Because the former is assigned and defined by the pupil and the latter required by the teaching task, these roles are performed, consciously or unconsciously, by all teachers, regardless of the teacher's "assigned" professional functions. Considering the broad responsibilities inherent in these roles, in addition to the innumerable professional roles ascribed to the teacher, one wonders why teachers are not more scarce. The answer is that teachers define their role, not so much according to what others expect of them, but according to their own perception of their role. It is the teachers' perceptions and values that determine their role not only as disciplinarians, model citizens, and dispensers of knowledge, but also as significant/salient others to their students.

To function positively in the role of significant or salient other, the teacher must be able to accurately perceive and reflect the developing self, to adequately interpret events, and to convey information correctly. And this perceptual ability and the quality of the teacher's performance can be significantly influenced by the teacher's self-concept.

In an early study of effectiveness in the helping professions, Combs (1969) compared the perceptual abilities of teachers, counselors, and nurses who were rated "effective" and "ineffective." He observed some important perceptual differences between the two groups in four major categories. Here are his categories and some of the questions that discriminated more effective from less effective human service providers:

1. *General perceptual organization.* Is the individual more interested in people or things? Does she look at people from the outside, or try to see the world as they see it? Does she look for the reasons people behave as they do here and now, or does she try to find historical reasons for behavior?
2. *Perceptions of other people.* Does he see people as generally able or unable to do things? As friendly or unfriendly? Worthy or unworthy? Dependable or undependable?
3. *Perceptions of self.* Does she see herself as with people or apart from them? As able or unable? Dependable or undependable? Worthy or unworthy? Wanted or unwanted?
4. *Perceptions of the professional task.* Does he see the job as one of freeing people or controlling them? Does he see his role as one of revealing or concealing? Being involved or uninvolved?

The perceptual differences emerging in each of these categories reveals a positive/negative dichotomy characterizing the five senses of self and their effect upon a teacher's perception of his or her job. The sense of bodily self is reflected in the general attitude of trust (positive) or mistrust (negative), which stems from a positive (safe) or negative (threatened) sense of self. Similarly, the propensity toward inclusion or exclusion of others, toward affiliation or isolation may result from, respectively, a positive or negative sense of self-identity. These perceptual differences also reflect a positive/negative dichotomy characterizing the senses of self-esteem and self-extension (performing self). Considering the five senses together, a positive or negative image of self as "helper" emerges.

As one might expect, Combs (1969), and Sparks and Lipka (1992), found that the perceptions of "effective" helpers fell on the positive side of the dichotomy. Teachers identified as effective helpers exhibited consistent and decisive classroom behavior and "positive," "realistic" self-concepts. And, according to Beane and Lipka (1986), a positive self-concept is a necessary prerequisite to the creation of a supportive classroom environment. Their conclusion is corroborated by the work of others (Combs & Soper, 1963; Bullough et al., 1989; Purkey & Novak, 1984) that suggests self-confident teachers generally exhibit classroom behavior that fosters positive pupil self-concepts. Effective teachers, as these authors have described them, and effective salient others, as described above, appear to share a positive perception of self and others that has a positive effect on pupil self-concept.

CONCERNS OF TEACHERS

While the studies of Combs, Sparks and Lipka, and Purkey and Novak suggest that perceptual "set" is associated with teacher effectiveness, other researchers at the University of Texas have identified a similar kind of set that may affect the teacher's performance as a salient other. In a series of studies (Fuller, 1969; Fuller, Bown, & Peck, 1966; Fuller, Pilgrim, & Freeland, 1967), researchers found that the concerns of preservice and beginning teachers could be grouped into definable developmental stages.

According to Fuller (1969), Borich (1997, 1993), and Borich and Tombari (1995), the preservice teacher's transition to the real world of teaching ushers in the first stage of teacher development, called the survival stage. The distinguishing feature of the survival stage of teaching is that the teacher's concerns focus on his or her own well-being, more than on the teaching task or learners. Bullough et al. (1989) describes this stage as "the fight for one's professional life" (p. 16). During this stage, teachers' thoughts typically turn to concerns such as:

Will my learners like me?
Will they listen to what I say?
What will their parents think of me?
Will I do well when my principal observes me?

In the classroom it is the teacher who functions as significant or salient other. And it is the teacher's concerns that shape the behavioral dialogue and influence the pupils' sense of self. Teachers who feel personally or professionally inadequate, or who dislike their role as teachers may be overly controlling, authoritarian, and defensively hostile toward their pupils. Or they may be excessively nondirective, easily diverted from teaching tasks and indifferent to their impact on pupil performance and products. In other words, extreme self-concerns can produce extreme behavior of one type or another. We might see verbal hostility toward pupils or unmerited praise and flattery; we might also anticipate low acceptance of pupil ideas or the reverse—unstructured pupil independence. A high frequency of convergent questioning (when divergent queries would be more appropriate) or an unstructured effort to resolve pupil misconceptions might also occur. And, finally, we might expect extreme patterns in the teacher's use of social and spatial distance.

Teachers who view pupils as an extension of themselves or proof of their adequacy have an equally negative effect on the classroom dialogue. They may, for example, ignore challenged or passive pupils or offer them excessive assistance in order to maintain the appearance of learning progress. In any case, teachers' preoccupation with self-concerns, typical at the beginning of teaching, can affect their interpretation of the pupil role and, in so doing, confine or expand the pupil's opportunity to learn and to establish a behavioral dialogue that promotes the pupils' sense of self in the classroom.

For most teachers, survival concerns and concerns about self begin to diminish during the first months of teaching, but there is no precise time when they are over. What signals the end to concerns for self and self-survival is the transition to a new set of concerns and a gradual diminishing of concerns about one's own well-being. This new set of concerns focuses on how best to deliver instruction. Various labels have been used to describe this second stage, such as the master stage of teaching (Ryan, 1992), consolidation and exploration (Burden, 1986), and trial and error (Sacks & Harington, 1982). Fuller (1969) described this stage as one marked by concerns about the teaching task.

At this stage the teacher begins to feel confident that he or she can manage the day-to-day routines of the classroom and deal with a variety of behavior problems. Now the teacher is at the point where he or she can plan lessons without an exclusive focus on managing the classroom. Focus turns toward the improvement of teaching skills and achieving greater mastery over the content being taught. During this stage the teacher may express concerns such as:

> *How good are my instructional materials?*
> *Will I have enough time to cover all the content?*
> *How can I add variety to my lessons?*
> *What's the best way to teach my subject?*

The final stage of teacher development is characterized by concerns that have to do less with management and lesson delivery and more with the teacher's impact on learners. Fuller (1969) refers to this stage as the impact stage. At this time, the teacher views learners as individuals and is concerned that each student fulfill his or her potential. During this final stage the teacher's principal concerns are:

> *How can I increase my learners' feelings of accomplishment?*
> *How do I meet my learners' social and emotional needs?*
> *What is the best way to challenge unmotivated learners?*
> *What skills do my learners need to be prepared for the next grade and the*
>   *world outside the classroom?*

According to Fuller (1969), the beginning teacher's thoughts and concerns first focus on his or her well-being and only later on the teaching task and students. Fuller found that during the early, middle, and late phases of student teaching, there was a shift in teaching concerns expressed by preservice teachers from a focus on oneself (Will the students like me? Can I control the class?) to concerns that emphasize the teaching task (Are there sufficient instructional materials? Is there enough time to cover all the content?) to concerns that emphasize the needs of pupils (Are the pupils learning? Can they apply what I've taught?). Fuller speculated that concerns for self, task, and impact are the natural stages that most teachers pass through, representing a developmental growth pattern extending over months and even years of a teacher's career.

Although some teachers may pass through these stages more quickly than others and at different levels of intensity, Fuller suggested almost all teachers can be expected to move from one to another, with the most effective and experienced teachers expressing student-centered (impact) concerns at a high level of commitment. Furthermore,

Fuller speculated that the lack of adequate emotional support during the critical student teaching experience and first year of teaching can result in a slower, more labored shift of focus to the teaching task. This, in turn, can result in failure on the part of the teacher to reach a concern for his or her impact on students.

Fuller's concerns theory has several other implications. Some teachers might return to an earlier stage of concern, for example, from a concern for their impact back to a concern for task as a result of suddenly having to teach a new grade or subject. Or they might move from a concern for task back to a concern for self as a result of having to teach in a different and unfamiliar school. Thus, teacher concerns may not always be determined developmentally but can be context dependent as well. The time spent in a stage the second time may be shorter than the first. Finally, the three stages of concern need not be exclusive of one another. A teacher may have concerns predominately in one area and still have concerns of lesser intensity in one or both of the other stages.

Fuller concluded that teachers who were preoccupied with personal concerns and self-protection, or who were worried primarily about their image as authority figures (concerns for self and task), did not have sufficient freedom from "self" to allow them to perceive or address the needs and concerns of their pupils. Teachers with positive self-concepts and self-confidence, however, exhibited a flexibility that allowed them to foster pupil autonomy, accept pupil ideas, and to teach toward the application of learned skills in as well as outside of the classroom.

TEACHER CONCERNS AND THE ROLE OF SIGNIFICANT/SALIENT OTHER

> I never knew what my difficulty was until you pointed it out to me. When I came to your class last October, I was trying with all my might to be like everyone else, to forget as entirely as possible my limitations and peculiar environment. . . .
>
> I have always accepted other people's experiences and observations as a matter of course. It never occurred to me that it might be worth while to make my own observations and describe the experiences peculiarly my own. Henceforth I am resolved to be myself, to live my own life and write my own thoughts.
> —Helen Keller, *The Story of My Life*

Teachers with positive self-concerns, whose concerns for pupils are greater than their concerns for self, can be expected to function within the teaching role as effective significant or salient others and to use the classroom environment to foster positive self-concepts in their pupils. A negative self-concept rooted in any of the five senses of self may limit the teacher's role by limiting the structure of the behavioral dialogue between teacher and pupil, transforming the classroom into a place for the reflection of teacher rather than pupil needs.

When teachers structure their roles to serve their own concerns and reinforce their own perceptions and values, this structuring is carried over to the behavioral dialogue, where it can color the psychological experiences of pupils engaged in that dialogue. The positive or negative reflections that pupils receive are based on the teacher's interpretations and are subject to the teacher's own perceptions of self. The pupils who consider the teacher a significant/salient other—who value these reflections—will incorporate them into their developing self-concepts, whether or not those perceptions of self are distorted or dysfunctional in the behavioral dialogue of the classroom.

Suppose that a teacher's basic psychological state is one of mistrust, resulting from an inadequate sense of self-image. As a result, this teacher may be fearful and suspicious of other's motives in his or her relationships with pupils, parents, and colleagues. To cope, the teacher might take on an authoritarian role, adopting and imitating negative and controlling behaviors while at the same time seeking approval from those in authority. Or the teacher might identify with pupils as the "victims" of authority, unable or unwilling to assume or perform any authoritarian behavior.

The teacher who adopts a controlling, authoritative model often is reinforced by conforming and compliant pupil behavior. Successful control of pupils' threatening behavior may reinforce the teacher's self-image as an authority figure and encourage him or her to continue acquiring and using control and power-seeking behaviors. Perceived threats to this teacher's control and authority, however, may provide cause for enlisting the authoritative support system of the school, further meeting the teacher's needs to identify with authority.

Thus, those pupils for whom the controlling, authoritarian teacher functions as a significant other will find their teacher a source of positive self-reflection only when their behaviors are compliant and compatible with the teacher's interpretation of the pupil role as an indicator of the teacher's own authority. Those pupils unwilling to accept this interpretation of their role, or who do not consider the teacher a significant or salient other, will select behavioral options other than compliance. Depending on the value system and self-concept of the individual pupil, the option chosen may be withdrawal, or disruptive, authority-confronting behavior, or even intermittent compliance redefined in a way that preserves the integrity of the pupil's self-concept.

Teachers who cope with an inadequate self-image by identifying with their pupils are unlikely to exert control or initiate authoritative behaviors. But they may enter the classroom seeking acceptance and approval from their pupils at the expense of their leadership role. Such teachers may encourage dependency rather than conformity in their pupils and may be inclined to interpret the products and performances of their pupils as demonstrations of their pupils' appreciation of them. Dependent pupils, who need role interpretation and direction, easily conform to the authoritarian teacher's demands for compliance. In order to get such direction from the approval-seeking teacher, however, dependent pupils may abandon responsibility for their own academic and social behavior. And for doing so they are rewarded with the teacher's attention. Reinforced for dependent behavior, they continue to reflect the teacher as accepted, needed, and approved. From this kind of interaction, dependent pupils can acquire effective manipulative skills by which to maintain dependency in future dialogues.

DIRECTIONS OF TEACHER-PUPIL INFLUENCE

Whether teachers influence pupil behavior more than pupils influence teacher behavior is best considered in the context of the behavioral dialogue. The nature of this dialogue and its impact upon the participants depends on the goals of the teacher. In most cases, the direction of behavioral influence is determined by the individual who initiates interaction—generally the teacher. The other participants in the behavioral dialogue assume a responsive stance by accepting the teacher's interpretation of their role. But the teacher who initiates controlling behavior may also define and limit the responding role of pupils. Even a seemingly noncontrolling but approval-seeking teacher can create a responding role for students in an apparent, but not actual, reversal of the teacher's natural position as initiator of the behavioral dialogue. In either case, it is the teacher who determines the initiating and responding roles in the classroom dialogue.

The teacher's power to interpret and control the dialogue in some classrooms may be so complete and pervasive that it may be difficult to find many pupil behaviors—except those in defiance of teacher directives—that are truly autonomous, independent, or initiating. Pupil behavior perceived as positive demonstrates acceptance of the teacher-interpreted pupil role, while that considered negative reflects either overt rejection of the teacher-assigned role, or simply a misunderstanding of that role. A pupil whose report card shows high marks for "initiative" will more than likely have had jump starts on all the teacher's assignments, added color to the social studies map, and gone to the library when faced with free time. "Shows initiative" rarely contradicts "follows directions well."

We may assume, however, that in a productive classroom, the teacher tends toward controlling behaviors under certain conditions and responding behaviors under other conditions. In other words, at times teachers should alter pupil behaviors and pupils, in turn, should alter some teacher behaviors, with neither teacher nor pupils demonstrating a discernible or consistent dominance over or influence on classroom activity. Klein (1971) reported an increase in the number of positive teacher behaviors following the occurrence of positive pupil behavior, a higher incidence of negative teacher behavior in response to negative pupil behavior, indicating that the flux of classroom climate is a two-way action. Groups of students or individual students, high-achievers, low-achievers, underachievers, creative pupils, conforming pupils, males and females, economically advantaged and disadvantaged pupils, student leaders and classroom disrupters can all serve as valued reflectors of the teacher's image, and in that capacity can reinforce or challenge the teacher's self-concept.

THE EFFECT OF SIGNIFICANT OTHERS ON TEACHER SELF-CONCEPT

The effect of significant/salient others on teacher self-concept can be illustrated from an ongoing study of school principals. Three behavior patterns of school principals were identified and related to teacher self-concept as part of a study by the author, based on work by Blase (1991) and Marshall and Mitchell (1991). From the findings of their work and some tentative results from the study in progress, we can (1) infer a relationship between principal behavior patterns and teacher self-concepts, and (2) hypothesize the behavioral dialogues that may occur between principals and teachers. Three patterns of principal behavior were identified.

Pattern I principal behavior could be described as independent but social, explorative, and realistic. These principals exercised strong and consistent guidance, but respected the independent decisions of their teachers. They were directive, but they usually accompanied directions with reasons. They demanded a good deal of their teachers, but were supportive and conscientious, and self-assured in their role as principals. In the process of acquiring prescribed behaviors through their training as school administrators, they may have received approval and eventually come to value their learned behavior as a source of independence and autonomy (self-reliant, competent), indicating a positive sense of self-extension. They may have also experienced a positive reflection of self, first as a teacher and then as an administrator, suggesting a positive sense of self-esteem. Finally, they may have satisfied their needs and achieved their goals through the impact of their behavior or through its indirect effect on others, evidence of a positive sense of self-image.

In summary, these principals appeared to exhibit behavior characteristics of significant others. They gave their teachers positive self-reflections. They allowed their teachers an active role in the behavioral dialogue of the school. They provided a consistent interpretation of their teachers' behaviors, thus establishing clear understanding and communication. They supplemented their directions with interpretation and information so that their teachers could construct a sense of approved behaviors and self-direction. They also attended to positive classroom practices and discouraged negative ones, allowing their teachers to acquire more "mature" teaching styles.

Pattern II principals, on the other hand, appeared less secure, more apprehensive, and more likely to become hostile or regressive under stress than Pattern I principals. Furthermore, their behavior was more conforming, less autonomous, and less social. These principals were less nurturing and less involved with their teachers than Pattern I principals. They were firm, used power freely, sometimes offered little or no explanation of their wishes, and encouraged no disagreement. They tended to use power as a controlling device and to exhibit less sympathy toward and less approval of their teachers. Their participation in the behavioral dialogue of the school seemed limited primarily to compliant behavior, while at the same time sometimes excessively censuring noncompliance. These principals tended to offer little interpretation and information about their behavior, which was dependent upon moment-to-moment rather than systematic interpretation, a condition that may have inhibited their role as salient other to their teachers.

A third pattern of principal behavior also emerged. Principals in Pattern III could be described as dependent, compared with Pattern I and II principals. They showed less restraint and self-reliance than principals in the other two groups. These principals were less demanding of their teachers and less controlling than Pattern I and II principals. They would also "baby" their teachers more. These principals appeared to be somewhat lax in setting standards and used warmth more manipulatively than did principals in the first two groups.

Since these principals tended to "play up" to their teachers and were less demanding, the role they perceived for their teachers was one of dependency on them. It may also be that the self-reflections and interpretations of their behavior these principals received from others failed to give them a realistic concept of themselves, their behavior, or their environment, leading to a lower level of social and communicative behavior.

These latter two patterns, if projected to their logical extremes, could limit development of a teacher's sense of self. For example, principals (like those in Pattern II) who failed to affirm appropriate classroom practices, while at the same time attending to inappropriate practices (without explaining why it is inappropriate), may only provide beginning teachers with information about what not to do. Given little or no information about appropriate and positive classroom practices, beginning teachers may have difficulty determining desired values and standards of the school environment and conclude that any behavior or practice that does not provoke a response is approved.

On the other hand, principals (like those in Pattern III) who fail to differentiate the teachers actions with regard to appropriateness and impact, may provide little cognitive information from which the new teacher can develop appropriate classroom goals. Under these circumstances, the beginning teacher's actions can become neither the source of recognition and approval (and eventually independence and autonomy) nor the basis of communication.

Somewhere between these extremes (similar to Pattern I) lies a course of principal behavior that encourages positive development of their teachers' self-concepts. The teacher's sense of self is acquired from psychological events within the behavioral dialogue of the school that transmit positive reflections of the development self and realistic, consistent interpretations of the self's behavior not only to the classroom but to the school. Typically, these reflections and interpretations are valued first as a means of gaining approval (concerns for self), subsequently as a tool for achieving independence (concerns for the teaching task), and eventually as a method for achieving competence (concerns for pupil impact).

THE ROLE OF SIGNIFICANT/SALIENT OTHERS IN THE TRAINING OF TEACHERS

> For thou has granted to man that he should come to self-knowl-
> edge through the knowledge of others, and that he should believe
> many things about himself on the authority of the womenfolk.
> Now, clearly, I had life and being; and, as my infancy closed, I was
> already learning signs by which my feelings could be communi-
> cated to others.
>
> —St. Augustine, *Augustine: Confessions and Enchiridion*

Some recommendations follow for how school administrators, supervising teachers, and teacher educators, as significant/salient others, can communicate a positive self-concept to teachers. A summary of the five components of self and some recommendations pertaining to each are:

Sense of Bodily Self

Every teacher-to-be carries with them several physical character-istics that may evoke responses from pupils that can influence the formation of self-concept. These characteristics, which may be considered "givens," are gender, body build, race, physical appearance, physical anomalies, and age. When teachers believe that a significant/salient other's response to them is determined by some physical or social characteristic, they will incorporate that perception into their self-concepts. They will conclude that a condition, over which they have little or no control, influences their acceptance or rejection. Even when the significant/salient other reflects a positive value for a particular phys-ical or social characteristic, a value is being expressed and a condition irrelevant to teaching may still be established, and therefore a self-concern is introduced into the teacher/significant other relationship. If the developing teacher feels accepted regardless of these character-istics, a sense of trust can emerge free from the concern for self that otherwise may influence the nature of their self-concept and their pro-fessional development. Yet, unconditional acceptance does not pre-clude the rejection of certain asocial behaviors. Such rejection by salient others allows the beginning teacher to see their behavior (something within their control), and not their "self," that is unac-ceptable. The developing teacher's sense of bodily self can be best nurtured by school administrators, supervising teachers, and teacher educators who:

1. Communicate the historical significance and value of individual differences in gender, body build, race, physical appearance, and age.
2. Establish a professional climate that encourages acceptance and trust in a personally nonevaluative environment.
3. Examine their teaching or administrative practices for physical, social, or cultural preferences, standards or values that may favor some individual differences over others, even if expressed positively, and that may create mistrust and an increased concern for self.

Sense of Self-Identity

The role of the significant/salient other in the development of a teacher's self-identity cannot be overemphasized. It is the significant other who either nurtures or inhibits the developing teacher to talk freely, ask questions, and learn from the dialogue between the significant/salient other and teacher. However, because the behavioral dialogue is, in part, determined by the self-concept of the teacher, it can become distorted if he or she is preoccupied with self-concerns. The predominance of such self-concerns may be grounded in the fear of responsibility and feelings of inadequacy that reduce the behavioral dialogue to a monologue delivered by the significant/salient other. The absence of a dialogue, or the intrusion of the significant/salient other's own self-concerns into the images reflected to the developing teacher, can also affect the quality of the dialogue. When significant others (in this case, teacher educator, supervising teacher, or school administrator) are excessively concerned with their own adequacy and perceive their relationship with a developing teacher as a test of competence, they will reflect the teacher as a product or extension of themselves, acceptable only when the teacher's behaviors affirm the significant/salient other's capability. Or, in order to ensure that they are seen as adequate and responsible, significant/salient others may anticipate and carry out both sides of the behavioral dialogue. And in so doing, they may obscure the image of the developing self, negating both the process and product of identify formation.

The value of unconditional acceptance is essential to a positive self-concept. To accept the beginning teacher is to acknowledge differences in ability, interests, and preferences and to recognize and respect the differences that may lie between the developing teacher and significant/salient other. To encourage this acceptance and promote the teacher's sense of self-identify, the significant/salient other can:

1. Acknowledge and teach the social and psychological phenomena responsible for individual differences among teachers.
2. Identify the typical sources of bias in a professional environment that may influence the acceptance and valuation of individual differences.
3. Use small groups and individual conferencing for acknowledging and responding to teacher differences.
4. Create a climate of group work and shared decision-making that encourages communication and a sense of relationship to others among developing teachers.

Sense of Self-Extension (the Performing Self)

The objective of the performing self is to achieve a positive self-reflection from significant/salient others and the environment. Along with the response to the developing self's physical presence, the self begins to experience a reaction to his or her behavior, which becomes the basis of communication. When behavior becomes mutually understood, it also becomes a source of approval or disapproval. When performance has a positive impact, it increases the value of the performance, modifies the subsequent estimate of risk, and increases anticipation of reward for the behavior performed. When a behavior has negative (or less positive than expected) impact, it will be performed less often and at greater estimated risk in the future. The developing teacher's efforts to acquire skills and to explore and test the environment comprise the performing self.

The beginning teacher is initially motivated to acquire behaviors that they have learned to value in their academic environment (for example, a high score on an exam). However, once beginning teachers perceive that they can perform newly acquired behaviors that influence the responses of their pupils, they begin to shift their values. They begin to diminish the importance of knowledge for its own sake and begin to prize impact over knowledge. This is when the student teacher's or first-year teacher's concerns for knowledge in coping with the teaching task are complemented with concerns for their impact on pupils. Teacher concerns, then, play an important part in determining the behavior of their performing selves. In order to foster the teacher's performing self, significant/salient others can:

1. Communicate that a teacher's impact on pupils is an important source of self-reflection, interpretation, and information about one's own behavior.

2. Emphasize the teacher's role as a valued significant or salient other to their pupils, particularly with regard to the guidance and information they provide to their pupils in achieving mastery of skills and independence and autonomy.
3. Provide feedback that allows teachers to realistically perceive their progress and share an appropriate amount of responsibility with their students, thereby moving them away from teacher authority, external control, and extrinsic rewards toward internalized standards, an internal locus of control, and intrinsic reward.

Sense of Self-Esteem

Self-esteem is acquired through a process of self-evaluation, during which teachers judge the effect of their impact according to acquired values and standards. Self-evaluation begins long before the teacher reaches the first-year classroom, and the high or low self-esteem that becomes apparent in a teacher's first year of teaching generally has its roots in the student teaching environment. This environment offers new psychological experiences that ultimately can affect the beginning teacher's self-esteem for years to come. Teachers who have not acquired a sense of self-esteem from their student teaching experience may encounter problems their first year, if their previous experiences have not equipped them with a process of self-evaluation for judging their impact in the classroom. In order to foster the teacher's self-esteem, significant/salient others can:

1. Communicate and interpret the standards used for evaluating the developing teacher's performance in the classroom.
2. Establish a clear relationship between the standards and the methods used to observe the expected performance.
3. Model in their own teaching and relationships the proper use of self-criticism and self-reward and show how to acquire and actively use self-evaluative skills.
4. Make individual improvement the value that underlies public performances.
5. Associate praise and criticism with specific elements of performance, reinforcing the positive and providing a basis for improving the negative.

Sense of Self-Image

We have defined the sense of self-image as a concept of self formed by attributes, behaviors, and beliefs that are assigned a value according to the self's perception of their impact on others and the environment. Valued standards become ideals and goals. Principals and teacher educators in their role as significant or salient others, and the school, acting as an influence, provide reflections, interpretations, and information that are internalized and incorporated into the teacher's sense of self-image. In order for teachers to acquire a positive perception of self, principals and teacher educators must provide them with acceptance and positive reflections. In order to acquire a realistic construct of self and therefore a realistic self-image, teachers must receive accurate and complete feedback from significant/salient others in the environment, which enables them to associate their attributes and behaviors with their consequent impact on pupils. In order to foster the teacher's sense of self-image, significant/salient others can:

1. Communicate and interpret the values and standards of the school and identify specific behaviors or examples by which the developing teacher can implement those values and standards.
2. Provide sufficient opportunities to observe values of the school and practice linking those values and standards to expected behaviors in the classroom.
3. Create an environment that encourages teachers to discuss their concerns about values and standards in a context of their own professional responsibility and provide opportunities for them to develop and exercise their capacity to make judgments about values and standards on their own.

REFERENCES

Allport, G. W. (1961). *Pattern and growth in personality*. New York: Holt, Rinehart and Winston.

Beane, J., & Lipka, R. (1986). *Self-concept, self-esteem, and the curriculum*. New York: Teachers College Press.

Blase, J. (1991).The micropolitical orientation of teachers toward closed school principals. *Education and Urban Society, 23,* 356–378.

Borich, G. (1993). *Clearly outstanding: Making each day count in your classroom*. Boston: Allyn & Bacon.

Borich, G. (1995). *Becoming a teacher: An inquiring dialogue for the beginning teacher*. Bristol, PA: Falmer Press.

Borich, G., & Tombari, M. (1997). *Educational Psychology: A contemporary approach* (2nd ed.). New York: Longman.

Bullough, R. V. Jr., Knowles, G. J., Crow, N. A. (1989). Teacher self-concept and student culture in the first year of teaching. *Teachers College Record, 91,* 209–33.

Burden, P. (1986). Teacher development: Implications for teacher education. In J. Raths and L. Katz (Eds.), *Advances in teacher education* (vol. 2). Norwood, NJ: Ablex.

Brophy, J., & Everston, C. (1975). *Learning from teaching: A developmental perspective.* Boston: Allyn & Bacon.

Brophy, J., & Good, T. (1986). Teacher behavior and student achievement. In M. C. Wittrock (ed.), *Handbook of research on teaching* (3rd ed.) (pp. 328–375). New York: Macmillan.

Combs, A. (1969). *Florida studies in the helping professions* (Social Science Monograph No. 37). Gainesville: University of Florida Press.

Combs, A., & Soper, D. (1963). The helping relationship as described by "good" and "poor" teachers. *Journal of Teacher Education, 14,* 64–68.

Erikson, E. (1963). *Childhood and society* (2nd ed. rev.). New York: Norton.

Erikson, E. (1974). *Dimensions of new identity: The 1973 Jefferson lectures on the humanities.* New York: Norton.

Fisher, C., Filby, N., Marliave, R., Cahen, L., Dishaw, M., More, J., & Berliner, D. (1979). *Teaching and learning in the elementary school: A summary of the Beginning Teacher Evaluation Study.* (Beginning Teacher Evaluation Study Report VII-I). San Francisco: Far West Laboratory for Educational Research and Development.

Fuller, F. (1969). Concerns of teachers: A developmental conceptualization. *American Educational Research Journal, 6,* 207–226.

Fuller, F., Bown, O., & Peck, R. (1966). *Creating climates for growth.* Austin: University of Texas, Research and Development Center for Teacher Education. (ERIC Document Reproduction Service, ED 013 989)

Fuller, F., Pilgrim, G., & Freeland, A. (1967). *Intensive individualization of teacher preparation.* Austin: University of Texas, Research and Development Center for Teacher Education. (ERIC Document Reproduction Service, ED 011 603)

Gage, N. (1985). *Hard gains in the soft sciences: The case of pedagogy.* Bloomington, IN: Phi Delta Kappan.

Ginott, H. (1972). *Teacher and child.* New York: Macmillan.

Kash, M., & Borich, G. (1978). *Teacher behavior and pupil self-concept.* Boston: Addison-Wesley.

Klein, S. (1971). Student influence on teacher behavior. *American Educational Research Journal, 8,* 207–226.

Marshall, C., & Mitchell, B. (1991). The assumptive worlds of fledgling administrators. *Education and Urban Society, 23,* 396–415.

McDonald, F., Elias, P., Stone, M., Wheeler, P., & Lambert, M. (1975). *Final report on Phase II: Beginning Teacher Evaluation Study.* Princeton, NJ: Educational Testing Service.

Mead, G. (1934). *Mind, self, and society from the standpoint of a social behaviorist.* Chicago: University of Chicago Press.

Purkey, W., & Novak, J. (1984). *Inviting school success.* Belmont, CA: Wadsworth.

Rogers, C. (1959). A theory of therapy, personality and interpersonal relationships, as developed in the client-centered framework. In S. Koch (Ed.), *Psychology: A study of science* (vol. 3). New York: McGraw-Hill.

Ryan, K. (1992). (Ed.). *The roller coaster year: Essays by and for beginning teachers.* New York: HarperCollins.

Sacks, S., & Harrington, C. (1982, March). *Student to teacher: The process of role transition.* Paper presented at the meeting of the American Educational Research Association, New York.

Sparks, R., & Lipka, R. (1992). Characteristics of master teachers: Personality factors, self-concept, locus of control and pupil ideology. *Journal of Personnel Evaluation in Education, 5,* 303–311.

St. Augustine. (1955). *Augustine: Confessions and Enchiridion,* vol. VII. Albert Cook Outler (Ed.). Philadelphia: The Westminster Press.

PART III

The First Years of Teaching

CHAPTER 5

TEACHER SELF-APPRAISAL
AND APPRAISAL OF SELF

Les Tickle

In Britain, defining what a teacher or a good teacher is or is supposed to be has become a preoccupation in recently renewed mechanisms of control over, and approval of, initial teacher education programs; of expectations placed on newly qualified teachers; and in government definitions of experienced teachers' duties. Assumptions about teachers and teaching that seem to abound in these arenas are predominantly based on a tightly defined, technical view of practice in which observable actions and supposedly consequential results and outcomes (in behavior management, or measured student performance, for example, are almost the only focus of attention. They are manifest most clearly through government agency–defined competences in the realm of efficient rules of classroom control and management, instruction for the transmission of externally defined knowledge content, and knowledge of the curriculum (mostly this means *the* government-prescribed national curriculum). In this scheme of things, success in teaching (for entry into the profession; for inservice training in the first few years; and for later stages of career development through teacher appraisal and national curriculum training) is judged by levels of individual competence, skill, and knowledge, as observed and recorded by more powerful supervisors, or by teachers themselves, working under such supervision. Zimpher and Howey (1987) define this realm of teaching as *technical* competence. It has evident associations with behaviorist principles and with curricula defined according to prespecified and measurable objectives and outcomes

This is not new. I have suggested (Tickle, 1987) that it stems from a reactionary reinforcement of conservative concepts of teaching and schooling. But it is powerful. It represents a constantly reforming managerial category, if not a social identity, of the teacher and related identity of the student, into which individuals might be inducted, and within which identities may be formed. I have also argued (Tickle 1987, 1989b, 1991, 1992, 1993a, 1993b, 1994) that in a broader educative sense, this technicist view of teaching—which is predominantly concerned with the acquisition and onward transmission of government-specified subject knowledge, attitudes, and values, and with the differentiation of pupils into occupational routes through assessment and testing—is a limited and limiting view. My critiques accept the importance of practical efficacy in teaching, though not simply in terms defined according to didactic instruction and assessment in prescribed behaviors. But they also seek to promote forms of teacher education that would be educative for teachers, and that stem from a more encompassing view of teaching. In that view I have in the past meant to foster a revisionist perspective of personally reflexive and socially critical-active teachers— whom I describe as tacticians capable of bringing about personal, educational, and social change, rather than instructional technicians who implement policies devised by others, polices that might result in the continuation of social inequalities, discrimination, injustices, and narrow worldviews. That is the broad mission of my teacher education.

In the past decade I have drawn extensively upon evidence from new teachers that shows how they initially came to seek identities largely within the technical conception of teaching. I have shown how they use and develop *clinical* competence, in the form of practical problem-solving, which involves reflective action for the improvement of instructional strategies (Zimpher & Howey, 1987; Tickle, 1992, 1994, 1995). From that evidence I demonstrated how subject knowledge and pedagogical skills are crucial to self-identity in teaching, especially among student and beginning teachers.

Among those with whom I carried out research, one of the features of their work was a lack of opportunity to make explicit, let alone review, their own educational aims and values. This realm of reflection, which Zimpher and Howey called *personal* competence, was not in the frame of consciousness. Nor, by and large, were the aims and values of colleagues, or of the formal policies of schools as social institutions. I have suggested though, that far from simply being self-induced, this feature is a response to the intensity of circumstances, with the demands of sometimes overwhelming social interactions and complex responsibilities in the job of teaching. I argued that as a result, beyond "efficacy" as it is commonly defined, and certainly as it is managerially defined, there is a need for and desire among new teachers to develop qualities and capabilities that will sustain long-term critical enquiry and learning—about their knowledge, their pedagogical practices, and the personal/educational aims, attitudes, and values that underlie them. These needs and desires are not necessarily universal, nor are they universally pursued and satisfied (Tickle, 1994, 1995). But they are the focus of attention in attempts to develop critical inquiry qualities and capabilities, the common ground of educational action research (Carr, 1995; McKernan, 1991; Tabachnick & Zeichner, 1991). This is the nature of the broad strategy that I have adopted over many years in pursuit of my mission in teacher education.

My research with new teachers also led me to suggest that there is an even deeper need among them, and in teacher induction programs, to take aspects of *self* in teacher development seriously. There appears to be a dearth of interest among policymakers and teacher education curriculum planners in such self aspects of teaching, which are additional but closely related to other aims and values. In policy and practice the identification and development of *personal qualities*, at the interface between aspects of one's personal virtues and one's professional life, between personhood and teacherhood if you will, has had scant attention. My initial focus in this respect was the failure of the technicist and clinical views of teaching to acknowledge, let alone provide for the development of, the emotions associated with being a teacher and with the intense social interactions of teaching (Tickle, 1991, 1994). Here, in my current view, there is a need to extend the substance and methods of teacher development, and it goes beyond the emotions, to other aspects of character and attitude. What I have in mind are qualities such as empathy; compassion; the ability to manage frustration and impatience; understanding and tolerance of, if not the celebration of, cultural variations or sexual orientations; love; the capacity to assess social situations; a mastery of reflective thinking; flexibility in the application of teaching techniques; tolerance of ambiguity and of conflicting interests and expectations; sensitivity to the needs of others; assertiveness in the face of abuse; an ability to share others' grief, sorrow, pleasure, or delight; the capacity to manage guilt, anger, and contempt; ambition; and so on. That is at the heart of my recent mission for teacher development and the basis, by way of this chapter, for my recommended reorientation.

My personal and self-consciously idiosyncratic list of contenders is not presented as a prescribed and complete set of alternatives to a command of knowledge or the technical skills of instruction. Rather, it is offered to open the gate of consideration, in a concrete and illustrative way, to the affective realms of teaching, which have a bearing on the educative experiences of the teacher-self and student-self, and on the development of individual identities. This is in my view the more problematic realm of being a teacher, one that has not been adequately attended to in discussions of, and proposals for, teachers' professional development. The perceived dearth of attention is in some contrast to the recent growth of research into the lived experiences of teachers, conducted through life histories, biography, and autobiography, drawing on symbolic interactionism, phenomenology, and hermeneutics as bases for both substantive and methodological concerns with the broader lives of teachers. (For example, Beynon, 1987; Denzin, 1989; Elbaz, 1983; Goodson, 1992; Goodson & Walker, 1991; Huberman, 1993; Nias, 1989; Sparkes, 1994; Tickle, 1994.)

Those developments, in part, corresponded with this current focus of my work with new teachers, and my concerns with the self and teaching, as they emerged through both research- and teaching-interests. What has transpired is a recognition that while "Capital T Teaching" (Tickle, 1993) in the technical and clinical senses of practice are of primary concern to new teachers, there is extensive evidence of concerns with *being* a teacher in the broader sense, with the "me" as well as the "I" of teaching. I will seek to explore these matters more fully here, from the point of view of a practicing, reflective teacher educator who has sought to extend the parameters of action research toward a reorientation of professional development that puts aspects of self at the center. The ideas of action research have never been a homogeneous set. They can be read, for instance, as serving the instrumental needs of instructional efficiency; the needs of personal fulfillment as educator and self-educator; the social-critical purposes of both individuals and professional groups; or some combination of these (see also McKernan, 1991; Tabachnick & Zeichner, 1991). Like others who promote action research, I have stressed different dimensions on different occasions, as I also do in this chapter.

CHRONOLOGY AND TEACHER APPRAISAL

The timing of external events and the refocusing of my personal perspectives are important. In the mid to late 1980s, after many years of doing research as a teacher and encouraging it among others as a teacher educator, I took on responsibility for researching the professional development experiences of newly qualified teachers. The research was a base for devising, and with colleagues delivering, professional development programs separately for teachers in their first few years of teaching. These were intended to promote principles of reflective practice and action research, informed by notions of the professional empowerment of individual teachers and their professional self-development. They were publicly oppositional to the prevailing political Right as it sought to rein in and, as I see it, to regiment and de-personalize teaching and learning. That has been done mainly through national curriculum legislation, national assessment, the prescription of teacher education courses based on behavioral competences, and teacher appraisal and career tracking (Tickle, 1987, 1994). The implementation of our new inservice programs corresponded almost exactly with changes in government control of initial teacher education; with the national implementation of teacher appraisal; and with changes in government-sponsored training for teachers to implement the national curriculum. From this vast array of events I will attend briefly here to teacher appraisal, the most pertinent for present purposes, and one I have not commented on elsewhere.

In teacher appraisal in Britain the idea of self-appraisal became a central feature, its widely accepted principle being that teachers take personal responsibility for engendering reviews of their practice and bringing about improvements in it. This idea is related to notions of reflective practice, action research, teacher autonomy, and professional self-development—ideas that, mainly through the activities of the organized teaching profession (i.e., the unions) contributed to the formally constituted, legislated framework of appraisal that has formed part of teachers' conditions of service since 1989 (see Elliott, 1991). Self-appraisal in this sense, however, can still be read as an instrument by which another strand of teacher assessment can be achieved—the managerial dimension, derived from the political promise to improve standards in education through the monitoring of teachers' classroom performance. That element of teacher appraisal was and is promoted largely by local education authorities (LEAs) as employers, and by the government through its Department for Education and Employment (DFEE), and its Office for Standards in Education (OfSTED) headed by Her Majesty's Chief Inspector of Schools. Its premise, like that of parallel developments in the assessment and monitoring of new entrants to teaching and of the initial teacher education programs they attend, is one that asserts that teaching is constituted by a range of identifiable and measurable instructional competences (Tickle, 1992). OfSTED is so confident of this behaviorist view of teachers that it now grades them on a scale of 1 to 7 against its own norms of excellence and incompetence.

The imposition upon the teaching profession of a legislated curriculum and national assessment regime, with a presumed set of instructional skills that define teaching, or the willing compliance of teachers to assess (and possibly identify) themselves against prescribed measures of technical efficiency, are potentially potent mechanisms, in terms of the impact on the self in teaching and teacher development. Such mechanisms play a part in defining what counts, and what does not, as legitimate matter for development, as well as defining who might manage it. Teacher assessment and appraisal in this form, when seen in the light of the self in teaching and teacher development, have a number of disturbing possible consequences. For example, they could:

- leave teachers and the act of teaching respectively depersonalized and dehumanized, framed in terms only related to technical skills of instruction;
- encourage individualized self-blame for deficiencies in teaching and learning rather than the identification of collective social responsibilities that might foster the pursuit of excellence in education (which I define, after Bruner, as the maximization of individual potential);
- substantially reinforce the difficulties teachers have in exploring and exposing their own values and attitudes, or the predominant ones of their institutions (Nias, 1989; Tickle, 1993, 1994);
- increase the power of the split between public and private lives and attitudes, which is sometimes experienced negatively and detrimentally by some teachers (Beynon, 1987; Sparkes, 1994);
- leave important aspects of teachers' personal values potentially beyond the reach of professional development;
- sanitize curricula (especially the humanities and arts) from extra-school social participation, individualism, and the celebration of personhood by both teachers and students.

Appraisal became the focus of attention with regard to newly qualified teachers when, in 1992, the managerially assessed probationary first year of teaching was abolished, and new teachers were included in the formal appraisal scheme. Contemporaneously with this series of events I sought to establish a case for a humanistic and holistic notion of teacher self-development, more problematic than that which was presumed in the formal scheme of appraisal. My notion is based on a comprehensive image of *self*-appraisal—not as appraisal of practice by one's self, but of appraisal of aspects of one's self as professional. The reason for seeking a broader view of self-appraisal stems from a concern for a more tolerant, humane, and person-centered kind of inservice education for new teachers than the technologistic form that has come to pervade much of teacher training. It is a bid for a more inclusive notion of teacher development, in which the essentials of being a teacher, and the bases of personal growth, perspective, and identity, can sit legitimately alongside subject knowledge, instructional strategies, and curriculum organization as worthy of educational and educative attention. That is the context of my current submission.

SELF-APPRAISAL FOR PROFESSIONAL GROWTH

I am conscious that this is an uninvited search on behalf of others, as well as a personal exploration of the bounds of the role of self in teacher development. At the heart of the exploration is a push at the parameters of what it means to be a teacher and of what the idea of developing as a teacher could and should entail. This is complex terrain—theoretically *and* in the lived experience of individuals becoming teachers. It has its own landmarks in sociology, social psychology, teacher-thinking, life-histories, teacher education, fiction, and autobiographical literature (see Nias, 1989). Recently its importance, at least for my present project, was summed up by Swanson (1989):

> The newer studies of "emotion" are broader than the word suggests. They have also to do with values and attitudes, motives and motivation. More generally they concern the meaning of social relations for people's fulfillment as persons or selves; a renewed interest in affective connections between personal functioning and social structure. (Swanson, 1989, p. 4)

In order to be faithful to the conception I want to convey, let me for the moment share the hope that my earlier comments locate me ideologically, theoretically, and professionally within the symbolic interactionist, and more lately hermeneutic, corner of the qualitative research/practice field (Tickle, 1994). That is necessary in order to make explicit some of the assumptions of teacher research and teacher education on which this section of the chapter is based. They set the paradigmatic context for the extension to teacher professional development I am proposing, and particularly for legitimizing and promoting the place of character, the emotions, and other aspects of personhood within it (see Clark, 1992; Denzin, 1984; Franks & McCarthy, 1989; for recent developments in the field of "emotion").

Teacher research and reflective practice, and their potentials for understanding and developing the role of self in teaching, were reformulated in the conduct of the inservice bachelor of philosophy (teaching) degree program at the University of East Anglia, Norwich, for teachers in their first few years of teaching (Tickle, 1989, 1992). Here, I will draw upon one unit of study in the program: *Self-Appraisal for Professional Growth*. The intentions and working practices of the unit, the substantive personal research topics defined and pursued by teachers in it, and the research methods they used in pursuit of appraisals of self have not previously been reported. In presenting a summary of the work here I will leave to readers the responsibility of further locating my research and professional practice from various published accounts listed in the references. Let it suffice for now to declare my celebration of persistent personal growth and constant development of identity within teaching. That celebration is not value-free of course, as I have already made plain. It does not permit the growth of homophobia and pedophilia, or the development of bullies, racists, or chauvinists, for example.

In presenting the work as a summary I hope that I can successfully "speak for those who cannot openly speak for themselves in particular forums so that the reader can achieve solidarity with them as fellow human beings" (Sparkes, 1994, p. 97). Individual teachers are protected by the use of a journalistic style of writing for reasons that will be partly evident from the substantive nature of some of their concerns. Equally to the point, the ethics and procedures of our collaborative endeavors gave me limited rights to use only some of their voices directly, and only within the tutorial team. Negotiating an amended contract with them all would take more time than I have. More pragmatically, I want to include a range of cases within this limited textual space, so I need to use summaries of extensive conversations and documentary data that were recorded in the form of diaries and student assignment reports.

The B.Phil (Teaching) degree was an innovative two-year inservice part-time program (unique in Britain) introduced in 1988 for teachers in their postinduction years. Its cohorts of twenty or so students in each intake between 1988 and 1994, on which this report is based, have included teachers of all age groups within the 5 to 18 years range, from primary, middle, high, and special schools, and sixth-form (secondary education for college bound students 16–19 years of age) college. Among high school teachers almost all school subjects have been represented: science, math, English, religious education, physical education, art, home economics and child care, geography, history, economics, music, technology. The whole program is organized in five units of study: Analyzing Children's Work; Teaching and Its Different Patterns; Curriculum Modification for a Context; Self-Appraisal for Professional Growth; and Developing Curriculum Leadership. It is based on engendering what Sockett (1994) has described as the characteristics of professionalism: character (virtues or personal qualities); commitment to continuous self-improvement; subject knowledge and pedagogical expertise; and educational leadership, as part of the social/community enterprise of education (Sockett, 1994, pp. 6–8).

In *Self-Appraisal for Professional Growth*, I have sought to explore with the teachers, and have them explore through their own teacher-research projects, the problematic nature of opening up dimensions of the self-as-teacher/teacher-as-self to scrutiny and potential development. These teacher-researchers have worked with support from their peers in defining and refining meaningful and realizable matters for, and methods of, inquiry in pursuit of the appraisal and development of aspects of self. The intention has been to extend the boundaries of my own participation in, and contribution to, professional development in direction of personal competence (Zimpher & Howey, 1987). It has also been to open up opportunities in this dimension of development to new teachers. In that form of capability, the conception of the teacher is one who has an understanding of self, has a sense of self-actualization, and "uses the self as an effective and humane instrument" (ibid., p. 104)— both in their own and their students' development. The collaborative explorations of the Self-Appraisal unit have sought to:

- take seriously the interests, cited earlier, in a more comprehensive and humanistic notion of teacher appraisal;
- address the need for a curriculum in teacher preparation that takes personal qualities, values, attitudes, and the emotions associated with being a teacher into account;
- confront the difficulties teachers have in getting beneath matters of technical and clinical expertise, and identifying dimensions of the ideals, beliefs, and perspectives that underlie their practice;
- provide opportunities to identify, make public, and seek to develop aspects of self, within principles of procedure set by the group, such as maintaining confidentiality when individuals request it; asking critical questions in supportive, nonthreatening ways; and negotiating partnerships to establish mutual trust in order to encourage risk-taking.

The aims and practices of the unit are consistent with, and a subset of, those of the B.Phil. program as a whole. The main general aim is the development of the capacity to make sound professional judgments in practice. Its presumption is that the search for prudence, or practical wisdom, that is, "the ability to discern the most suitable, politic, or profitable course of action" (Stenhouse, cited in Rudduck & Hopkins, 1985, p. 52), must encompass a search for evidence, within professional situations, that will form a basis for judgment and guide actions. Criteria for the assessment of students' work, which apply throughout the program and which are known to them, are:

- demonstrating a capacity for generating and gathering information/evidence upon which to make judgments in teaching;
- displaying effective modes of analysis of the evidence;
- taking justifiable practical action based upon the analyses;
- evaluating the effects and effectiveness of the actions by way of supplementary evidence.

The application of that general aim and these criteria to self-appraisal presumes that there is room for action in the development of self, as well as a willingness to act, initially in the pursuit of a research issue/problem, and of evidence related to it. What constitutes the most suitable, politic, and profitable *subject* for potential action, the sources of evidence available, and the methods that might be used for soliciting, recording, and analyzing that evidence as prerequisite to deciding upon courses of development action, are determined by individual teachers. The problematic nature of the unit is set out in a printed, tutorial, opening statement that displays something of its value-orientation and the potential substance of the teachers' inquiries and matters for development:

> This unit is designed to provide a better awareness and understanding of teaching as a personal commitment and professional activity from a humanistic perspective. The work within it is designed to make explicit an assumption that the prospect of formal appraisal offers only limited (if any) educational opportunities for teachers. It will consider the nature of appraisal, but emphasise self-appraisal—its principles, purposes, procedures, climate, criteria, and consequences. This will be done through a mode of collaborative enquiry within the group, seeking to construct experiences of an educative kind. It will be assumed such experiences might result from modes of self-appraisal partly by addressing the relationship and the possible tension between appraisal of aspects of one's teaching by oneself, and the appraisal of self in teaching, either by oneself or others. This relationship will be explored as a segment of problems which exist in defining professional competence, and professional growth. The "official" view of teacher knowledge being made up of personal qualities, subject knowledge and teaching skills as a triad of "expertise" will be used as a starting point for the exploration. (Course Handbook)

This trio of teacher knowledge, which informed policy from the mid-1980s, has become a duo, with the exclusion in recent listings of competences of the concern with "personal qualities." It is difficult to locate a reason for the demise, but it corresponded with a veritable growth industry in the assessment of competences in many levels of employment, training, and occupations, and predated the 1995 merger of the government's Departments of Education and Employment. In itself this is a matter for critique introduced to the students. They also consider the need to explore research methods that they may not have encountered before. Support for carrying out exploratory research, and ways of doing so, are provided in course materials:

> There will be opportunity to discuss, develop and use research methods appropriate to self-appraisal. These may be more autobiographical, reflective, and introspective than methods used in previous units, since the process of self-appraisal is seen as comprising four possible elements:
>
> - an understanding of self as a professional—a teacher's experiences, perspective, strategies and actions are all influenced by the way s/he sees her/himself in the role of teacher. The unit will begin by focusing on your perceptions of self: your good points; your biases; your blind spots; your dreamer spots; and your untapped reservoirs of unknown potential—in the context of self, appraisal, and professional growth.
> - appraisal of practice and the aims, values and beliefs on which it is based.
> - analysis of the working environment—it will be argued that if teachers are to modify their practice or aspects of their self effectively, then they must understand the environment in which they work, including the political and ideological environment, and the constraining forces which act upon them. Each student will be encouraged to consider their relationship to the circumstances in which they work, including their place among others who are significant in their life and work.
> - evaluation and prospects—students will be encouraged to evaluate their venture in self-appraisal and to devise proposals for their further professional self-development. (Course Handbook)

From the tutorial perspective, these aspirations are pursued partly through such descriptions and discussion of the aims of the unit itself, and the possibilities of self-appraisal at the level of principle. Through tentative proposals for avenues of research, and through consideration of a range of kinds of evidence and research methods that might attend personally significant issues, a process of sifting leads to individualized research plans and strategies for carrying them out. The sites of research are sometimes outside the tutorial group meetings, but often also within them, where critical friendship agreements may be used to elicit and record evidence of a personal kind. A set of conditions, theoretical support, working procedures, and expectations is negotiated with the teachers. These include:

- the establishment of conditions for learning thought necessary to explore aspects of self in teaching, through the concept of negotiated principles of procedure;
- exposure to theoretical matter on the self, on teachers' competences, and on appraisal, in order to provide a metaperspective on personal/professional development for the teachers;
- the identification and negotiation of substantive topics of personal research that have significant meaning to individuals and the potential for development of the self;
- taking of risks in the teacher-research methodologies adopted, and the data sought by the teachers, in pursuit of self-understanding and self-development.

SEARCHING AND SUBSTANCE

The unit also has guidance materials and criteria for the conduct of a research assignment that is expected to culminate in a report of the experience of self-appraisal. The assignment task forms the focus of most of the tutorial group activities, and is worded so as to encourage a dual level of evidence handling—on the substantive aspects of self chosen by each teacher, and on the processes involved in undertaking an appraisal of self. The latter equates, in research terms, with a methodological critique and is intended to help each person to improve the means by which aspects of self are appraised. There is of course the possibility of fusion (if not confusion) between the two elements of substance and method. The task/guidance is presented as follows:

- define and justify an aspect of teaching for self-appraisal;
- devise appropriate methods to examine this aspect;
- use these methods to identify strengths and/or weaknesses in the aspect of teaching appraised;

- set realistic aspirations in the light of available evidence and plan appropriate courses of action to meet these aspirations;
- evaluate the process and effectiveness of the research undertaken, against its original aims. (Course Handbook)

These are worded so as to encompass teaching in its broadest sense, to include aspects of classroom practice, which have been the mainstay of previous units, but to open up the wider possibilities I have discussed. As tutor I am clearly (and happily) open to the charge that my printed statement and my predispositions encourage students to orientate their research in certain ways. My summary defense, if one is needed, is that most have expressed their surprise at having, and have grasped, the opportunity to deal with matters that seemed unreachable in their initial training and in their schools' agendas for their professional development. I will summarize briefly what some of the teachers have deemed significant research topics, in order to illustrate the qualitative nature of their self-appraisal. The examples, in their kind, appear to warrant my earlier assertions that this realm of activity lies at the interface between the personal and the professional, an interface in which aspects of the development of identity as a teacher are critically felt. They also imply that the development of professional identity has that much broader scope which I discussed earlier. Furthermore, they suggest that opportunities to bring the role of the reflexive self to bear upon issues of personal and professional importance, in addition to more conventionally conceived matters of practice, has significant potential for enhancing the development of identities among teachers. The subjects have included (among others):

- an overtly seemingly self-confident woman teacher whose public presentation of confidence deliberately masked an inwardly deep insecurity, leading to identity conflicts, and the self-closing of avenues to advice and support that she wanted;
- teachers whose practices are governed largely by an overriding desire to be personally popular with students, sometimes to the detriment of other goals, and who sought to understand the origins of this desire and its impact on their practice;
- a self-defined and self-consciously introvert teacher in adult company, who is mainly secure with this characteristic, but who recognizes it as professionally idiosyncratic, and who is under pressure especially from administrators to talk more among colleagues;
- a self-declared "humane" teacher who seeks to acknowledge individuality and personal rights among adolescents, and who is at odds

with a school regime based on what she regards as perpetual retribu-
tion toward students for minor manifestations of individual behavior
involving initiative, decision making, and choice (such as taking jack-
ets off in class);
- teachers plummeted into low self-worth, either through interpretations of comments from colleagues, students, or parents, or from
their own deliberations about the efficacy of individual actions or
their practice in general, and despite their awareness of "external"
counterevidence that should promote self-esteem;
- a secretly gay male teacher fearful, because of that fact, in his
staffroom relationships with other teachers, and even in conversation
with them, such that he did not regard himself as functioning effectively, and certainly not confidently, as a professional colleague or as
a person with integrity and courage;
- a "new age" teacher of religion whose moral code excludes conventional school notions of punishment and of social control, and who
wishes to institute his ideas by example in the way he responds to
students;
- a young female teacher experiencing explicit sexual comments from
male students and male colleagues, seeking to understand her reactions to these, and to develop constructive strategies of response that
will help both her and them;
- a teacher who perceives herself as regularly, unjustly, and unnecessarily, being short-tempered and irritable with young pupils, and
fractious in her responses to their questions and persistent requests
for help with their learning;
- a teacher who is self-conscious about her desire to treat boys and
girls equally in every respect who is suddenly made conscious of a
tendency in her practice to actually treat them very differently;
- a teacher who reacts to even casual and insubstantial criticisms with
severe self-deprecations, and the temporary but frequent formulation
of herself as a "crap person," seeking to understand the phenomenon
and to devise mechanisms for managing her responses;
- a male teacher who believes he is wonderful in every respect and that
the students adore his every move, and who wants confirmatory evidence to support this perspective.

The methods employed by the teachers in the initial pursuit of evidence has often focused on explicating the issues and the reasons they
are issues. Sometimes this has meant adopting autobiographical en-
quiries or supportive searches to uncover key or even core values (Nias,
1989), and perhaps the reasons for attachment to them. It has meant

generating plausible and trustworthy methods for gaining access to, and recording, the perspectives of significant others in the teaching context or among family and friends. In some instances it has involved monitoring the teacher's own responses to situations and to the actions of other people. And it has meant triangulating evidence in search of possible, multiple interpretations of those actions and in seeking the perspectives of others.

Sometimes the risks of adopting such methods have been what I will call merely academic ones—that is, this is an award-bearing program, subject to assessment and external moderation, and not all professional educators and examiners sit in the same paradigmatic camp. More importantly for me and the teachers, the risks have been a further severalfold. One risk is that of opening up to others the nature of the research, by looking for necessary evidence, and by doing so exposing the very vulnerabilities that it is intended to help overcome. The case of the gay teacher's relations with colleagues is an example of this. The data from this case showed that, like Sparkes' lesbian subject Jessica (Sparkes, 1994), the inquiries were helpful in developing a deeper understanding of the situation and of personal responses to it, though the course of action chosen left the circumstances unchanged.

Another is that of shaking the foundations on which professional action and conduct has formerly been dependent, of displacing what were deemed sound values and judgments, without yet formulating replacements. The displacement of self-presentation as a seemingly confident professional by the "real" self-doubting teacher illustrates that risk. Data in that example show a teacher wrestling with a deep conflict. It resided between career ambition, which was deemed in part to depend on self-confidence being noticed by her superiors, and inner acknowledgment of novicehood. The teacher's inquiries unearthed a previously subconscious dilemma: public display of (false) self-confidence was preventing her from seeking access to help, advice, support, and professional development opportunities involving more senior colleagues. That in turn was, potentially, thwarting the career ambition. Through supported self-management strategies a resolve to develop different attitudes to potential sources of her own learning was brought about.

A third, emergent risk is the possibility of residual loyalties to beliefs and values cohabiting with newly forming ones. This can be manifest as conflict when deeply held values are confronted by new experiences and changes in perception. Tensions can exist as conflicting desires are calibrated gradually and judged against further evidence of changes in practice. Attachment to existing ideas and previous experiences or ways of doing things are possible, as illustrated in data from the (originally) self-elected introvert teacher. Her responses to the expectations of colleagues to be more outgoing among adults was accompanied by inquires into those expectations themselves, and appraisal of collective "norms" for teacher conduct, as well as the reasons for her being "different." The accommodations that she reached were complex and subtle responses to the data that she gathered.

These few examples indicate that like the individual cases reported by Dadds (1995), Nias (1989), Sparkes (1994), and others the presentation of the subtleties and details of data in each of the many cases within the B.Phil. (Teaching) degree deserve major space that is not currently available. However, my general point here is that in the conduct of self-appraisal inquiries of this kind, the need for professional esteem and self-approbation is evident, yet I recognize that perpetual self-growth intrinsically involves the possibility of self-challenge and disapprobation of the self in some respects. That tension deserves careful attention.

SELF, IDENTITY, AND PROFESSIONALISM

These directions and foci of self-development differ radically from the prevailing mentalities of teacher training and formal appraisal, which concentrate solely on subject knowledge and classroom practice. They do so, in all modesty, because of an opportunity to open up these directions for the teachers, through a program in which the tutorial focus was permitted and chose to hone in on self-awareness, on identity formation, on "self-confrontation in the explication and clarification of values" (Zimpher & Howey, 1987, p. 104), and on aspects of personal commitment and interpersonal involvement in teaching and in learning as a teacher.

My concerns with the personal dimensions of teaching might be regarded as blind allegiance to the "Romantic preoccupation" with "the teacher as a person," an individual whose personality, perceptions, and predispositions influence judgments and behavior, and form the core "by which education itself takes place" (Nias, 1989, pp. 13–15). That is a very powerful image, one that Nias shows to have affected influential educators, researchers, commentators, and policymakers over the past century and a half. It is one that seems to be perpetuated by research analyses and inspectorial assessments of "master teaching," by the persistence of students in elevating some tutors to almost idol status, and by parents whose summations of "good teachers" often include the prioritizing of personality characteristics. The allegiance, however, is not blind, nor is it, I hope, even blinkered. It is developed partly from awareness of, and fear of a return to, an apprentice-teacher system adopted in England by the Quakers in the 1780s, and later promoted by Joseph Lancaster on their behalf, and by Andrew Bell for the Anglicans. This was training for systems of teaching in which each school was organized and administered, and the curriculum derived from intricate centralized planning, under strict regulation and license, through local superintendence.

My analysis of data showed that the induction of new teachers into *only* the technical and clinical dimensions of teaching was commonplace. That constitutes a mild version of such a system, and fails the new teachers and those who follow them into the profession. It also signaled a crucial deficiency in my thinking about the inservice professional development of teachers at this early career stage. That was the recognition that my approach to reflective practice and action research was itself largely centered on the development of practice in the instructional sense of that word. Yet there was evident need to attend to the empowering possibilities of the development of aspects of the self as teacher. To do so at this early career stage holds out the chance of developing personal identities in constructive ways, potentially subverting those disturbing managerial consequences of teacher assessment and appraisal.

As a result, the search for an alternative psychology of teaching led, for me, to a reconceptualization of teacher development in the direction of *personal* competence (Zimpher & Howey, 1987). It is a direction in which the education of teachers, and the qualitative improvement of the education of pupils, is one along the lines suggested by Salmon (1988). She points out that which ought, perhaps, to have been self-evident—the personal constructs of teachers are crucial to the kind of education on offer to pupils (Salmon, 1988, p. 22). However, she argues, while psychology focuses on the individuality of pupils, teachers usually get lumped together, their knowledge and capabilities assumed to be standard, and their training standardized and finite. In her view of self, identity, and teacher development, personal constructs are the seed corn of the education of teachers themselves, and their openness to transformation is a condition of professionalism as Sockett (and others) has defined it. If that can be achieved in the first years of teaching then a humane and person-centered sense of professionalism might be possible.

In adapting this educative stance for teacher professional development, it follows that the personalities, perceptions, and predispositions of individual teachers are somehow to be nourished. This is not a bid from a perspective of teachers as deficient in some respects, nor does it imply that self-scrutiny necessarily will lead to self-promoted changes in the constructs that individual teachers explore. It is a search for a developmental and constructionist approach to teacher education that is capable of handling such matters.

That was the basis of my plea for a curriculum for the emotions for new teachers (Tickle, 1991, 1994). But where teaching is unique and personal, in this sense of being individualistic, it is also an activity and profession in which isolation from other adults, a sense of autonomy, and dependence upon self-help are predominant characteristics (Lortie, 1975; Nias, 1989; Tickle, 1994; Waller, 1932). That being so, the need for and the means of gaining nourishment for the personality, perceptions, and predispositions will have to be appreciated by teachers themselves, and by those who might provide for their professional development. In the case of the newly qualified teachers I have referred to, this point is crucial, in several respects. First, the time—either for support of those who seek to address these personal qualities of their own volition, or for intervention strategies for the development of those who do not—seems, in the light of my research with beginning teachers, to be from the very beginning of their induction into the profession. But there may be a particular case for strengthening the support/intervention in those first few years of full-time teaching, when routinization of practice and the firming of identity as a teacher seems to occur.

This is a time when the preoccupations of new teachers certainly include deeply personal matters, as well as many more practical problems that need solving—housing, transport, lack of social life and even sleep, and so on. The immediate experiences of becoming a teacher include many dimensions of self—that is well demonstrated by my research, and within the Self-Appraisal unit of the B.Phil. This is a career point when habituation of practice is not yet established, and when, perhaps, the values and attitudes of both "situational selves" and "substantial selves" (Nias, 1989, p. 21) are less than static, and when individuals might take on a metaperspective of self-appraisal processes. However, I have argued (Tickle, 1993, 1994, 1995) that it is unreasonable to expect new teachers at one and the same time to seek to establish their credibility as teachers and also to tear up their own foundations of practice by overly self-questioning without carefully managed support. I have also demonstrated and argued that the number of topics that present themselves as possible candidates for introspection and self-examination leaves perceived classroom efficacy (in technical and clinical senses) a likely and reasonable priority contender at that stage. But the danger in this is that the preoccupations with inservice training of the technicist and behaviorist kind, and the interpretations of self-appraisal as part of teachers' conditions of service, will leave the other kinds of opportunities unexplored, and teachers potentially underdeveloped in important dimensions of self.

REFERENCES

Beynon, J. (1987). Ms. Floral mends her ways. In L. Tickle (Ed.), *The arts in education*. London: Croom Helm.

Carr, W. (1995). *For education: Toward critical educational inquiry*. Milton Keynes, UK: Open University Press.

Clark, M. S. (Ed.). (1992). *Emotion*. London: Sage.

Dadds, M. (1995). *Passionate enquiry and school development: A story about teacher action research*. London: Falmer Press.

Denzin, N. (1984). *On understanding emotion*. San Francisco: Jossey-Bass.

Denzin, N. (1989). *Interpretive interactionism*. London: Sage.

Denzin, N. (1992). *Symbolic interactionism and cultural studies*. Oxford: Blackwell.

Elbaz, F. (1983). *Teacher thinking: A study of practical knowledge*. London: Croom Helm.

Elliott, J. (1991). *Action research for educational change*. Milton Keynes, UK: Open University Press.

Ellis, C., & Flaherty, M. (Eds.). (1992). *Investigating subjectivity: Research on lived experience*. London: Sage.

Franks, D. D., & McCarthy, E. D. (Eds.). (1989). *The sociology of emotions*. Greenwich, CT: JAI Press.

Goodson, I. (Ed.). (1992). *Studying teachers' lives*. London: Routledge.

Goodson, I., & Walker, R. (Eds.). (1991). *Biography, identity and schooling: Episodes in educational research*. Lewes, UK: Falmer Press.

Huberman, M. (1993). *The lives of teachers*. London: Cassell.

Lortie, D. (1975). *Schoolteacher*. Chicago: University of Chicago Press.

McKernan, J. (1991). *Curriculum action research*. London: Kogan Page.

Nias, J. (1987). Teaching and the self. *Cambridge Journal of Education, 17*, 178–184.

Nias, J. (1989). *Primary teachers talking*. London: Routledge.

Okely, J., & Callaway, H. (Eds.). (1992). *Anthropology and autobiography*. London: Routledge.

Peters, R. S. (1972). The education of the emotions. In R. F. Deardon, P. Hirst, & R. S. Peters (Eds.), *Education and the development of reason*. London: Routledge and Kegan Paul.

Rudduck, J., & Hopkins, D. (Eds.). (1985). *Research as a basis for teaching*. London: Heinemann.

Salmon, P. (1988). *Psychology for teachers: An alternative approach*. London: Hutchinson.

Sockett, H. (1994). *The moral base for teacher professionalism*. New York: Teachers College Press.

Sparkes, A. C. (1994). Self, silence and invisibility as a beginning teacher: A life history of lesbian experience. *British Journal of Sociology of Education, 15*, 93–118.

Swanson, G. E. (1989). On the motives and motivation of selves. In D. D. Franks & E. D. McCarthy (Eds.), *The sociology of emotions*. Greenwich, CT: JAI Press.

Tabachnick, B. R., & Zeichner, K. (Eds.). (1991). *Issues and practices in inquiry-oriented teacher education*. London: Falmer Press.

Tickle, L. (1987). *Learning teaching, teaching teaching*. Lewes, UK: Falmer Press.

Tickle, L. (1989a). New teachers and the development of professionalism. In M. L. Holly & C. S. McLaughlin (Eds.), *Perspective on teacher professional development*. Lewes, UK: Falmer Press.

Tickle, L. (1989b). On probation: Preparation for professionalism. *Cambridge Journal of Education, 19*, 277–285.

Tickle, L. (1991). New teachers and the emotions of learning teaching. *Cambridge Journal of Education, 21*, 319–329.

Tickle, L. (1992). Professional skills assessment in classroom teaching. *Cambridge Journal of Education, 22*, 91–103.

Tickle, L. (1993a). Capital T Teaching. In J. Elliott (Ed.), *Reconstructing teacher education*. London: Falmer Press.

Tickle, L. (1993b). The first year of teaching as a learning experience. In D. Bridges & T. Kerry (Eds.), *Developing teachers professionally*. London: Routledge.

Tickle, L. (1994). *The induction of new teachers: Reflective professional practice*. London: Cassell.

Tickle, L. (1995). Reflective professional practice: Embrace or elusion? In R. McBride (Ed.), *Teacher education policy*. London: Falmer Press.

Waller, W. (1932). *The sociology of teaching*. New York: Russell and Russell.

Wilson, S. M., Shulman, L. S., & Richert, A. E. (1987). 150 different ways of knowing. In J. Calderhead (Ed.), *Exploring teachers' thinking*. London: Cassell.

Zimpher, N., & Howey, K. (1987). Adapting supervisory practices to different orientations of teaching competence. *Journal of Curriculum and Supervision, 2*, 101–127.

CHAPTER 6

IDENTITY AND INDUCTION: ESTABLISHING THE SELF IN THE FIRST YEARS OF TEACHING

Paul G. Schempp, Andrew C. Sparkes, and Thomas J. Templin

Finding ourselves in unfamiliar places requires that we look around to understand what the situation demands of us, and that we look within to determine our abilities and willingness to accommodate those demands. Beginning teachers undertake this same process during their first years in schools. It is during the induction period that new teachers must prove themselves in the workplace by executing their duties within the conventions of accepted practice while displaying a proper demeanor. But they also must find themselves. They must discover who they are and understand what they must become in order to not only remain a school member, but thrive and derive personal satisfaction in such a membership. Beginning teachers must search for and establish the self in school.

Novice teachers often find their beliefs vigorously challenged as they attempt to meet the demands and expectations pressed upon them by schools (Veeneman, 1984). The dialectical process of induction reshapes the actions and beliefs of both the individual and institution (Schempp & Graber, 1992). New members change as they affiliate with an institution, and the organization changes as new members usher in fresh ideas and unique ways of acting. Dialectical tensions emerge as practices, perspectives, and convictions are tested by the potent demands of life in school. Neither individual or institution is completely transformed, however, because induction is a process of synthesis and adaption for both.

The dialectics of induction instigate a shift in the social relations of the group. Popkewitz (1987) noted that "the notion of power relates not to ownership but to the understanding of changing social relations and innumerable vantage-points from which power is exercised" (p. 5). Underpinning, directing, and defining the shifting social relationships found in teacher induction is social power. In shaping their role in schools, beginning teachers struggle to both understand and exercise power within the school culture. As new members function in the worksite culture, value is given to their opinions and services as their status in the school becomes defined. The greater the status achieved by a member, the greater the influence in shaping the thoughts and actions of the group. For the inductee, social power is a necessary prerequisite for both their daily functioning and their long-term acceptance in the school.

The importance of teacher induction has attracted the attention of the scholarly community in recent years. The research activity in this area has revealed insights into the process beginning teachers undergo as they become members of a school community. The authors' research in this area has focused particularly on the social processes that meld new teachers with established schools (Schempp, Sparkes, & Templin, 1993). We shall use our findings as a platform to examine the establishment of self in the first years of teaching. We shall also identify the trends in research in teacher induction to examine the development of identity in induction.

In any professional practice, one must undergo a rite of passage. In this rite, one must prove oneself worthy of becoming a member. Other members of the group will assess the initiate's character, service, and ability to contribute to the common good. During this rite of passage, it is, however, equally important for the new member to determine who they are, and if they belong. Several factors influence, challenge, and sustain the perspectives and practices of beginning teachers. It is within the context of these elements that beginning teachers must establish their identity—the self. These components vary in importance depending on the circumstance and situation. No one element stands omnipotent, nor is it possible to predict which factor weighs most heavily in the teacher's thoughts or actions at any given moment. None of these factors are, however, ever very far from a new teacher's thoughts or decisions. It is from three interrelated elements that teachers establish their identities in schools: (1) biography, (2) establishing the self in teaching, and (3) establishing the self in schools.

These three factors do not represent an exhaustive list of influences shaping and sustaining the self in teaching, but rather, they encapsulate the influences and experiences common to many beginning teachers. While commonalities in the development of self exist, ultimately identity is a unique and personal phenomenon for each person. Based upon our research, and the work of others, we are reasonably confident that these three factors represent the primary elements in the chemistry of school life for teachers and, therefore, may serve as our guideposts for exploring the establishment of self during the early years of teaching.

Biography

Beginning teachers carry three sets of experiences to their new place of employment: (1) experiences that exercised similar or related pedagogical skills, (2) experiences as a pupil, and (3) university coursework. The experiences become used or ignored depending upon the interests of the teacher and the demands of the institution.

Teaching-Related Experiences

When describing resources for skills and knowledge used in teaching, teachers most easily recalled related experiences. For example, student teaching is often cited as the most beneficial of university education because it represents actual time with the students. Athletic coaching, working in summer camps, and even child-care experiences often supply beginning teachers with experiences in interacting with children, organizing activities, providing directions and instructions, and managing groups of people. Such experiences have the dual purpose of allowing beginning teachers to develop teaching skills, and confirming their occupational choice. For potential teachers, these experiences form a foundation upon which future skills, orientations, and knowledge will be built.

It is also in these early experiences that future teachers begin forming their identities as teachers (Lortie, 1975). A child with aspirations to teach will begin screening the activities, practices, and dispositions of their own teachers in an effort to construct the persona of the teacher they would like to be. The successes and failure they experience in their early "teaching" roles (e.g., babysitting, teacher helper, tutoring, camp counselor) also help shape their identities as future teachers. By the time future teachers entered teacher education programs, they have a wealth of experience in occupationally relevant experiences. And these experiences have taught them that they are well suited to a pedagogical profession. They see themselves as teachers.

Apprenticeship-of-Observation

Lortie (1975) theorized that students serve an apprenticeship-of-observation that later becomes an important information source for teachers practicing the craft. In studying this theory, it was found that teachers began identifying, selecting, and evaluating pedagogical routines and practices while students in public schools (Schempp, 1989). During the apprenticeship period, teachers become acquainted with many pedagogical tasks and skills. Prospective teachers learned effective strategies for motivating and disciplining students, presenting and demonstrating sport skills and subject content, organizing and operating a classroom, and developing interpersonal relationships with students, and, in general, they learned how to act like a teacher (e.g., dress, speech, demeanor). Surprisingly, assessment criteria distinguishing good and poor teachers (and their practices) appears firmly established during the apprenticeship period, and the belief that teachers' work is individualistic rather than collective and professional can be directly traced to this period of socialization. The lessons learned in the apprenticeship period are often recalled during induction as teachers attempt to define themselves as teachers in the classroom.

Particularly strong in the shaping of one's identity as a teacher is the influence of previous teachers. The teachers in whose classrooms we sat as students not only taught us much about the routines and duties of a teacher, but they also taught us how to interact with students, and inspired us to love a certain subject and to become teachers ourselves. This influence is often subtle, but it remains powerful and pervasive. Previous teachers not only influence the decision to become a teacher, but often inform teachers as to what to do, and why (McEvoy, 1986).

University Coursework

Educational background, specifically university coursework, appears to have its greatest value in supplying subject-matter content. In particular, it is the activity or "practical" courses that allow beginning teachers to construct pedagogical routines and rituals fit for public schools. Translating philosophy into policy or extruding a teaching plan from a theory is more difficult and less economical. The press and grind of public school pedagogy requires beginning teachers to adopt professional perspectives that are practical (Clandinin & Connelly, 1986; Elbaz, 1983) rather than intellectual (Giroux, 1988).

Portions of the preparation program that required contact with students in public schools appeared the strongest contenders for most useful aspect of education. One teacher familiar to the authors, who, in his first year of teaching taught three different subjects, drew heavily from his university teaching methods classes (Schempp et al., 1993). The methods classes had required him to teach in public schools and then reflect upon and judge those experiences. Learning to reflect helped him work through the strategies he uses today. He also found the feedback received from his peers, his professor, and his students useful in formulating a variety of teaching approaches.

The university education brought to schools by new teachers, unfortunately, holds little currency with their seasoned peers, in most cases. Many veteran teachers believe they learned most, if not all, their professional practice from the trial and error of classroom instruction rather than the lecture halls of universities. The low status of a university preparation often leads beginning teachers to suppress and devalue their education in favor of lessons gained from classroom experience or from the stories and suggestions of veteran colleagues.

Even with the best education, there are times when education fails beginning teachers, and they often described these occasions as the difference between the university "ivory tower" and the "real world" of public schools. These events reinforce the low status of professional preparation and elevate experience as the real teacher of teachers. Further, expectations and perspectives on professional practice may be strikingly different between those shared by university-based teacher educators, and those needed for survival in public schools (Etheridge, 1989). When this occurs, novice teachers often experience "transition shock" (Corcoran, 1981), or what Huberman (1989) describes as painful beginnings.

Biography plays an important role in establishing the self in teaching. Teacher histories provide the foundational beliefs, knowledge, perspectives, and skills that they bring with them to teaching. Biography, thus, is the beginning point from which teachers begin to establish their identity in schools. Further, it appears that some of the sources of influence found in the teachers' past will continue to shape their identity as they move through their careers.

ESTABLISHING THE SELF IN TEACHING

A profession such as teaching is often defined by the services it provides as well as the tasks it undertakes (Schön, 1983). Therefore, while teachers may serve different students, schools, communities, and even subjects, the fact they are of the same profession means that they share similar occupational demands. Similarities can also be found in their reactions and responses as they meet the demands of their new role as teachers.

Role demands are embodied in the expectations teachers face in school (i.e., what they are supposed to do and how they are supposed to do it). Some of these demands are explicit (e.g., classroom management, grading) while others are more implicit (e.g., committee assignments, instructional style). Teachers have little choice but to meet the required demands, for failure to do so means risking the loss of their job. The development of self in teaching is strongly influenced by the context of teaching. As teachers are required to perform particular tasks and meet the challenges of teaching, they must constantly call upon their personal resources, and test their knowledge, perspectives, and beliefs to accomplish their occupation mission. In this regard, knowing who one is cannot be disassociated from what one does.

Zeichner, Tabachnick, and Densmore (1987) delineated the impact of school experience on teacher development as occurring on two levels: interactive (classroom) and institutional (school). These contexts hold distinct and unique tasks for the teacher, and, therefore, the role demands of teaching can be seen to influence the beginning teacher's establishment of self at these two levels of classroom and school. We also speculate that teachers must further establish their identity in the context of the community, but little work has been undertaken in this area to date.

Classroom

The majority of a teacher's professional life is lived out in the classroom. What a teacher does, knows, believes, and values can easily be seen in the artifacts of their classroom. The routines and rituals of the classroom represent the daily lived experience of the teacher. While teachers may, at times, be able to separate themselves from the classroom, it is quite impossible for a classroom to be separated from a teacher.

Doyle (1986) portrayed classroom tasks as revolving around two central structures: student learning and classroom management. And as Lortie (1975) noted, the duties of a teacher are the same on the first day of teaching as they are the last. Lacking routines worn comfortable by long practice and without the benefits of knowledge gained in years of experience, beginning teachers must quickly discover efficient and economical practices for negotiating daily life in the classroom. Novice teachers often find the weight of their responsibilities heavy, and at times crushing. One teacher recounted the events of his first day like this:

> The first day there was not much teaching going on. Our building has three levels. I have a basement class first period. Second period I have a class on the main floor. Third period I'm out in the gym. Fourth I'm back inside on the main floor. Fifth and sixth I'm in the gym again and seventh period I'm back down in the basement. So this is my first day of taking attendance, learning the kids names, laying down basic rules and regulations, picking up everything I need and getting to all my classes. Kids have all sorts of questions on the first day: "When do I eat lunch?" "When is this and when is that?" I'm still trying to figure out all those rules and regulations myself. My first class had 14 Spanish-speaking kids and 2 English-speaking kids. I was trying to explain class rules to a bunch of kids that didn't understand English. This is my introduction and I'm thinking "Oh God! I'm not going to make it!" (Schempp et al., 1993, p. 458)

The first order of business and primary classroom responsibility for most beginning teachers is quite clearly classroom management. In a comprehensive summary of research on the perceived problems of beginning teachers, Veeneman (1984) identified classroom discipline as the most serious and consistent problem among beginning teachers. Classroom management appears at the top of concerns for beginning teachers in almost every study of teacher induction (Huberman, 1989; Bullough, Knowles, & Crow, 1989; Schempp, Tan, Eldar, & Nabel, 1995).

Classroom management is so essential to teaching that it often serves as a gate for screening teachers in and out of schools. The acquisition and effective implementation of classroom strategies for beginning teachers is a powerful demand that can escape no new teacher. Those who can adopt ways of managing students are well on their way to successful and satisfying careers, while those who fail to do so are doomed to either miserable or short careers (Huberman, 1989). As an example, a third-year teacher tells this story:

> I was half-time, and there was a particular math and science teacher who was really having trouble. I have a pretty good management style, so the principal asked if I would take over this teacher's class. Mainly what they needed was a classroom manager to get the class back under control. They had pretty much

driven this guy to a nervous breakdown. I taught the last six weeks of that term and had the same assignment next term. It went great and now I'm full-time. (Schempp et al., 1993, p. 459)

More than simply managing children, the primacy of classroom management reflects the reality of school life and becomes part of the teacher's identity. Teachers are expected to establish themselves as authority figures over students (Waller, 1932). It is incumbent upon new teachers to demonstrate the power and authority they hold over students to those outside the classroom (Feinman-Nemser & Floden, 1986; Hoy, 1968; Ryan, 1970). Success or failure in the beginning years, bluntly put, resides in the teacher's control over students; the greater the level of control, the greater the level of success one can expect in the classroom.

While gaining power over students may be an important role demand, and an essential part of who a teacher is in the classroom, controlling and disciplining students does not bring a sense of personal satisfaction for most beginning teachers. Yes, they must manage students, but no, they don't have to like it, seems to summarize the feelings of most new teachers. Forging meaningful personal relationships with students brings teachers their greatest rewards and personal satisfaction (Lortie, 1975; Jackson, 1968; Sarason, 1982). While others in the school and community may define teachers in terms of their ability to control a class, beginning teachers (and perhaps all teachers) see the essence of their role, and define themselves as teachers, in an almost contradictory way. Rather then controlling students, teachers define themselves in terms of their ability to know, understand, and help their students. Teachers measure their success in terms of their students' success. And student success and achievement is broadly defined. Helping students to understand math can stand right alongside motivating students to come to school, assisting them in controlling their anger, or planning their future. Teachers must establish themselves in multiple ways and through multiple roles: counselors, social workers, babysitters, friends, and even surrogate parents. Many teachers believe they are sharing, caring people, and derive a deep sense of satisfaction when they establish their teaching roles in ways that permit them to exercise those qualities (Lacey, 1989; Schempp et al., 1993).

If teachers derive their greatest satisfaction from caring for students and not dominating them, gaining power over students would classify as part of the "regime of truth" (Foucault, 1970) in schools. Put another way, teachers' control over students is taken for granted in schools. Administrators, parents, peers, and even students see the teacher as the central authority figure in the classroom. Student control rests as the cornerstone of professional competence. This "truth" influences the perspectives and actions of novice teachers, making it necessary to acquire tactics for student control (Huberman, 1989; Schempp et al., 1993).

The primacy of management and the importance of interpersonal relationships has the side effect of marginalizing subject matter. The classroom responsibilities facing inductees may have less to do with teaching children and more to do with juggling the multiple demands of a functioning institution. Reflecting on and articulating a given body of knowledge become secondary obligations for many beginning teachers as other priorities take precedence.

Knowledge of the subject matter and the ability to demonstrate this knowledge can serve as an avenue for gaining status in the school, particularly among students. Subject expertise (when available) is, however, more often used for establishing authority in the classroom than it was for furthering the education of students (Feinman-Nemser & Floden, 1986). Although important, subject-matter expertise is still, for beginning teachers, a distant second to the need for student control. Being a competent classroom manager is an essential element in establishing one's identity as a teacher in schools.

School

While the central tasks of teachers are found in classrooms, skillfully undertaking duties of a schoolwide consequence is also a consideration in defining the self as teacher. Teachers' participation or lack of participation in schoolwide activities is critical to the development of their identity. These activities represent one of the few arenas in which teachers can interact with other adults, specifically administrators, peers, and parents. Their performance in these activities may, therefore, hold serious consequences for career development.

Because their work in classrooms isolate them (Templin, 1988), meetings and school functions offered an opportunity to be viewed by colleagues, administrators, and others as part of the school culture. These events give teachers a visibility they cannot achieve in their normal, daily course of duties. The tasks they undertake, their level of involvement in student activities, their interactions with staff, parents, and administrators, and their committee work are platforms upon which teachers can establish themselves as school members.

School meetings are a primary domain for executing school duties and forging an identity. Teachers attend numerous meetings with varying purposes (e.g., curricular, informational) and with various individuals (e.g., faculty, parents, administrators). School meetings serve as important locations in the establishment of self in teacher induction. It is in these meetings that new teachers begin to tell others who they are. Also within many of these meetings, teachers can shape their identity and the roles they wish to play in the culture of the school. To this end, new teachers are very often careful as to how they dress and what they say, to whom, and when during schoolwide meetings.

Extraneous duties conspire, at times, to make the newcomer's life difficult. It is not one single duty that is troublesome, but the multitude thrust upon them. The number of decisions, the variety of tasks, and the immediacy of the demands force beginning teachers to use instinctive reactions, adopt time-honored traditions and management routines, and import lessons from related experiences (Schempp et al., 1993). The fluid, immediate, and dynamic pressures of school life do not permit teachers time to reflect deeply on a problem before attempting a solution. The reflexive responses required to maintain class momentum, satisfy the needs of a diverse student body, and adapt to schedule and procedural changes leaves no time for teachers to recall university lectures, consult their colleagues, or review pertinent professional literature. The role demands of the school create a situation where beginning teachers feel they succeed or fail alone (Burlingame, 1972; Lortie, 1975).

ESTABLISHING THE SELF IN SCHOOLS

The traditions and trademarks, the codes of culture, that give meaning and purpose to the established practices and patterns of daily school life are learned by teachers in their induction period. It is within this culture that they must locate themselves as individuals and establish their identities. The school culture is comprised in the rules that define what is normal, acceptable, and legitimate in terms of acting and thinking in the school.

Culture codes distinguish the important from the unimportant, and identify the sources of power within the school. Within the codes of culture, teachers learn both the distribution and appropriation of power within their school. In the process, teachers learn who has power (e.g., administrators, "involved" teachers) and the ways and means of appropriating the necessary power to secure their position in the school culture. Sparkes (1989) viewed the nature of school culture as contested and dynamic:

> The patterns of understandings, which newcomers must grasp, make up the various cultures of teaching and form a process of reality construction that enable individuals to see and understand particular events, objects, language and situations in distinctive ways. Hence, teacher cultures are embodied in the work-related beliefs and knowledge that they share, which includes beliefs about the appropriate ways of acting on the job, what is rewarding in teaching, and the "craft knowledge" that enables teachers to do their work. Importantly, these patterns of understandings also provide a basis for making the individuals' behavior meaningful, and culture should be viewed as an active living phenomenon through which teachers create and recreate the worlds in which they live. (pp. 319–320)

While biography may serve as the foundation of a teacher's identity in school, and the classroom serves as the place where one defines the self as teacher, the workplace culture takes on an increasingly important role as inductees attempt to gain veteran status and establish themselves in the school. Cultural codes become particularly pronounced in situations where job security is an important consideration. These codes or "regimes of truth" (Foucault, 1970) are informally passed to the newcomer by other members of the culture, usually during informal contacts during the school day. Bearers of cultural messages included administrators, colleagues, and students. The causal, interactional nature of these "culture lessons" tell the novice "how things really work in the school."

Embedded within the codes of school culture are ways of thinking and acting that are intended to serve beginning teachers as they attempt to establish the self in school. To successfully establish themselves as teachers in the institution, beginners must learn the roles played by the other members, comprehend the messages these people bear, and adopt and devise strategies for gaining the influence necessary to insure their acceptance, and survival, in the school. And survival in the school is the prime concern for many beginning teachers (Pataniczek & Isaacson, 1981).

In order to establish the self during induction, a teacher's identity must accommodate three dimensions of school culture: (1) established school members, (2) the value of their subject matter as perceived by others, and (3) the events and activities of daily life in the school. These shall be addressed in turn.

Established School Members

The established school members with whom the beginning teacher must learn to interact include administrators, staff members (peers and support personnel), and students. It is in the eyes of these individuals that a teacher shapes their identity and establishes the self in school. The hierarchy of power in the school quickly becomes clear to new teachers. Principals and administrators hold the greatest power, followed by teachers and staff, and then students. The beginning teachers' status is fixed within the teacher group, but teachers negotiate their identity with all three groups.

Administrators. The individuals holding the greatest power over the inductees are administrators. The principal is often instrumental in obtaining employment for beginning teachers, and satisfying the expectations of these individuals is usually a prime contingency for maintaining employment as a teacher. Because beginning teachers are often grateful for the position, and because a principal is a key to a satisfying work experience, teachers are normally grateful and loyal (Huberman, 1989; Feinman-Nemser & Floden, 1986; Schempp et al., 1993).

Administrators use the codes of the school culture to select and retain new teachers. Teachers are well aware of these codes and attempt to remain within these expectations regarding behavior, appearance, and attitude. Expressions of individuality and assertions of self must fall within these boundaries in order for the beginning teacher to be accepted by the larger school community. Often these codes have less to do with educating students and more to do with what Ginsberg (1987) termed the "ideology of professionalism" (i.e., looking and acting professional).

Feinman-Nemser and Floden (1986) identified buffering as a role administrators often play for teachers. That is, administrators served as brokers between influences and regulations from outside the school and the beginning teacher. For example, a mandate or information from the school board, state educational agencies, and sometimes even parents is screened by administrators and then passed along to the teacher, usually with a comment regarding its relative importance.

Largely due to the enormous power of administrators, beginning teachers seldom approach them for help or support, at least initially

(Schempp et al., 1995). The principal, in particular, is critical to the success or failure for the first-year teacher for the principal plays a central role in determining if the new teacher stays or goes. For neophyte teachers to bring their problems or concerns to the principal is to run the risk of admitting a lack of competence. In a recent study, we found that in the first few months a teacher is in a new school, the principal is the last individual they will approach for help or advice (Schempp et al., 1995). It does appear, however, that as a relationship of trust and respect begins to develop between a first-year teacher and his/her school principal, the principal can become an important source of support for the teacher. In the absence of a trusting relationship, the principal remains a person to be avoided.

Staff Members. Teaching colleagues and support personnel represent an influential group for the beginning teacher. Peer teachers in particular play active roles during induction by helping newcomers make the transition into the culture of the school in ways that preserve their own sets of interests (Ball, 1987). Colleagues identify important tasks, guide curricular decisions, and inform the beginning teacher of his or her status in the school. Veteran teachers have established traditions and perceptions that the novice must accept, reject, modify, or accommodate as they establish themselves in school. The newcomer risks alienating established teachers when they inject their own brand of pedagogy or offer a professional opinion on a topic of discussion.

For the most part, however, it seems beginning teachers found "uncaring colleagues"—teachers who are burned out or simply too busy to discuss matters pertaining to the education of children (Schempp et al., 1993). The pressure of a myriad of duties, the concerns of the classroom, and the isolated nature of teaching appear to conspire to leave beginning teachers much to their own devices in navigating the professional decisions and problems they encounter in the early years on the job. Although new teachers may find it necessary to appease their peers and demonstrate a willingness to conform to institutional norms and standards, peer teachers do not seem a particularly powerful socializing agent in terms of pedagogical practice or beliefs (Lortie, 1975). The characterization of collegial relationships as "supportive but independent" is a consistent finding in teacher socialization research (Burlingame, 1972; Zeichner et al. 1987).

Students. Teachers spend more time with students than any other members of the school community. It is logical, therefore, to recognize that students play a important role in teachers' identities. As Waller (1932) recognized long ago, winning over student respect and gaining acceptance are critical to the establishing of the self in teaching. Besides reinforcing the primacy of classroom management, students convey their perceptions of subject-matter importance. Teachers must come to grips with both pedagogy and management, and the more effective ones are able to fold the two together (Huberman, 1989; Schempp et al., 1993). Learning to manage student behavior and motivate student learning are two important tasks facing the new teacher.

In their study of beginning high school teachers, Blase and Greenfield (1982) found students to be the most powerful socialization agents new teachers encounter. Students, they concluded, "shape the development of teachers and have a major influence on how teachers actually behave in classroom settings" (p. 269). Students provide important input regarding the beginning teachers' level of success. Teachers receive immediate and continuous feedback regarding their policies, practices, and perspectives from students. In the isolated confines of a classroom, this feedback strongly influences a young teacher's sense of competence and professional value.

Given the pressures and problems facing many beginning teachers, the need for support and guidance is natural and necessary. Beginning teachers often experience physical exhaustion, mental and emotional stress, as well as related social and personal problems (Schempp et al., 1995). That support is not necessarily found in the workplace for many beginning teachers. Therefore, inductees turn to family members and friends to help them find their way through their first years of teaching. Parents, siblings, spouse, and friends provide a receptive ear, a word of encouragement, a bit of advice, or even a shoulder to cry on for teachers struggling to establish themselves in school.

The Value of Subject Matter

A subject matter is accorded status and prestige in accordance with the norms of the school culture. Teachers' behavior and beliefs influence others' perceptions of their subject area. That is, the way teachers perceive their subject and convey those perceptions, influences the perceptions others have of their subject. And as teachers are identified with the subject area in which they teach, their identity is inextricably linked to how others in the school identify and define their subject.

During induction, teachers learn that in the scheme of school culture, subject matter is not among the higher priorities. Classroom management, school politics, and meeting the childrens' social and emotional needs all take precedence over subject knowledge. Lacey (1989, p. xv) described this cultural norm as teachers "emphasizing the welfare of the child above the interest of their subject."

Beginning teachers often look to their subject-area or grade-level colleagues first when attempting to seek answers to questions. Subject-area peers can further serve as professional mentors, and later are looked to for advice on other concerns relative to teaching (Galvez-Hjornevik, 1986). It is within the group of subject-area specialists that the beginning teacher forms an important segment of their school identity, for the status of their subject is often directly related to the status its teachers carry in the school (Schempp et al., 1993).

The Self in School Life

Teachers spend their time in a multidimensional and often frantic venture called a school day. Pressed by time constraints, curricular demands, the competing and contradictory needs of individual students, limited resources, and a relentless schedule, teachers must establish themselves in a caldron of activity. Peers, students, and administrators can exert enormous pressures on beginning teachers (Zeichner et al., 1987). These groups, collectively and individually, inform teachers about the cultural codes, "regimes of truth," or "standards of the profession" that drive the form and function of daily life in school. Within the boundaries of these standards and before these individuals, beginning teachers must forge their identity in terms of the actions, attitudes, and demeanor they assume and use to guide their conduct in the everyday experience of school life.

The self becomes established in schools in a dialectical tension between the norms of school culture and the teacher as individual. Thus, understanding and adapting to school culture can be quite apart from (although certainly related to) learning to teach children in classrooms. Every established group has certain cultural norms, for it is within these norms that a group achieves identity and distinction. Newcomers are expected to learn and subscribe to the prevailing ways of the group.

The induction period reveals to teachers that professional survival and success is contingent upon their ability to prove that they understand and embrace the cultural norms of the school. This is not to say that teachers must learn to agree with every policy or philosophy encountered or attempt to follow every directive or suggestion given. Rather, beginning teachers find it necessary to demonstrate their uniqueness as an individual, while at the same time not violating the cultural norms of the school. In short, teachers feel compelled to prove they fit with the group (Schempp et al., 1993).

Several strategies used by beginning teachers to fit the self in school life have been identified (Lacey, 1977; Huberman, 1989; Schempp et al., 1993). A common strategy among new teachers is the joining of committees. Curriculum committees are preferable, for they allow novices to learn the routines and requirements for classroom life while simultaneously providing a stage for demonstrating their eagerness to fit. Lacey (1977) termed this strategic compliance. Being seen as an integral part of the school is an important consideration for the beginning teacher. Joining committees allows them to gain visibility and recognition as a vital, contributing school member. Committees also provide the inductee with an opportunity to better understand precisely how the school functions. Committee activities take the neophyte out of the confines of the classroom and bring them into the larger arena of the school. Such work is also done in concert with other teachers and administrators and thus reinforces the beginning teacher's identity as a school member. Interestingly enough, neophytes are quite diligent in attendance and quick and efficient in performing any assigned tasks, but their role during the meetings is a quiet one.

Remaining silent is, by far, the most prevalent and dominant strategy used by new teachers to fit in (Schempp et al., 1993). To exhibit their willingness to "fit in" and accept the status quo, beginning teachers form a society of the silent. That is, they are afraid to express opinions to peers and administrators that might be considered controversial and thus jeopardize their chances for success and survival in the school. Convinced that teachers do not want to change, afraid of demonstrating a lack of knowledge or competence, and fearful of being perceived as troublesome, the society of the silent choose to restrain their voice as a means of demonstrating passive acceptance of the norms of the school culture. To do otherwise is to, at best, lower their status in the eyes of their peers, and at worst, risk their job. Beginning teachers bide their time as they learn the ways of the school, weigh their options for action, and wait for the time when they can assert the self in school.

CONCLUSION

Establishing the self in the first years of teaching can be a challenging experience as the newcomers find their long-held beliefs challenged, their perceptions of the work of teachers incomplete, and their preparation inadequate for the tasks of teaching. As much research has recognized, teachers experience induction in different ways (Bullough, Knowles, & Crow, 1989; Huberman, 1989; Zeichner, Tabachnick, & Densmore, 1987). The conditions of the school, the individual variations of students, and the unique expectations of each teaching position create a singular induction for every new teacher. Likewise, each teacher brings with them a distinct and different constellation of personal factors—background experiences, education, beliefs, motives, and the like. It is in the dialectical tension between the external factors unique to the school and the internal factors unique to the teacher that one searches for his or her identity as a teacher.

In the current economic conditions in North America, new teachers are often so pleased to have a teaching position that they are not inclined to complain about the conditions of employment or their induction. And they are certainly not inclined to suggest or initiate sweeping institutional reforms. We are, therefore, pessimistic about improving schools with a fresh tide of teachers. When employment is difficult to obtain, having a job, regardless of the conditions, in generally preferable to no job at all. Economic conditions appear likely to continue pressuring new teachers to forsake their ideals and practices learned in preparation programs in favor of accepting the present conditions and standards of the schools. Until induction periods encourage teachers to think reflectively and critically and to experiment with reform proposals, the new corps of teachers entering schools cannot be expected to carry a reform agenda into schools. The development of self as a teacher in schools today does not, unfortunately, permit one to develop educational institutions as well. Until new teachers are freed from old traditions, this is not likely to change.

One possibility for initiating change would be to change teacher induction. Encouraging, or even allowing, beginning teachers to express themselves more freely without fear of condemnation, reprisals, or job loss is one such change. The knowledge and beliefs veteran teachers have won through years of service and experience should not be summarily dismissed. However, new teachers must be encouraged to develop an identity that does not simply "fit in," but rather is based upon experimentation and characterized by pedagogical practices and responsive perspectives that place student learning and welfare at the forefront of concerns. They also must be encouraged to reflect critically on what it means to teach in public schools, to interrogate, challenge, and change the structures of schooling that constrain the essential missions of schools (Sparkes, 1991). As teachers develop their identity, they need to see themselves as change agents and should come to realize that they can change the conditions in which they teach. That realization must begin during induction.

As unique and individual as each teacher in each school may be, there are commonalities shared among all teachers who attempt to establish an identity in their induction. Recognizing these commonalities provides important insights for both teacher educators and those preparing to join the ranks of teachers. Understanding the process by which the self is established in the first years of teaching is an important prerequisite for identifying successful transition strategies as teachers move into schools and seek to establish themselves. Understanding the process by which teachers establish the self in school is also important for those currently in schools who seek to accommodate and capitalize on the unique talents, experiences, and energies new teachers bring to schools.

References

Ball, S. (1987). *The micro-politics of the school*. London: Methuen.

Blase, J. J., & Greenfield, W. (1982). On the meaning of being a high school-teacher: The beginning years. *The High School Journal*, May, 263–271.

Bullough, R. V., Knowles, J. G., & Crow, N. A. (1989). Teacher self-concept and student culture in the first year of teaching. *Teacher College Record, 91*, 209–233.

Burlingame, M. (1972). Socialization constructs and the teaching of teachers. *Quest, 18*, 40–56.

Clandinin, D., & Connelly, F. (1986). Rhythms in teaching: The narrative study of personal practical knowledge of classrooms. *Teaching and Teacher Education, 2*, 377–387.

Corcoran, E. (1981). Transition shock: The beginning teacher's paradox. *Journal of Teacher Education, 32*, 19–23.

Doyle, W. (1986). Classroom organization and management. In M. C. Wittrock (Ed.), *Handbook of research on teaching* (3rd ed., pp. 392–431). New York: Macmillian.

Elbaz, F. (1983). *Teacher thinking: A study of practical knowledge*. London: Croom Helms.

Etheridge, C. P. (1989). Acquiring the teaching culture: How beginners embrace practices different from university teachings. *Qualitative Studies in Education, 2*, 299–313.

Feinman-Nemser, S., & Floden, R. (1986). The cultures of teaching. In M. Wittrock (Ed.), *Handbook of research on teaching* (3rd ed., pp. 505–526). New York: Macmillian.

Foucault, M. (1970). *The order of things: An archaeology of the human sciences.* New York: Vintage Press.

Galvez-Hjornevik, C. (1986). Mentoring among teachers: A review of the literature. *Journal of Teacher Education, 37,* 6–11.

Ginsberg, M. (1987). Reproduction, contradiction and conceptions of professional: The case of pre-service teachers. In T. Popkewitz (Ed). *Critical studies in teacher education* (pp. 86–129). Lewes, UK: Falmer Press.

Giroux, H. (1988). *Teachers as intellectuals: A pedagogy for the opposition.* South Hadley, MA: Bergin & Garvey.

Hoy, W. (1968). The influence of experience on the beginning teacher. *School Review, 76,* 312–323.

Huberman, M. (1989). The professional life cycle of teachers. *Teachers College Record, 91,* 31–57.

Jackson, P. W. (1968). *Life in classrooms.* New York: Holt, Rinehart, & Winston.

Lacey, C. (1977). *The socialization of teachers.* London: Methuen.

Lacey, C. (1989). Foreword. In T. Templin & P. Schempp (Eds.). *Socialization into physical education: Learning to teach* (p. xv). Indianapolis: Benchmark Press.

Lortie, D. C. (1975). *Schoolteacher.* Chicago: University of Chicago Press.

McEvoy, B. (1986, April). *"She is still with me": Influences of former teachers on teacher practice.* Paper presented at the American Educational Research Association annual meeting, San Francisco.

Pataniczek, D., & Isaacson, N. (1981). The relationship of socialization and the concerns of beginning teachers. *Journal of Teacher Education, 32,* 14–17.

Popkewitz, T. S. (1987). Ideology and social formation in teacher education. In T. S. Popkewitz (Ed.), *Critical studies in teacher education* (pp. 2–33). Lewes, UK: Falmer Press.

Ryan, K. (1970). *Don't smile until Christmas: Accounts of the first year of teaching.* Chicago: University of Chicago Press.

Sarason, S. B. (1982). *The culture of the school and the problem of change* (2nd ed.). Boston: Allyn & Bacon.

Schempp, P. G. (1989). The apprenticeship-of-observation in physical education. In T. Templin & P. Schempp (Eds.), *Socialization into physical education: Learning to teach* (pp. 13–38). Indianapolis: Benchmark Press.

Schempp, P. G., & Graber, K. C. (1992). Teacher socialization from a dialectical perspective: Pretraining through induction. *Journal of Teaching in Physical Education, 11,* 329–348.

Schempp, P., Sparkes, A., & Templin, T. (1993). The micropolitics of teacher induction. *American Educational Research Journal, 30,* 447–472.

Schempp, P., Tan, S., Eldar, E., & Nabel, N. (1995, June). *Induction: First steps in teaching-difficulties and small successes. Data from an international study and initial recommendations.* Symposium presented at the Association International des Écoles Supérieures d'Éducation Physique World Congress, Netanya, Israel.

Schön, D. A. (1983). *The reflective practitioner: How professionals think in action.* New York: Basic Books.

Sparkes, A. C. (1989). Culture and ideology in physical education. In T. Templin & P. Schempp (Eds.), *Socialization into physical education: Learning to teach* (pp. 315–338). Indianapolis: Benchmark Press.

Sparkes, A. C. (1991). The culture of teaching, critical reflection and change: Possibilities and problems. *Educational Management and Administration, 19,* 4–19.

Templin, T. (1988). Teacher isolation: A concern for the collegial development of physical educators. *Journal of Teaching in Physical Education, 7,* 197–207.

Veeneman, S. (1984). Perceived problems of beginning teachers. *Review of Educational Research, 54,* 143–178.

Waller, W. (1932). *The sociology of teaching.* New York: Russell & Russell.

Zeichner, K., Tabachnick, B., & Densmore, K. (1987). Individual, institutional and cultural influences on the development of teachers' craft knowledge. In J. Calderhead (Ed.), *Exploring teachers' thinking* (pp. 21–59). London: Cassell Educational.

PART IV

Reexamining and Affirming: The Master Teachers

CHAPTER 7

CARING: THE WAY OF
THE MASTER TEACHER

Karen J. Agne

A new word has come on the scene in today's educational community. It has found its way into the language of every facet of the profession. It is being regarded as the essential ingredient for excellence
in instruction, classroom management, classroom and school climate,
student motivation, administrative leadership, and parent and community support systems. It pervades the educationese of the nineties.
It is the theme to which a multitude of new books on education and
teaching, and entire educational journals are devoted. The word is
caring.

This treatise will consider the concept of caring as it relates to the
self of the master teacher and excellence in the classroom. The principles of caring and its effects on teachers, students, and others are
demonstrated by research that supports the concept that caring is the
way of the master teacher.

MY EXPERIENCE AS THE DEVELOPING CARING TEACHER

Twenty-eight years ago I walked into my first classroom, filled
with my own students, for the first time. Like most new teachers I carried with me every notion I had accumulated about schools, classrooms, students, and learning, everything I had personally experienced
and learned in the past and many assumptions about the future. This
was my classroom. I was responsible for its atmosphere and control.
These were my students, my charges, and my job was to teach them, en-
lighten them, "fix" them. And I was fully equipped, confident, and capable of succeeding, or so I thought.

Those first few years of teaching turned out to be the most difficult venture I had ever attempted. In those days, foremost in my teacher mind was the belief that I was the captain of this ship. A good captain should be in charge. I had to control my class or they would control me. It soon became evident that I was losing the battle. I recall even questioning whether I possessed adequate resilience to pursue this career.

It was a kindergarten class that gave me my first glimpse of the error in my battle strategy. Here I was taught by five-year-olds that they would learn everything I meant to teach them and a host of other things about which I was completely unaware. Indeed, a parent informed me that her daughter "became me" each weekday evening, while the family was obliged to play the role of the class. She had learned and mimicked well both my verbal and my body language, aped my distinct demeanor.

I was witnessing what Bandura had proclaimed years before, that children learn by modeling (1977). They learn by absorbing who you are to them, not by memorizing what you say. They will become you, like it or not. And although many other pronouncements would prove to be accurate about teaching and learning, this idea was fundamental and was also, it seemed to me, the single component of this process that was most directly dependent upon my own immediate and future choices and actions. The person I projected in the classroom could have direct implications for the success of a thousand future students.

It would be necessary, therefore, to reflect deeply upon who I was and who, as a result, my students would be learning to become. The first responsibility of a teacher, I surmised, was to work consciously and diligently toward reaching self-actualization; that is, to aspire to become the highest potential me. This was a tall order, but a worthy one. And, like most new teachers, I was an idealist and believed my classroom could be exemplary.

As I contemplated the many positive role models I had encountered either through personal observation or literature, a single common attribute defiantly emerged again and again. Each seemed consciously willed to service to others, to graciousness, to love. I determined that in order to pursue this paradigmatic goal I must resolve to define love, think love, indeed, realize how to *be* love to my students. As a result, I became very aware of the classroom events and situations in which I felt frustrated, angry, or impatient. I learned to recognize the student attitudes and behaviors for which I had the least tolerance. These became my personal challenges.

I would soon realize that I was working as hard as ever, but enjoying the classroom more and more. I would find myself exhausted, but nevertheless smiling at the end of the day. I had ceased being hoarse because I no longer shouted over or at the class. I was listening more, both to my students and to myself. It was imperative to know them and myself better in order to realize my goal. Consequently, my students and I became very good friends. We grew to trust each other, to depend upon one another. My students depended upon me to guide their understanding and I depended upon them to show me how.

I was not *the* teacher; *we* were *the* teacher. Some inexplicable change had occurred. There was a subtle difference in the chemistry between my students and me, a higher flow of interaction, an obvious jump in the quality of the classroom experience. My students and I had become a teaching/learning unit, a kind of perpetual learning, growing machine. We had become an example of a model of teaching/learning effectiveness that could be described by five causal links, which I would discover later (Agne, 1991): (1) teacher belief, (2) teacher behavior, (3) student belief, (4) student behavior, and (5) student achievement. My beliefs about myself as teacher/learner predisposed my behaviors in the classroom. These behaviors were being modeled by my students. My beliefs had influenced their beliefs, which predisposed their learning behaviors and led ultimately to their achievement.

Future classes brought further wisdom taught by first graders, third graders, and finally gifted learners of all ages. My students molded me into a well-seasoned teacher. I had experienced most of what to expect from students and much of what to do about it. I had accumulated my own list of classroom do's and don't's, exhibited obvious savvy, and clearly exuded "withitness" (Kounin, 1970).

I was beginning to internalize the wisdom of early masters who proclaimed that "the teacher . . . gives not of his wisdom but rather of his faith and his lovingness." No one can give another understanding. All one can do is "lead (him) to the threshold of (his) own mind" (Gibran, 1923). We do not teach; we facilitate the learning of another. And apparently we facilitate best by presenting ideas in a setting that we have prepared to be the most conducive to each student's highest level of focus, a setting that offers the most care.

As years passed, classes changed, new and different concepts of instruction and curriculum came and went, colleagues changed, and the society changed, locally, nationally, and globally. But one thing remained the same. One thing still happened every year, with every class, regardless of other inconsistencies. I discovered that each year, after a period of time, the same kind of synchronicity occurred within the classroom. Somewhere along the way in the day-to-day routine of school something clicked; we became one. My students and I became a unit, a whole, like a well-oiled machine that seemed to perpetuate itself. No, my job did not become easier. But I ceased to notice its difficulty, its stresses. I enjoyed this experience. I was thriving in it and so also, I observed, were my students.

When I analyzed what was happening, in reflection I realized that at some point in each school year, I had always fallen in love with my students, even as my earlier philosophical inquiry had predicted. I had become committed to the well-being, growth, and happiness of each one. I was no selfless saint. There was no preconceived plan to acquire an attitude of student adoration; it just happened. Somewhere along the line, I had quite serendipitously, quite unconsciously, experienced this change, a committedness, an attitude of love, and it worked.

As soon as I consciously confirmed to myself what was occurring, I was compelled to study this phenomenon, because I wanted to believe that this transformation had more to do with student learning and effective teaching than anything else related to education.

Now the greatest problem with understanding, interpreting, and implementing such a concept is that it is at once too simple, fundamental, and profound. To further complicate things, the notion of love has received more interpretations, varied descriptions, synonyms, and treatments than any concept known to, or felt by, humanity. How do you study an idea that is completely subjective? How do you assess the presence or depth of caring? Nevertheless, love, commitment, or some associated principle appeared to be closely related to successful teacher/student interaction and learning. There was obviously more to effective teaching than a scholarly command of required curriculum and a well-stocked bag of instruction and classroom management tricks.

Further study led me to discover that over a hundred years of teacher effectiveness research had addressed primarily teacher behaviors, what teachers "do" in the classroom. In addition, the effectiveness of these behaviors was generally determined by measuring student differences on standardized test scores. Instinct and experience suggested a flaw in this research approach; a major factor seemed to be missing from the teacher effectiveness equation.

Researchers have pointed out a number of problems with measuring teacher effectiveness through student test scores (Shavelson, Webb, & Burstein, 1986). Comparing student gain scores is not reliable because such measures preclude individual differences among students' beginning achievement and self-motivation levels (Rosenshine & Furst, 1973). Moreover, this approach presents teaching as chiefly a technical rather than deliberate, thoughtful, human occurrence (Shulman, 1986).

Teachers' behaviors are clearly a very important and vital aspect of the nature of teaching expertise. But while dozens of effective teacher behaviors filled the pages of classroom management texts, little was offered in the way of clues to teachers' thought processes, intentions, beliefs, and feelings. No one was asking, "What generates these behaviors?"

It made sense, of course, for colleges of education to study teacher behavior. Behaviors, after all, can be described, implemented, and taught as methods to would-be teachers of the future, unlike personality, for instance. Teacher personality research (Coopersmith, 1967; Ryans, 1960) was interesting, but society could not legally screen teacher candidates by personality, even if we did discover a link. Nor could teacher candidates emerge from educational studies as masters of a new teaching personality.

So we taught preteachers about withitness, positive reinforcement, motivation, grouping, pacing, questioning skills, and the myriad of other critical behaviors that fill the classrooms of effective teachers. But by 1969, Hamachek had reminded us that we still could "not tell the good guys from the bad guys" (p. 341). This sentiment was echoed years later as more researchers concluded that little was really known about effective teaching (Ornstein & Miller, 1980; Rosenshine & Furst, 1971).

No, it was not just the behavior, not the personality. So, what was responsible for the transformation that inevitably occurred, sometimes early, sometimes later, in my classroom each year? What precursor? What precipitated the shift?

Further probing revealed that some researchers were beginning to consider the internal and cognitive aspects of the teacher's effect to be equally valid and important in the search to understand teaching expertise. These researchers were declaring that for the first time we were coming to realize that "teaching is complex, demanding, and uniquely human" (Clark & Peterson, 1986, p. 293), and further that "What makes a good teacher is a highly personal matter having to do with the teacher's personal system of beliefs" (Combs, 1982, p. 3). It is the internal, feeling, thinking, believing aspect that determines which behaviors will occur. So that "if our purpose and intent are to change the practices of those who teach, it is necessary to come to grips with the objectively reasonable beliefs of teachers" (Fenstermacher, 1979, p. 174).

I had worked beside dozens of excellent teachers over the years, most of whom emitted unique and quite individual behavior. And to all appearances, those behaviors that were different among these masters likely had more to do with their expertise than those that were the same. Indeed, I believe any preservice teacher could learn to exhibit the majority of behaviors deemed necessary for effective teaching and remain a poor to mediocre teacher. Perhaps this explains the common notion that good teachers are born and not made. Clearly, good teaching seemed to have more to do with certain intentions and beliefs, factors that may or may not already exist within a teacher candidate, than with education or experience.

Literature searches uncovered a model for conceptualizing teacher effectiveness in the form of a familiar A-B-C-D link model. This model described a causal chain of four interconnecting links that included teacher beliefs, teacher behavior, student behavior, and student achievement (Rose & Medway, 1981). This model appeared to closely match what was happening in the classroom with one exception. I had envisioned five links. The missing link was student beliefs (Agne, 1991).

If teacher beliefs and intentions predisposed my behavior, so also did student beliefs and intentions, modeled from and influenced by me, predispose their behavior and subsequent achievement. There, encompassed in the A link of this familiar model, was that component which years before had made such an impact on my perception of the teaching/learning process—teacher beliefs. What could be discovered within the A link that ultimately afforded positive impact on student achievement? Which teacher beliefs ultimately resulted in student success and growth?

Researchers have established that teachers' thoughts and behaviors are guided by their belief systems (Clark & Peterson, 1986). Further, certain teacher belief systems have been found to correlate with student achievement. Among these are teacher efficacy, teacher locus of control, and pupil control attitudes.

In 1991, a study was conducted to determine whether there were differences in teacher effectiveness as a result of teacher beliefs. Teachers of the Year and inservice teachers were surveyed on a set of four teacher beliefs (Agne, Greenwood, & Miller, 1994). The four beliefs, thought to be highly related to teacher effectiveness, were teacher efficacy, teacher locus of control, pupil control orientation, and teacher stress.

Teacher efficacy may be defined as the teacher's belief in his/her ability to affect student learning (Ashton & Webb, 1986; Gibson & Dembo, 1984). Self-efficacy beliefs "affect people's choice of activities, how much effort they expend, and how long they will persist in the face of difficulties" (Bandura & Schunk, 1981, p. 587). Teachers with high self-efficacy are more likely to perceive low-achievers as teachable and worth their time and effort (Ashton & Webb, 1986). Berman, McLaughlin, Bass, Pauly, and Zellman (1977) pronounced teacher efficacy to be the "single most powerful explanatory variable" related to teacher behavior and student achievement.

The importance of teacher locus of control for academic achievement is also well known (Murray & Staebler, 1974). Teacher locus of control may be defined as the degree to which the teacher believes his/her own actions or behavior determine and contribute to classroom events and student performance (Rose & Medway, 1981). The relationship between locus of control and student achievement was first determined in 1962 by Crandall, Katkovsky, and Preston.

Teachers' attitudes toward their students and the resulting classroom climate have also been found to affect student achievement (Brookover, Schweitzer, Schneider, Beady, Flood, & Wisenbaker, 1978). Pupil control orientation among teachers may range from custodial, defined as punitive, autocratic, and moralistic, to humanistic, which is described as friendly, respectful, and flexible (Willower, Eidell, & Hoy, 1973).

Finally, schools have been named among the most stressful ecologies in our society (Samples, 1976), and teaching among the most seriously high-stress occupations (Cox & Brockley, 1984). Teachers' beliefs that result in fear, indicated by high levels of stress, have been found to correlate with diminished tolerance, patience, and interaction with students (Koon, 1971), reduced efficiency and loss of caring (Eskridge & Coker, 1985).

The major result of the Agne study of beliefs among Teachers of the Year and other inservice teachers (1991) was that Teachers of the Year were significantly more humanistic in their beliefs about pupil control than were other classroom teachers.

Apparently, teachers who have been selected from among the teachers in their states to receive awards as Teacher of the Year hold more caring beliefs about students than do other classroom teachers. That is, the Teachers of the Year, a group of teachers who embody high levels of teaching expertise and who have been identified as master teachers, tend to be significantly more trusting, accepting, friendly, respectful, flexible, democratic, nonpunitive, nonmoralistic, self-disciplined, and student-empowering than other teachers with equivalent experience, education, and teaching situations.

Furthermore, Teachers of the Year were found to hold beliefs that spring from higher levels of self-efficacy and from an internal locus of control. These belief systems (humanistic pupil control, high self-efficacy, and internal locus of control) were found to be interrelated and may certainly, en masse, be considered to be descriptive of the caring aspect pervading expert teachers' classrooms.

Presumably, these beliefs were responsible for generating the ideas and decisions that manifest in the behaviors expert teachers model to their students. It now appears that the key to the classroom is much more a function of who teachers are and of what they believe than of what teachers do. The key to the classroom is caring.

THE PRINCIPLES OF A CARING BELIEF SYSTEM

Human beings very early in life come to understand the notion of caring. Even in the most abusive circumstances, it is safe to assume that a person need only be born for someone to have cared for him. Indeed, the chances are good that someone has paid attention to or taken an interest in her, cared if she has survived.

Caring may be thought of as having degrees or levels. It is possible to care deeply, to be unconditionally committed, or to barely care at all. In fact, "careless" is the commonly used term for expressing a lack of concern, making mistakes, or not giving one's best efforts.

At the most fundamental level people may talk about caring as having someone or something matter to them. In order for caring to occur, one must be focusing on another rather than on oneself. Caring may be assumed, therefore, to be "other-oriented."

Other-orientedness should not be construed to mean that a person neglects himself. For when people care for others, they put into operation a chain of events that ultimately cares for all others, including themselves. Each time someone helps another, she automatically helps all. Caring has a generally contagious effect. It ripples out from one to many.

Caring has been described as trusting, accepting, friendly, respectful, flexible, democratic, nonpunitive, nonmoralistic, self-disciplined, and other-empowering. Caring is the orientation of those who tend to express a high sense of self-efficacy and who are internal in their locus of control. That is, people who care usually believe that they are personally capable of attending to another and making a difference. They choose to depend on themselves and on their own initiatives to solve problems in these efforts, rather than to rely mainly upon others. Caring people are less inclined to blame others for failure in these initiatives or to blame factors outside of themselves or their control.

Most people operate in a caring state to a greater or lesser degree, according to some part of the foregoing definition, at least some of the time. In fact, most would probably rather be a caring person than an uncaring person. Caring affords harmony. People would rather live with harmony than with disharmony. The concern here is not to inspire the desire to be caring. Rather the concern is to understand what it is that stops that caring state. What distorts caring? What keeps people from remaining in that giving state in spite of how much they may aspire to be there? If caring is the most important belief system related to student achievement, then it behooves teachers to understand which phenomena support and enhance this state as well as which contribute to its demise.

Fear and Control in a Consumer Society

This period in history could well be labeled "The Age of Consumptopithecus." People in today's society have come to equate happiness and success with getting the things that they want. Since people can never get enough to be completely satisfied, they keep producing more things to want and need. People's lives revolve around consuming. In order to get the things they think they need, people try to control and fix everything and everyone around them. When people desire to get something from another person or from the world and they are not successful, the result is fear and stress. Since they must inevitably fail to get everything they want, people find themselves revolving in a continuous circle of control, fear, and stress.

Students and teachers alike bring with them into the classroom the attitudes and beliefs that result from life in a society based on consumerism. The only difference is the form that the commodities and needs take. In the classroom, for the student the need is a sense of successful achievement; the commodities are generally grades, promotions, and degrees, but may also include a multitude of other day-to-day requirements depending on the age or grade level of the student.

For the teacher the needs may take the form of student cooperation, attention, and motivation to learn; the commodities include everything the teacher deems necessary to assist him in facilitating understanding for the student and all products that provide evidence of student learning and achievement.

Fear dominates people's lives much more than most realize. It comes in many forms, which are subcategorized as worry, anger, frustration, jealousy, greed, and many other terms. Attention to self-talk during fear states reveals that a person's thinking generally runs along the lines of, "What about me? What if I don't get my way? What if I don't get my share? I may be inconvenienced. Are they better than me? What's wrong with me? Why won't they listen to me? What if I fail? Will I be hurt? Will I be alone?" The focus is on oneself, not on others, and on getting, not giving.

The principal concern with fear states is that they prevent or replace compassion, or caring states. People cannot focus on the needs or pain of others if they are focused on their own needs or pain. If a person is full of fear, her reactions reflect that fear. She will show signs of stress, disrupted concentration, irrational perception, inattention, and generally decreased levels of achievement and productivity. The result of fractured concentration, perception, attention, achievement, and productivity in the classroom for all concerned goes without saying.

The danger in recognizing that people may function in either a fear state or a caring state, a getting state or a giving state, is that values are immediately attached to these states. "Caring is good; fear is bad. I must be caring. I have to stop my fear." Therefore, the first step is to let go of the idea of opposites. There is no maximum level of caring, generosity, or harmony. Nor is there a zero point of fear, selfishness, or disharmony. There is a spectrum. And anyone may find himself at any point on that spectrum at any time. There can be no sense of, "I should feel this. I shouldn't feel that."

Of course, this is not to say that it is okay to be harmful or uncaring to others or to ourselves. But as soon as the labels of "good" or "bad" are applied, a motivation for judgment is created, followed by tension and, ultimately, the very fear we are attempting to control.

Fundamentally, control is not even possible, because human beings are always functioning in a harmony/disharmony continuum. Much of life experience is the result of environmental happenstance and our response the result of reaction rather than proactive will. There is no perfection. In fact, human beings are perfectly imperfect. Caring directs people to find acceptance as expressed by compassion and forgiveness, the deferral of judgment, and patience.

In order to internalize a belief system of caring, it is necessary to develop gentle awareness. There is nothing to control . . . nothing to "fix." There is only accepting, even adoring, the magnificent complexity of humanness.

Realizing the Illusion of Control

Through deep awareness and introspection, people bring the source of their reactions into conscious focus. Each may now ask herself, "What am I afraid of? What fear is generating my tension?" The more someone practices introspection, the more she learns to know herself and the areas of life to which she attaches fears, and why.

People may also discover, to their surprise, that there is no basis in the present situation to justify many of their fears, that these are fears left over from old past experiences, modeled to them by their parents, learned from others, taught by society, or based on false assumptions.

With greater awareness of their fears, people gain better understanding of their reactions. They discover that much of their behavior is a function of their efforts to protect themselves from what they believe may be painful.

If people care about themselves, then it is expected that they will choose to defend themselves from harm. This perception not only invites people to have compassion for themselves for being vigilant, but also encourages them to evaluate the usefulness or validity of their fears, lower their shields, and allow their focus to shift to others and to the matter at hand.

There will always be fears, shielding, judging, and closing off of ourselves. But people can learn to work skillfully and benevolently to recognize when their walls go up and their energy and concentration shuts off, and then have the courage and commitment to study what triggered the mechanism and choose to reopen to compassion and caring for themselves and others, or for the task for which they are responsible.

Likewise, as people grow to understand the mechanism within themselves that allows them to grow or that shuts them down, to have patience, and to let go of their need to control, they will recognize that others struggle with the same problem and they can now perceive others' reactions differently. They can respond to others with care instead of fear.

Before a person can be caring, he must be able to perceive others and their behaviors in a way that affords compassion within him. Through realization of his own fear structure, he can now be patient, defer judgment, and feel compassion for others, knowing that they, too, struggle with fears. The perception becomes, "I am one who is worthy of love," rather than "I am one who needs to be defended to feel safe." This is the basis of a caring belief system.

When the caring belief system described here is fully realized, it may be instrumental in promoting the highest levels of human communication, interaction, health, and well-being. It offers an explanation for the inattentiveness, stress, and lack of the ability to concentrate that affects human achievement, creativity, and productiveness.

THE COMING OF AGE OF THE CARING ETHIC

Research into teacher effectiveness concludes that teachers' behaviors are major factors in the success of the teaching/learning process.

The premise presented here is that these behaviors are driven by belief systems and that certain beliefs differentiate the most effective teachers.

Researchers have stated that superior teachers are more intuitive, personally committed, and other-oriented, and that the fundamental system of beliefs upon which expert teachers base their decisions and behaviors is founded in caring (Agne, 1992; Berliner, 1988).

The notion that caring is important to teaching is not new (Rogers, 1958; Combs, 1965). Caring has been advocated for as long as educational research has existed. Much educational literature proclaims the need for caring teachers, administrators, parents, and communities (Combs & Gonzalez, 1994; Rogers & Freiberg, 1994). Recent reform writers are naming caring as the ethical aid and solution to the problems of crime and apathy that plague our society. Indeed, they advocate caring as the addition to the curriculum that may pave the way to educational reform through the production of caring citizens for the future (Kohn, 1991; Noddings, 1992).

Caring: A Way of Being

One reason why many new perceptions in education become new editions to the bandwagon category is that the educationists will attempt to implement them. But caring is a mode of thinking, a belief system whose antithesis is fear and stress. When this mode is blocked by states of fear and the resulting stressors, effective teaching and modeling is thwarted. Therefore, adding the subject of caring to the curriculum as a solution to the ills of society is itself a strategy based in fear, the opposite of caring.

Caring, as it functions within the expert teacher, is not a topic that may be internalized through instructional methodology, but rather it is a way of being, perceiving, thinking, and believing, a state of mind that directs effective teaching behaviors. It is the precursor to the decision making and the performance that produces the master teacher.

This is not to say, however, that the caring belief system may not be acquired. It is just that one does not become a caring person by replicating the behaviors of caring people. Caring is a subjective experience that comes from within; it must be "felt," not objectified. The caring belief system may be defined by a predisposition toward other-orientedness. It is, therefore, possible to understand and internalize caring by recognizing that the root of self-orientation is fear, the opposite of the caring state.

Most people experience a constant conflict between self-orientation and other-orientation, if they experience other-orientation at all. The magnitude of this conflict may be determined, in most cases, by the extent to which each is exposed to human interaction in the daily existence.

Self-awareness is the key to recognizing these states. Internal dialogue and external physical reactions are cues to the changes in these modes of functioning, and vigilance to the onset of these changes may be learned by anyone, in time.

It is important to realize that the goal is not to stop the fear states that periodically or, in some cases, constantly occur within. It is a vital part of human functioning to armor and protect the self from perceived harm. Often, however, fear states occur without need, out of habit that has become conditioned in perception and behavior. One common example of fear conditioning may be observed in those who find themselves compelled to be in constant control of themselves and others, a situation in which many teachers may easily find themselves because of the nature of the teacher/student relationship.

In the case of the classroom, human interaction is the name of the game. The teaching/learning process is defined by human interaction. Since fear posturing will inevitably occur whenever a threat to the self is perceived, students cannot learn readily in a setting where they feel attacked or a lack of support and acceptance. Likewise, teachers cannot be effective if they feel the need to be in constant control of themselves and their students, or if they perceive their students' reactions to themselves to be anything other than acceptance, respect, and caring.

CARING AND THE MASTER TEACHER

The level of caring that has developed within many master teachers is much more than simply acceptance of students and some measure of fearlessness within the self. The level of caring within a master teacher has, I believe, become expanded to a state that, much of the time, may be experienced as adoration.

This deep state of caring may occur in a number of ways. It is likely that many candidates came into the teaching profession already holding deep caring capacities, found success as a result, and perpetuated those states in the classroom. Others, however, may have acquired deep caring states because experience and careful observation, coupled with commitment to the understanding of the teaching/learning process, taught them that caring works. And, whether consciously or not, they simply became conditioned to repeat those behaviors and demeanors that brought about the highest rate of success, an expansion of the old adage that you can catch more flies with honey.

Teaching requires constant daily interaction with twenty-five or more unique and exquisitely complex individuals, each with the potential for hundreds of thousands of needs and concerns during the course the school year. The master teacher becomes a creative problem-solver.

Becoming the master teacher may well result in a very scholarly individual as a result of the multitude of hours spent by the teacher in search of solutions. But we need not assume that all master teachers are bookish highbrows. What we will likely find instead is a committed zealot, in terms of the approach and demeanor with which she seeks ways to serve the needs of the student. The level of commitment to the growth of each student is unsurpassed, in most cases, even by the efforts of parents of those individuals in her charge.

This phenomenon is the result of the belief held by the expert teacher that the responsibility for the quality and depth of each student's mental growth and emotional well-being lies squarely on his shoulders and with his ability to discover and effect creative solutions to the problems that inevitably arise with each student on a daily basis.

Clearly, experience and familiarity with the many categories of problems that commonly arise in the teaching/learning process effectively sharpen that capability more and more over time, but experience alone is not enough. It is the care-driven commitment and dedication common among experts that forces the creative edge witnessed among the masters, a devotion, unconfined by classroom walls and school bells, that lives constantly within the mind and thoughts of the analyzing teacher. The master teacher possesses an unsinkable will. The way is inevitable.

This level of will, of course, presupposes an unusual capacity for patience, for the best way may take time to discover. And the measure of patience springs from the trust that develops between the master teacher and his students as a result of adoration that is already in place.

Embracing Fear

Aspy and Roebuck (1977) proclaimed that "You can't learn from someone you don't like." I would like to proffer that "nor can you expertly teach someone you don't like." Herein lies the connection between the teaching/learning process and personal fear (stress). The capacity to like, indeed to adore, the other is strongly related to recognizing and accepting the fear within the self and the other that blocks that capacity to care, to focus, and ultimately, to learn and achieve.

The caring teacher makes the assumption that students whose behaviors are counter to those that promote focus and learning are driven

by the normal fear states that occur within us all. The student is, therefore, perceived by the caring teacher as acting out of fear. From this
place of compassion the teacher is then able to respond to the student
with acceptance, trust, and patience.

The armored teacher, on the other hand, reacts to fear with fear
and resents the student's actions because they are perceived as a personal affront against the teacher. The result will be a breakdown in the
teaching/learning process.

These occurrences need not be perceived as overt, obvious
episodes. They are rather more likely to be quite subtle or even hidden
from the immediate awareness of both the student(s) and the teacher to
which they occur in any interaction. This explains, in part, why intermittent observations of teachers in classrooms fail to provide researchers with accurate, comprehensive data on the basis of effective
teaching.

Caring: The Leavening Agent

Caring acts as leavening because a small amount may serve to
cause expansion in each person encountered by it or engaged in it. With
the development of deep caring states comes the intense level of attention and dedication common among expert teachers.

As the seed of caring grows within the teacher, more and more
mental activity is devoted to the incubation of thoughts and ideas con-
cerning the teaching/learning process. Ever increasing mental time-on-
task is given over to issues of classroom problem-solving. It is these
thoughts that guide the behavior of the expert teacher. These thoughts
and resulting perceptions are the precursors to the personal sense of responsibility to professional knowledge and preparation, the expert decision-making skills, and the effective teaching behaviors that occur in
the classrooms of master teachers.

The caring beliefs and resultant behaviors that allow the master
teacher to emerge are now constantly modeled to and ultimately ab-
sorbed by the students. Students, in turn, begin to adopt caring beliefs
and model the consequent behaviors to each other. The caring set in
motion by the expert teacher contagiously spreads, creating a new
group ambience.

Researchers have long suspected that the learning environment
has more impact on successful achievement than any set of established
teacher techniques, and further that superior learning environments result from a subtle and much more comprehensive mechanism. Joyce
(1975) concluded that "even where we find that increased learning is as-

sociated with the presence of certain kind of skill or style in teaching, it is very likely that the reason is because that skill or aspect of style is an index of a much larger complex of behaviors that signals the presence of a certain kind of environment."

A MINI VIEW OF THE CARING MACHINE IN THE CLASSROOM

Let us paint a mental picture of what one caring belief system looks like and the principles under which it operates.

Caring is first other-orientedness. The other, as opposed to the self, takes our focus. In serving the other, one becomes more and more sensitive to the needs of the other. Caring further entails some level of unconditional acceptance, a demeanor that requires the ability to reserve judgment and to exude forgiveness and general harmlessness.

Given that people differ extensively in terms of their personalities, styles, and energy levels, it is reasonable to assume that energy expended from each other-oriented person will vary considerably. We may say that the level of commitment is likely to be directly related to the level of other-orientedness in each. In the context of the classroom, where a teacher may have 25 or 30 other human beings to be oriented toward, how committed she is to each student affects everything that occurs.

Now at some time during the school year, each of the 25 to 30 charges will have some need for teacher attention. Most will seek this attention in one way or another each day and many dozens of times per day.

Most teacher/student interaction occurs according to the "squeaky wheel gets the grease" theory. Teachers will attend first to those with the concerns that have the greatest urgency, in addition to all of those other little things quickly corrected in between and on the way to greatest concerns. This operation is the same in most classrooms. What may be different in the caring classroom is how the teacher interprets the concern at hand.

Caring and committed behaviors are likely to be emitted most by those who most often perceive the other in ways that evoke their caring focus. If someone perceives others as always being in either a love state or a fear state, then he is likely to offer care or compassion rather than punitive reaction.

If, for instance, we perceive that each problem or need was initiated by, or is being maintained by, some form of fear, then we may more easily choose to react with compassion. "What is this child afraid of?

What is the fear that initiated this concern? What fear(s) are lurking within this frustrating situation?"

If we perceive fear states as the opposite of love states, then we allow for a compassionate place to start. What is the fear? If we can identify the fear(s), we are able to set into motion a problem solving mode that encourages creative, thoughtful steps toward resolution.

The caring belief may be guided by two questions: (1) What are the fears underlying the surface situation or problem? and (2) What are the most caring choices toward resolution of the fears in the situation? The caring approach asks, "Which would be the most loving actions, given the circumstances in this place, at this time and for all those involved?"

Gaining the answer to this question, determining possible choices, and taking action on the decision may take seconds, months, or years. The problem or situation that a teacher may be reacting to could be one that gets an instantaneous answer or one that takes many years to understand.

The number and type of problems encountered by teachers within each hour is stifling to most. Some may just need a gentle hint to discover an answer. Others may be problems that require long-range goals, like, "How do I see myself best serving in the years to come?"

Situation ethics requires us to ask, "What would be most caring to the majority in each situation?" A caring belief system might follow this initial step, caring for the majority. Further, it might be equivalent to Kohlberg's (1971) sixth (potential) stage of moral reasoning, the Universal Ethical Principle Orientation, which depends on abstract concepts of integrity and equity guided by individual conscience. The caring ethic diverges from these only insofar as it recognizes that just as soon as the majority's needs are met, the individual still requires time and energy.

Now is the time to ask, "What is the fear underlying this need?" again and again for each individual child. This is the behavior that seems to entail the commitment. Perhaps it is this level of committedness within each individual teacher that characterizes the major difference between levels of effectiveness in the classroom.

Recall that the principle concern with fear states is that they prevent or replace love states. And, insofar as love states allow personal tranquility, energy flow, and unobstructed focus, they are more likely to encourage unfettered learning and active achievement. Fear states, on the other hand, are more likely to promote stress, disrupted concentration, and scatterbrained, irrational perceptions and behavior—in general, decreased levels of achievement.

Researchers have reported that teachers' stress levels are correlated with diminished levels of tolerance, patience, caring, and involvement with their students (Blase, 1986). Moreover, research indicates that students of fearful teachers make significantly lower academic growth gain (Heil & Washburne, 1962; Osborne, 1968).

Students' Fears

Fears, of course, may be related to anything. However, in the classroom, they often follow a line of thinking, premature or immature, that goes like this: "What about me? Is anyone going to pay attention to me? Am I going to have my needs met? Am I going to be embarrassed? laughed at? left behind? chosen? ignored? accepted? successful? What about me?"

Fears among today's school children, may also include, "Is anyone going to be there when I get home? Is someone going to shoot at me on my way? Am I going to be hurt? Am I going to be alone? Am I going to be protected? What will happen to me if I say "No!" to my friends? To the neighborhood gang members? What will happen if I cave in? What will my parents/teachers do if they find out? What about me?"

These fears occur, to greater or lesser degrees and in different variations, depending upon the experiences to which a person has become accustomed. In the classroom any level or variation may be present at any time. A student may choose any number of behaviors that are distracting to his or others' focus and may choose to emit these behaviors on a more or less constant basis. Talking, fiddling or fidgeting, noise making, falling out of chairs, and teasing are common types of classroom behaviors that fall into this category. These ostentatious behaviors, especially if they are harmful to others, will most often gain a teacher's attention first.

The other end of the spectrum may include those behaviors that are much more concealed and abstruse, and may even go undetected. The behaviors or fears of the invisible student may never surface. Shy students often disappear in a classroom unless they fail to achieve. Yet shyness may be a clue to a much deeper fear or fears, which typically escape the attention of all but the caring experts.

Teachers' Fears

Paying heed to fear states within students is only half of the requirement for a caring classroom to occur. The teacher must be equally aware of the fear states within himself. This requires constant attention to one's own feelings, attitudes, and reactions. Most teachers would

readily agree that an ordinary and expected part of the profession includes daily frustrations, irritations, and concerns.

Fear questions for the teacher in many typical American classrooms will vary in type and range, depending on the experience of
the teacher. They may include worries such as, "Am I going to get
any help with the mental, physical, or emotional needs of individual
students in my class? How will I get this class to listen to me? What
if I don't find a way to motivate these students? What if this class
never settles down? How will students' scores on standardized
achievement tests affect me? What forms of neglect or atrocity occur
with my students when they leave this classroom? What can I legally
do about it? What abuses can I expect from students, parents, the
principal, the superintendent, the janitor, the school board, politi-
cians, the society?"

Such questions can be clues to teachers as to their personal professional health and well-being or hardiness. For instance, one's line of
self-questioning may often run in the direction of, "Am I ever going to
get used to this noise level? Am I going to be able to tolerate the personal abuse of this job for much longer? Can I seriously see myself con-
fined to the classroom five years from now? ten years from now? When
I'm sixty-five? Will I always be satisfied with the standard of living allowed by the teaching profession? Am I becoming a stodgy and boring
professional? Does this position offer challenge enough to ensure the
level of personal growth I desire?"

If the line of personal reflection frequently or constantly includes
many of the above, a teacher may be headed for burnout. Burnout in
the teaching profession is a serious issue (Kyriacou, 1987; Dworkin,
1985; Selye, 1976).

But this line of questioning may also reveal the basis for many
problems in the classroom. If caring means other-orientedness, there
must be a balance in the amount of energy and concern targeted on the
self as opposed to the other.

Other-Orientedness and the Self

This brings us to another topic of the caring approach that must be
clarified. How does one functioning in an other-oriented state regard
the needs of the self?

A belief system that focuses on the other as opposed to self might
easily be construed as one that likely fails to give attention to the self.
However, having compassion for the self seems to be prerequisite to
feeling compassion for others.

The capacity to care for others, which we have described as unconditionally accepting, nonjudgmental, forgiving, and harmless, may be directly related to the level of the capacity one has for caring for the self. This is not to say that a person who feels contempt, guilt, shame, or disrespect for herself could not care for another. However, for her to do so requires that the greatest capacity, depth, or wisdom be enhanced in direct proportion to her capacity to practice that belief with the self.

Perhaps something occurs when we do unto others as we would have them do unto us. We begin to feel better about ourselves. Here we may again think in terms of states of fear versus states of love, openness, or acceptance. It may be expected that those who experience more time in states of openness than in states of fear and stress will be more likely to also exhibit more periods of and perhaps higher levels of caring for others as well as for self.

Ultimately, to be the teacher, we must first be healthy, that is, not functioning in constant states of fears. For that upon which we obsess comes out in our behavior and is then modeled to our students. If one is full of fear, one's teaching reflects that fear. Additionally, it is generally well known among medical professionals today that the degree of happiness, joy, and laughter in an individual's life has direct positive relationship to the condition of his overall physical health. A stable personality is essential for expert teaching to occur.

The principles of caring are simple. Fear, which is responsible for stress, blocks or interferes with attention to the task at hand, and therefore also interferes with learning and achievement. Caring offers the understanding, patience, forgiveness, and acceptance necessary to encourage people to release the barriers that they construct to protect themselves when they feel afraid, and in so doing allows increased focus and concentration. Caring offers a model for human relations that promotes personal growth, healing, and productivity, transforming people and environments.

Though the principles of caring are simple, their successful execution is quite another, extremely complex matter. Caring mastery requires tremendous dedication, hard work, and commitment. Learning to acquire the level of awareness necessary for a caring state to be maintained and for caring classroom environments and teacher/student relationships to evolve demands personal vigilance, patience, and courage.

No surviving professional teacher is unaccustomed to or daunted by hard work, however. It is hoped, therefore, that comprehension and awareness of this way of perceiving and being in life and in the classroom will compel readers to discover caring, and through it the path to mastery.

REFERENCES

Agne, K. (1991). The relationship between teacher belief systems and teacher effectiveness. (Doctoral dissertation, University of Florida). *Dissertation Abstracts International*. vol. 52/10-A, p. 3557.

Agne, K. (1992). Caring: The expert teacher's edge. *Educational Horizons, 70,* 120–124.

Agne, K., Greenwood, G., & Miller, L. D. (1994). Relationships between teacher belief systems and teacher effectiveness among Teachers of the Year. *Journal of Research and Development in Education, 27,* 141–152.

Ashton, P., & Webb, R. (1986). *Making a difference: Teachers' sense of efficacy and student achievement.* (Research on Teaching Monograph Series). New York: Longman.

Aspy, D., & Roebuck, F. (1977). *Kids don't learn from people they don't like.* Amherst, MA: Human Resource Development Press.

Bandura, A. (1977). *Social learning theory.* Englewood Cliffs, NJ: Prentice Hall.

Bandura, A., & Schunk, D. (1981). Cultivating competence, self-efficacy, and intrinsic interest through proximal self-motivation. *Journal of Personality and Social Psychology, 41,* 586–598.

Berliner, D. (1988). *The development of expertise in pedagogy.* Paper presented at the annual meeting of the American Association of Colleges of Teacher Education, New Orleans.

Berman, P., McLaughlin, W., Bass, G., Pauly E., & Zellman, G. (1977). *Federal program supporting educational change: Vol. VII. Factors affecting implementation and continuation.* Santa Monica, CA: Rand.

Blase, J. (1986). A qualitative analysis of sources of teacher stress: Consequences for performance. *American Educational Research Journal, 23,* 13–40.

Brookover, W., Schweitzer, J., Schneider, J., Beady, C., Flood, P., & Wisenbaker, J. (1978). Elementary school social and school achievement. *American Educational Research Journal, 15,* 301–318.

Clark, C. & Peterson, P. (1986). Teachers' thought processes. In M. C. Wittrock (Ed.), *Handbook of research on teaching* (pp. 255–293). New York: Macmillan.

Combs, A. (1965). *The professional education of teachers.* Boston: Allyn & Bacon.

Combs, A. (1982). *A personal approach to teaching: Beliefs that make a difference.* Boston: Allyn & Bacon.

Combs, A., & Gonzalez, D. (1994). *Helping relationships.* Boston: Allyn & Bacon.

Combs, A., & Taylor, C. (1952). The effect of perception of mild degrees of threat on performance. *Journal of Abnormal and Social Psychology, 47,* 420–424.

Coopersmith, S. (1967). *The antecedents of self-esteem.* San Francisco: W. H. Freeman.

Cox, T., & Brockley, T. (1984). The experience and effects of stress in teachers. *British Educational Research Journal, 10,* 83–87.

Crandall, V., Katkovsky, W., & Preston, A. (1962). Motivational and ability determinants of young children's intellectual achievement behaviors. *Child Development, 33,* 643–661.

Dworkin, A. (1985). *When teachers give up: Teacher burn-out, teacher turnover and their impact on children.* Austin, TX: Hogg Foundation for Mental Health.

Eskridge, D., & Coker, D. (1985). Teacher stress: Symptoms, causes, and management techniques. *The Clearing House, 58,* 387–390.

Fenstermacher, G. (1979). A philosophical consideration of recent research on teacher effectiveness. In L. Shulman (Ed.), *Review of research in education* (Vol. 6, pp. 157–185). Itasca, IL: Peacock.

Gibran, K. (1923). *The Prophet.* New York: Knopf.

Gibson, S., & Dembo, M. (1984). Teacher efficacy: A construct validity. *Journal of Educational Psychology, 76,* 569–582.

Hamachek, D. (1969). Characteristics of good teachers and implications for teacher education. *Phi Delta Kappan, 50,* 341–344.

Hart, L. (1983). *Human brain and human learning.* New York: Longman.

Heil, L., & Washburne, C. (1962). Brooklyn College research in teacher effectiveness. *Journal of Educational Research, 55,* 437–450.

Joyce, B. (1975). Listening to different drummers: Evaluating alternative instructional models. In *Competency assessment, research, and evaluation: A report of a national conference* (pp. 61–81) Albany, NY: Multi-State Consortium on Performance-Based Teacher Education.

Kohlberg, L. (1971). Stages of moral development as a basis for moral education. In C. Beck, E. V. Sullivan, & B. Crittendon (Eds.), *Moral education: Interdisciplinary approaches.* Toronto: University of Toronto Press.

Kohn, A. (1991). Caring kids: The role of the schools. *Phi Delta Kappan, 72,* 496–506.

Koon, J. (1971). Effects of expectancy, anxiety, and task difficulty on teacher behavior. (Doctoral dissertation, Syracuse University). *Dissertation Abstracts International, 32,* 821-A.

Kounin, J. (1970). *Discipline and group management in classrooms.* New York: Holt, Rinehart, & Winston.

Kyriacou, C. (1987). Teacher stress and burn-out: An international review. *Educational Researcher, 29,* 146–152.

Lent, R., Brown, S., & Larkin, K. (1984). Relation of self-efficacy expectations to academic achievement and persistence. *Journal of Counseling Psychology, 31,* 356–362.

Murray, H., & Staebler, B. (1974). Teacher's locus of control and student achievement gains. *Journal of School Psychology, 12,* 305–309.

Noddings, N. (1992). *The challenge to care in schools.* New York: Teachers College Press.

Ornstein, A., & Miller, H. (1980). *Looking into teaching: An introduction to American education.* Chicago: Rand-McNally.

Osborne, M. (1968). The influence of teacher expectancy of anxiety behavior and pupil performance. *Peabody Journal of Education, 45,* 214–217.

Rogers, C., (1958). The characteristics of a helping relationship. *Personnel and Guidance Journal, 37,* 6–16.

Rogers, C., & Freiberg, H. J. (1994). *Freedom to learn.* New York: Merrill.

Rose, J., & Medway, F. (1981). Teacher locus of control, teacher behavior, and student behavior as determinants of student achievement. *Journal of Educational Research, 74,* 375–381.

Rosenshine, B., & Furst, N. (1973). The use of direct observation to study teaching. In R. M. W. Travers (Ed.), *Second handbook of research on teaching* (pp. 122–183). Chicago; Rand McNally.

Rosenshine, B., & Furst, N. (1971). Research in teacher performance criteria. In B. O. Smith (Ed.), *Research in teacher education; A symposium* (pp. 37–72). Englewood Cliffs, NJ: Prentice Hall.

Ryans, D. (1960). *Characteristics of teachers.* Washington, DC: American Council on Education.

Samples, B. (1976). Sanity in the classroom. *Science Teacher, 43,* 24–27.

Selye, H. (1976). *The stress of life* (rev. ed.). New York: McGraw-Hill

Shavelson, R., Webb, N., & Burstein, L. (1986). Measurement of teaching. In M. C. Wittrock (Ed.), *Handbook of research on teaching* (3rd ed., pp. 50–91). New York: Macmillan.

Shulman, L. (1986). Paradigms and research programs in the study of teaching: A contemporary perspective. In M. C. Wittrock (Ed.), *Handbook of research on teaching* (3rd ed., pp. 3–36). New York: Macmillan.

Willower, D., Eidell, T., & Hoy, W. (1973). *The school and pupil control ideology* (The Pennsylvania State University Studies, No. 24). University Park: Pennsylvania State University.

CHAPTER 8

EFFECTIVE TEACHERS: WHAT THEY DO, HOW THEY DO IT, AND THE IMPORTANCE OF SELF-KNOWLEDGE

Don Hamachek

To a casual observer, teaching may appear to be an easy task, easy, that is, until one begins to see the smaller units of behavior dynamics within the larger context of an operational classroom. What one observes is a stunning array of behavioral possibilities—some students are listening and learning, thinking and trying, while others are in various stages of resisting and refusing, defying and dissenting. Classrooms are seldom neat and orderly places where students move quietly and obediently from one activity to another with restrained enthusiasm. This does not mean that there is no order in the educational efforts of individual classrooms, but it does suggest that events cannot always be predicted before they happen, or be easily controlled when they do. In the course of ongoing classroom life, it takes savvy and interpersonal competence to keep up with the changing demands of instructional activities, students' needs, and one's personal goals. It has been estimated, for example, that in a single day, an elementary teacher might have up to 1,000 interpersonal exchanges with students (Jackson, 1968). Secondary school teachers may interact with as many as 150 students per day. This astonishing number of teacher-student encounters is one of the reasons that teaching can be an incredibly demanding and complex task.

Which leads one to ask: What kind of individual does it take to be an effective teacher under these circumstances? What sorts of behaviors and self-perceptions tend to distinguish expert or "master" teachers from the rest? The purpose of this chapter is to explore these questions in order to identify some of the behaviors and personal qualities that have come to be associated with teachers who are viewed as masters of their craft.

WHAT BEHAVIORS ARE ASSOCIATED WITH TEACHER EXCELLENCE?

Deciding where teachers fall along a continuum of effectiveness remains a daunting challenge. Fine distinctions have been made between "good" teaching and "effective" teaching along this continuum by researchers who study teacher behavior. Berliner (1987b), for example, makes the point that a teacher who begins class on time, reviews material with students, emphasizes important points, asks higher-order questions, and so on, might be judged to be a "good" teacher irrespective of whether students are learning anything. In this sense, good (or poor) teaching is determined by particular standards of practice, independent of effectiveness. Whether one is an "effective" teacher, however, is always tied to instructional outcomes, to students' actual learning. Thus, effective teaching is related more to students' academic performance, and "good" teaching is associated more with teachers' classroom behavior. I believe a strong case can be made for the idea that those who are designated as "master" or "expert" teachers are so labeled because their teaching behavior reflects a successful blend of the best qualities associated with "good" and effective teaching.

Sternberg and Horvath (1995) have gone a step further and have suggested that we need to "distinguish those teachers who are expert at teaching students from those who are merely experienced at teaching students" (p. 9). They assert that what is needed is a reconceptualization of teaching expertise, one grounded in a psychological understanding of how experts differ from nonexperts and how people think about expertise in their real-world encounters with it.

A central premise of their argument is that there exists no well-defined standard that all experts meet and that no non-experts meet. Rather, they suggest that experts reflect a family resemblance to one another that defines the category "expert." They go on to suggest that a convenient way of discussing such categories is in terms of a *prototype* that captures the central tendency of all the exemplars in the category. By definition, a prototype embodies specifically designated exemplars of a category, which allows it to serve as the basis for judgments about category membership. With this in mind, Sternberg and Horvath (1995) offer a reconceptualization of expert teaching, one that advances a "prototype" view of how an expert teacher behaves and thinks.

In support of their position, they point to empirical data to show that experts differ from nonexperts in three basic domains of teacher behavior and activity, which includes (1) *knowledge* (experts bring knowledge to bear more efficiently on problems), (2) *efficiency* (experts do more in less time in their areas of expertise), and (3) *insight* (experts are more likely to arrive at novel and appropriate solutions to problems within their areas of expertise). Thus, Sternberg and Horvath (1995) propose that teaching expertise should be perceived as a category that is structured by the similarity of expert teachers to one another rather than by a set of necessary and sufficient features.

RESEARCH METHODOLOGIES FOR
IDENTIFYING TEACHER EXCELLENCE

The question remains, how do we actually go about identifying those behaviors associated with good, or effective, or expert, or master teachers, depending on what they are called? Dunkin and Biddle (1974) and Good and Brophy (1994) have been instrumental in suggesting and designing research methodologies for answering that question. Some possibilities gleaned from their work include the following:

1. Ask students, experienced teachers, principals, and college professors to list characteristics they associate with good teaching.
2. Choose several classrooms and do intensive case studies on them over a long period of time, including in-depth interviews with students and teachers. Keep student performance records.
3. Observe a variety of classrooms, rate various teachers on specific traits, and then examine which traits are associated with teachers whose students are among the highly motivated and/or the highly achieving.
4. Identify teachers whose students consistently achieve at a higher level than other students; then carefully observe those teachers to see what they do.
5. Train teachers to use various strategies to teach the same lesson, and then determine which approach promotes the greatest student learning.

There Is No One Route to Being an Effective Teacher

When a teacher can be categorized as an effective or expert teacher, it is because that person is engaging in observable and specifiable behaviors that set him or her a cut above others. It is not easy research to do. Empirical research points to why this is so: there is no best way to be an effective teacher. This is true at the elementary level (Soar & Soar, 1978), at the junior high level (Evertson, Anderson, & Brophy, 1978), and at the high school level (Stallings & Hentzell, 1978). Indeed, there is no single pathway to good teaching because no one set of teaching behaviors is clearly related to student performance outcomes in all situations (Brophy, 1992; Leinhart, 1992) and, in any case, achievement is only one of many student outcomes that is important in assessing teacher effectiveness.

The past twenty years or so has produced an enormous mountain of research related to teacher effectiveness. With fewer dollars available for educational purposes, there has been increased pressure at local and state levels for better and more efficient instruction. Thus, questions about what constitutes effective teaching, or what makes for a master teacher, have become increasingly important. Although it is true that no single teaching behavior is associated with effective instruction, McDonald (1975) has observed from his review of teaching effectiveness research that there are certain "patterns" of behaviors that distinguish effective from ineffective teachers. As we work our way through this chapter, you will begin to see some of these patterns emerge as we examine four major dimensions of teacher behaviors and characteristics: (1) personal characteristics, (2) intellectual characteristics, (3) interaction styles, and (4) instructional approaches.

PERSONAL CHARACTERISTICS OF EFFECTIVE TEACHERS

When we talk about someone's personal characteristics, it is usually with reference to distinctive patterns of actions, thoughts, and emotions that characterize his or her overall behavior. Personality is the essence of one's personal characteristics. Although he or she may not be aware of it, each person has a unique personality, an overall personal attribute that contributes to the emotional tone of relationships that makes one either easy or difficult to get along with, which is why personality considerations are so crucial for teachers. There is probably no other profession in which one's personality is such an important factor as in teaching, in that it contributes so significantly to the interpersonal medium within which learning occurs.

Personality is part of the interactive aspect of teaching. That is, in our interactions we not only communicate what we know, we telegraph who we are. This might not be such an important consideration in professions where the contact between the "professional" and the client is typically brief and transitory. This is not, however, the case for teachers and students. Here, the contact is extensive and extended over long time periods, allowing the interactive aspects of the teacher-learner relationship to have, for better or worse, a greater cumulative effect.

Warmth and Interpersonal Responsiveness Are Apparent

Students have always been astute observers of the personality characteristics of their teachers and they are in generally high agreement about what it is they like about their teachers at a more personal level. For example, in an earlier research project, Witty (1967) found, from an analysis of more than 12,000 letters written in response to "The Teacher Who Helped Me Most," that the top-ranking personality traits associated with these teachers were the following: (1) cooperative, democratic attitude, (2) kindliness and consideration for the individual, (3) patience, (4) broad interests, (5) pleasant personal appearance and manner, (6) fairness and impartiality, (7) sense of humor, (8) pleasant disposition and consistent behavior, (9) interest in students' problems, and (10) flexibility.

More recent studies (Murray, 1983; Soar & Soar, 1979; Sparks & Lipka, 1992) support Witty's findings; that is, warmth, friendliness, and understanding are teachers' personal characteristics most strongly related to positive student attitudes.

What happens when these personal qualities are held to the more rigid test of whether having them makes any difference in the actual performance of students?

Sears (1940) found positive correlations between the extent to which a teacher reflected a personal interest in, and willingness to listen to, students' ideas and the creativity shown by elementary-level students. Tikunoff, Berliner, and Rist (1975) found that second- and fifth-grade students of teachers who, among other things, were accepting, cooperative, and involved, showed greater achievement gains in mathematics and reading than students whose teachers were rated lower on those characteristics.

It is worth noting that while research with K–12 students suggests that a teacher's personal characteristics *might* influence student achievement in either an up or down direction, this is less likely to be true for college students (Abrami, Leventhal, & Perry, 1982). Younger students' self-concepts are not fully consolidated, and their defenses less well constructed, which may be why they are more likely to be influenced by teachers' personal qualities.

A note of caution: the studies mentioned in this section are all cor-relational, which means that we cannot assume that particular aspects of a teacher's personal characteristics—warmth, friendliness, sense of humor, and so forth—*cause* positive student attitudes or student learn-ing, or creativity, only that these two variables are related to each other.

Although there is nothing inherent in a teacher's personal manner that, by itself, promotes learning, it does contribute to a positive or negative classroom climate. It can punctuate an emotional climate with what Purkey and Novak (1996) call an "inviting" or "disinviting" tone. It is the difference between being in a classroom and feeling invited, important, and valued and feeling uninvited, unimportant, and not valued.

Because a teacher's personality is an integral part of everything that he or she does, it is difficult to prove that it "causes" any changes in students' achievement or attitudes. I think, however, that this amor-phous dimension of one's being is a definite factor in every classroom that—for better or worse—sets an emotional tone to which students res-onate in various ways.

Enthusiasm Stands Out

Enthusiasm, like warmth, is difficult to define objectively. Yet it does exist and can have a quite positive effect on the overall emotional climate of a classroom.

Good and Brophy (1994) have suggested that teacher enthusiasm consists of at least two basic components, which include: (1) a sincere interest in the subject, and (2) vigor and positive energy. Effective teachers project these qualities. Teachers who are less dynamic, per-haps even shy, can compensate by funneling their enthusiasm through the subject matter, if not through their personalities. For example, a somewhat quiet, introverted fourth-grade teacher takes her class on frequent field trips, and has them thinking and talking about it as much as two weeks in advance. Before they visited the zoo, the stu-dents worked in small groups, with each group being responsible for reporting on a particular animal, which included classifying an animal as either—in the students' terminology—an "eater" of other animals or an "eatee."

Enthusiasm can be shown in many ways. It does not necessarily mean that a teacher has to bounce around with endless energy. It can show itself in quieter, more subtle ways. If you think of enthusiasm as an essentially positive energy capable of both kindling and capturing attention, there are endless ways to express it. Consider the following account offered by Bereiter, Washington, Engetman, and Osborn (1969), which reflects, I think, an enthusiasm, a positive energy that is conveyed in a more subtle, playful manner:

> When a good teacher pointed to a picture and said, "What's this?" she expected all children to respond. If they didn't respond, she would perhaps smile and say, "I didn't hear you. What's this?" By now all the children were responding. She would smile, cock her head and say, "I didn't hear you." Now the children would let out a veritable roar. The teacher would acknowledge, "Now I hear you," and proceed with the next task, with virtually 100% of them responding. Basically her approach was to stop and introduce some kind of gimmick if the children—all of them—were not responding or paying attention. She did not bludgeon the children, she "conned" them. It seemed obvious that they understood her rules; she would not go on until they performed. It seemed that they liked performing because when they performed well she acted pleased.

Does a teacher's enthusiasm make a positive difference in students' learning and attitudes? It seems to. For example, teachers who are trained to be more enthusiastic have students who are more attentive and involved in class, although they do not necessarily do better on classroom tests (Gillet & Gall, 1982).

Other researchers (Mastin, 1963; Rosenshine & Furst, 1973), however, have pointed to evidence suggesting that not only is teacher enthusiasm related to higher student achievement, but that students respond more favorably to material presented by enthusiastic teachers.

Proactive Behaviors Are Prominent

Proactive teachers tend to be those who are essentially positive, flexible, democratic, and capable of setting reasonable goals for the class as a whole, and for individual students. Good and Brophy (1994) note that teachers tend to fall along a continuum from *proactive* to *overreactive*, with the more effective teachers clustering toward the proactive end.

Overreactive teachers, found at the other end of the continuum, are among those who develop rigid, stereotyped views of students based on first impressions and students' prior records. Not surprisingly, they tend to treat students in terms of their stereotyped preconceptions rather than as individuals, and are among the most likely teachers to project negative expectations for their students' achievement.

Proactive teachers are likely to be effective teachers because of their essentially positive mindset about what is possible for students to accomplish. Rather than *reacting* to those times when students are not achieving, they are more likely to proactively plan their teaching-learning activities in such a way as to minimize that happening in the first place.

Humanness Is an Earmark

Effective teachers tend to be "human" in the fullest sense of the word. They are characterized by a sense of humor, a pleasant manner, and are viewed as friendly, fair, and enthusiastic by their students. They are not, however, always on top of their game. Porter and Brophy (1987), for example, pointed out that there is nothing in the literature to suggest that a teacher has to excel at all times in the qualities associated with effective teaching in order to be an effective teacher. Being fully human does not mean being totally perfect.

In fact, Morse, Bloom, and Dunn (1961) found that there are many acceptable personal characteristics that can go into making a good teacher. From their interviews of students in grades 3 and 10, two major trends were noted. For example, students tended to rate a teacher as good on such matters as "She helps us learn," even if she was considered tough, and "She cares about us," even if the lessons were somewhat confusing. Wide differences were found in the considerations students weighed in their judgments. However, should a teacher be too extreme in one dimension—for example, "mean" rather than merely "strict," or "chaotic" rather than merely "lax," or "arbitrary" rather than merely "quite demanding"—the student would more often than not overlook the teacher's more positive characteristics. In other words, a student's otherwise positive perceptions were frequently lost because of some overriding negative characteristic of the teacher that blocked his or her good points. The important point is that students were tolerant of a range of differences in a teacher's behavior unless the behavior became too extreme. Students do not expect perfection in teachers. They do, however, look for fairness, a personal quality consistently associated with good teachers.

Warmth, a sense of fairness, and humanness are important components of the personal characteristics of effective teachers. Qualities of this type help teachers to be sensitive and empathic. Intellectual strength and subject-matter competence give effective teachers substance and depth, an idea we examine next.

INTELLECTUAL CHARACTERISTICS OF EFFECTIVE TEACHERS

Teachers' breadth of knowledge, the clarity of their presentations, their preparedness, how well they think on their feet, how stimulating they are to their students are factors to be considered when looking at the intellectual dimensions of an effective teacher, especially those we may want to designate as master teachers. Shulman (1987) has identified three kinds of knowledge that should be part of the intellectual arsenal of effective teachers. First of all, they must have content knowledge, knowledge of the subject matter to be taught. Secondly, they need pedagogical knowledge, which includes knowledge of how to motivate students, how to manage groups of students in a classroom setting, how to design and administer tests, and so forth. Finally, effective teachers need pedagogical-content knowledge, which is knowledge of how to teach that is specific to what is being taught. There is evidence suggesting that effective teachers reflect these knowledge domains in at least six ways, and it is to these ways that we now turn our attention.

Subject-Matter Knowledge Is Combined with Specific Instructional Skills

Although being in command of one's subject matter is absolutely necessary, it is not, in itself, a sufficient condition to be an effective teacher. In addition to having a solid grasp of the important facts, concepts, and procedures of their own academic discipline, effective teachers are able to translate their knowledge of pedagogical practices—into assignments, explanations, lessons, tests, examples, demonstrations, and other teaching activities (Leinhardt & Greeno, 1986; Wilson, Shulman, & Richert, 1987).

Research is showing that effective teachers differ from novice and less effective teachers in much the same ways that expert physicists, physicians, or even chess players differ from novices in these fields (Chase & Simon, 1973; Chi, Feltovich, & Glaser, 1981; Sabers, Cushing, & Berliner, 1981). Skilled, effective teachers, for example, work from integrated, underlying principles for action, which allows them access to richer and more elaborate strategies for coping with problems in teaching. As an illustration of this, Leinhardt (1986) found that effective math teachers could review a previous day's work with students in two to three minutes, compared to the fifteen minutes or so taken by less effective teachers.

Thorough Preparation Is a Trademark

Research shows that, whether at the college level (Goldsmid, Gruber & Wilson, 1977) or in the public schools (Davis & Thomas, 1989; Wright & Nuthall, 1970), effective teachers prepare themselves thoroughly and carefully. Becoming an excellent teacher is not something that happens to a gifted few, but is, rather, the outgrowth of hard work and thorough preparation. Teachers' preparedness is responded to positively by both gifted and average students at all levels. Bishop (1976) and Milgram (1979), for example, found that both high school and elementary level students, regardless of level of intelligence or creative thinking, sex, or age, valued the intellectual preparedness of teachers more highly than teacher creativity and personality. Milgram (1979) found that girls emphasized personality more, and intelligence less, than boys, a finding consistent with the emphasis girls tend to place on personal-social relationships.

Organization and Clarity Are Well-Developed Traits

No outcome in teacher effectiveness research is clearer than the issue of teacher clarity and its effect on student learning. The evidence points to a consistent finding: teachers who are organized and who give clear presentations and explanations tend to have students who not only learn more but rate their teachers more positively (Davis & Thomas, 1989; Hines, Cruickshank, & Kennedy, 1985; Land, 1987; Murray, 1983).

Additionally, there is evidence showing that effective teachers, as opposed to less effective or novice teachers, have a better organized and more clearly integrated lesson plan (Borko & Livingston, 1989; Leinhardt & Greeno, 1986). According to Leinhardt and Greeno, a lesson plan includes global (content nonspecific) planning components, local (content-specific) planning components, and decision elements that build in the flexibility necessary to respond to expected and unexpected events. The superior organizational structure inherent in the lesson plans of effective teachers enables them to teach effectively and efficiently. For example, their superior organization and integration of content-nonspecific teaching knowledge, such as general class-management routines, maximizes the time that students devote to learning, rather than passing out materials or switching activities. Further, the clarity and breadth of their content-specific teaching knowledge, such as explanations to specific student questions, enables the effective teacher to relate student lesson objectives, thus keeping the instructional goals on track.

The more complex the material, the more necessary it is for the teacher to present it as clearly and as systematically as possible. A teacher's clear and organized explanation does for a student's mind what a light bulb does for a dimly lit room—it cuts through the darkness and shadows.

Greater Responsibility Is Assumed for Student Outcomes

Effective teachers, more so than less effective ones, are more likely to believe that when there is a breakdown in the teaching/learning machinery both the teacher and the student must assess the situation and make necessary adjustments. It has been found, for example, that when effective teachers are confronted with students who have continual personal adjustment difficulties, they see these as problems to be corrected rather than merely endured (Brophy & Rohrkemper, 1988). Effective teachers work on building relationships with problem students, rely on special education assistance, and socialization strategies (i.e., helping students to be involved with others), and seek the help of mental health professionals when necessary.

As an example of the benefits of this attitude, research in secondary science classes has shown that low-aptitude students achieve more if their teachers accept responsibility for seeing that all students learn science than they do if their teachers attribute degree of science mastery primarily to ability and motivation factors residing solely within the students (Lee & Gallagher, 1986).

Less effective teachers are more likely to turn the responsibility for dealing with problematic students over to persons such as the principal, school psychologist, or school counselor. Or they may try to control them through demands backed by threats of punishment.

Preparing Students for New Learning Is Skillfully Done

Effective teachers are particularly skilled at preparing their students for new learning. They are, for example, more likely than less effective teachers to give their students advanced organizers in the form of study questions, or perhaps overviews of relevant reading prior to a complex learning task (Mayer, 1984). In addition, effective teachers are more likely to see to it that students understand what is expected of them, and why, which not only keeps students on track, but helps them develop a sense of personal responsibility for their work (Anderson & Prawat, 1983). Teachers' instructions are sometimes vague, leaving students befuddled. For example, in a study done by Duffy, Roehler, Meloth, and Vavrus (1986), an ineffective reading teacher began her lesson on using context in reading by saying, "Today we are going to learn about context. This skill will help you in your reading" (p. 206). This is a fairly general statement, one that left many students confused about the goals of the lesson. Compare that statement with one expressed by a teacher judged to be more effective:

> At the end of today's lesson, you will be able to use the other words in a sentence to figure out the meaning of an unknown word. The skill is one that you will use when you come to a word that you don't know and have to figure out what the word means. (p. 206)

Effective teachers are also more skilled at giving explanatory directions at the beginning of an instructional sequence. Berliner (1987a), for example, noted that an ineffective teacher might introduce a lesson on understanding words with prefixes with an explanation like, "Here are some words with prefixes. Write the meaning of each in the blanks." A more effective teacher, on the other hand, would be more likely to explain (1) how to divide a word into a prefix and a root, (2) how to determine the meaning of a root and the prefix, and (3) how to put the two meanings together in order to make sense of the whole word.

An additional characteristic of effective teachers is their skill in giving verbal signals that indicate transitions from one topic to another with phrases such as "The next area we'll look at is . . . ," and "Now let's turn our attention to . . ." (Berliner, 1987b).

Effective teachers seem to understand a simple and basic truism when it comes to preparing students for new learning: When students know clearly what the expectations and directions are, the energy that might ordinarily go into worrying about *what* to do is more likely devoted to actually *doing* it.

Thoughtful Self-Examination Is a Continual Process

When considering the intellectual characteristics of highly skilled teachers, the overall picture that emerges from research is one that underscores a command of content area(s), a propensity for organizing and preparing carefully (behaviors that reflect a high value placed on academic achievement and learning), and a willingness to spend time preparing students for new learning. Doing these things requires planning and foresight, which are characteristic behaviors of effective teachers. They are, in a word, *thoughtful* about their practice. Porter and Brophy's (1987) review of teacher effectiveness research underscores why effective teachers are good at what they do: (1) they take time for reflection and self-evaluation, (2) they monitor their instruction to be sure that the subject matter is meaningful and worthwhile, and (3) they accept responsibility for guiding student learning and behavior.

INTERACTION STYLES AND INSTRUCTIONAL
METHODS OF EFFECTIVE TEACHERS

Effective teachers are effective not just because of particular personality traits and intellectual behaviors, but also because of the way they interact with students. It is not just what teachers do, but *how* they do it that matters. Depending on how they do it, teachers can either challenge and encourage students to go farther, to not give up, or dishearten and discourage students to the point where trying harder seems fruitless. We turn our attention now to what effective teachers do to promote positive interaction styles.

Feedback Is Specific, Discriminate, and Personalized

Effective teachers are skilled at giving feedback that is specific to a task and personalized to the student. The most effective feedback, whether it be praise or instructional, is that which students are able to apply directly to themselves.

An example of how this works can be seen in the results of Page's (1958) research with high school and junior high school teachers and students in which teachers graded objective tests taken by their students and then randomly assigned each paper to one of three groups. Group 1 students were given back their papers with only a grade but no comment. All Group 2 students were given a stereotyped, standard comment from "Excellent," if their scores were high to "Let's raise this grade." All C students, for example, received their grades with the notation, "Perhaps try to do still better." For those in Group 3, teachers wrote a personal comment on every paper saying whatever they thought might encourage that particular student. On the next objective test, Groups 2 and 3 outperformed Group 1. Personalized comments had a greater effect than standardized comments, and even a very short standard comment produced measurable achievement gains. Significantly, the greatest improvement was made by failing students in Group 3 who received the encouraging personal notes on their papers.

Good and Brophy (1994) note that effective teachers give feedback that is: (1) tailored to particular students (rather than delivered to the entire class); (2) given in a straightforward, declarative sentence (rather than in gushy exclamations); and (3) given when someone really needs

help or has done a particularly fine job (rather than delivered indiscriminately to either individual students or the class as a whole whether
it is needed or not).

Positive Rapport and Positive Expectations Are Practiced and Valued

The rapport existing between teachers and students is the interpersonal medium within which teaching and learning occur. Research supports the idea that one of the reasons effective teachers are effective is
because they are able to create an interpersonal medium that encourages positive rapport. How do they accomplish this? Research findings
suggest the following three overlapping possibilities:

1. Slavin's (1987) review of research indicates that positive-rapport
   teachers have as their important overall goals the improvement of
   their relationships with students and the nurturing of students' self-
   esteem.
2. Johnson, Skon, and Johnson's (1980) research suggests that one of the
   ways they do this is to emphasize cooperation, rather than competition in their classrooms, which usually results in a more positive
   learning experience for their students.
3. Another thing they do is emphasize the learning process, rather than
   its products (Slavin, 1990).

Activities of this variety seem to have the effect of creating classrooms that look more like cooperative enterprises than competitive con-
tests, where both teachers and students are sensitive to the human
components of the teaching-learning process, not just the academic benefits derived from it.

Does positive rapport result in improved achievement? There is evidence that it can. Good and Grouws (1975) found, in their study involving third and fourth graders, that the students' rapport-rating
scores were both descriptive and predictive of their achievement; that
is, the higher the rapport, the greater the achievement.

The process of positive rapport, coupled with high expectations, is
no better illustrated than in the results of a study reported by Pederson,
Faucher, and Eaton (1978). In the process of looking at the long-term
outcomes of fifty-nine adults who had attended a single school in a
poor neighborhood, one bit of information recurred; among the individuals being studied, those who had a particular first-grade teacher
(called Miss A in the study) were more likely to show IQ increases during elementary school, got better grades, finished more years of school-

ing, and were more successful as adults. Not one of Miss A's students whom Pederson was able to contact for interview (forty-four others were interviewed who had other first-grade teachers) was in the lowest level of adult success as defined in this study, despite the fact that most of the children in Miss A's classes came from poor, and often minority, families. Pedersen and his colleagues systematically ruled out other reasons for the success of Miss A's students. In race, religion, intelligence, and economic status, Miss A's pupils were similar to their schoolmates.

The reason for the difference was Miss A herself. She believed that all her students could learn, conveyed that message strongly to them, and got involved in the lives of her students in ways personally meaningful to them.

In the course of his research, Pedersen asked all of his subjects to name as many of their elementary school teachers as they could. Everyone who had Miss A for first grade remembered her. Most of those who had other first-grade teachers could not remember their teacher's name. Four of the subjects said Miss A was their first-grade teacher when, in fact, records showed she was not. Pedersen ascribed it to "wishful thinking."

Although this is only one study, and has a small number of subjects, the results are consistent with other research efforts we examined. Teachers who have a good rapport with their students, and who have high, but reasonable, expectations for them, can make a big difference for the better. As Pedersen et al. (1978) expressed it:

> If children are fortunate enough to begin their schooling with an optimistic teacher who expects them to do well and who teaches them the basic skills needed for further academic success, they are likely to perform better than those exposed to a teacher who conveys a discouraging, self-defeating outlook. (p. 11)

Students Are Allowed Sufficient Time for Learning

Two components of time are important in relation to classroom learning. There is *allocated time*, which teachers devote (i.e., allocate) to particular content areas on a given day; and there is *engaged time*, which is the actual on-task time that students spend on a particular subject.

Teachers vary widely in their time allocation to particular subjects. Berliner (1987a), for example, notes that his research indicated allotted time ranged from 16 to 50 minutes a day in mathematics instruction, and from 45 to 137 minutes a day in reading instruction.

In some instances, it may be that teachers are simply not aware of the discrepancies in time given to one subject over another. In other cases, there is evidence that some teachers allocate more time to their favorite content areas. For example, Schmidt and Buchmann (1983) found that teachers who enjoyed teaching reading more than writing stressed reading over language arts instruction, while teachers who enjoyed mathematics more than social studies allocated more time to mathematics.

Effective teachers, however, have been shown to be quite good about allowing sufficient allocated time and study-engaged time, or time on-task, for each subject. For example, classrooms generally range along a continuum from approximately 50 to 90 percent time on-tasks by students. Effective teachers are generally found at the higher end of that continuum (Berliner, 1987b). Their students are working on the tasks they are supposed to be working on from 75 to 90 percent of the time.

The relationship between allocated time and engaged time is clear. If students in Class A have been allocated forty hours for reading comprehension activities, and students in Class B have been allocated ten hours for similar activities, is there much question which group of students will probably do better on a reading comprehension test? If teacher effectiveness is measured, in part, at least, by how much students learn, is there any question which teacher will probably be judged most effective? Learning takes time, and teachers who allocate enough of it are more effective than those who do not.

Direct Teaching Is a Preferred Style

Direct teaching is a term coined by Rosenshine (1979, 1987) to serve as a label to cover six teaching behaviors associated with effective teaching. Essentially, direct teaching is a method that involves presenting subject matter in small, explicit steps, pausing periodically to check for students' understanding, and encouraging active involvement from as many students as possible. It is particularly well suited for teaching explicit, structured information and skills (e.g., science facts and concepts, mathematical procedures, grammatical rules, vocabulary, and special reading procedures). The six steps involved in direct teaching include the following:

1. Begin by reviewing and checking the previous day's work.
2. Inform students of the day's lesson goals.
3. Provide guided practice.
4. During guided practice, give students ample feedback.

5. Allow students time to practice using new information on their own.
6. Provide weekly and monthly reviews.

It should be noted that following these steps is less relevant when teaching in areas that are less structured and less well defined than others such as composition, analysis of literature or historical events, writing term papers, or discussion of social issues (Spiro & Meyers, 1984). Although effective teachers might begin their teaching in any of these areas by reviewing what was done on previous days and by stating the goals of the day's lesson, they would not necessarily break the instructional units into subunits that students had to master one step at a time. Rather, the emphasis would be on exploring a diversity of ways rather than one way, on exploring opinions and attitudes rather than memorizing facts and correct answers.

The conclusions reached by Rutter, Maugham, Mortimore, Ouston, and Smith (1979), after studying 1,400 students in twelve secondary schools in central London, support the idea of direct teaching as a route to effective teaching. Basically, their findings showed that students learned and behaved best in schools where teachers planned their lessons carefully, started teaching promptly when classes began (by not spending large amounts of time distributing books and papers), were less casual about letting classes out early, and put more emphasis on academic achievement. Additionally, they found that teachers in highly achieving schools gave and checked more homework assignments.

Achievement differences between students in good schools and bad schools were substantial. The researchers had grade-school records of many of the students and used them to make predictions of how well the children were likely to do in secondary school. Compared with what might have been expected from the students' past achievements, the least able students in the most effective schools scored as well on standardized tests as the most able students in the least effective schools.

It is important to keep in mind that the research related to direct methods of teaching, including Rutter's large study, does not show that teachers using these methods are detached, content-centered automatons insensitive to the more humanistic variables of classroom life (Arends, 1994; Davis & Thomas, 1989). For example, because a teacher uses a more direct style (i.e., lecturing, asking rhetorical questions, giving orders, and so forth) does not mean that indirect approaches (using students' ideas, giving open-ended assignments, praising, joking, encouraging, and the like) are never used by this type of teacher. Research suggests that these two methods of teaching *used in combination* are most likely to result in achievement gains (Davis & Thomas, 1989; Flanders, 1960; Rosenshine, 1979, 1987). Whereas direct-influence methods have more to do with a teacher's relationship to subject matter in terms of how it is conveyed, indirect-influence methods are more reflective of a teacher's relationship to students in terms of their interaction with them. Effective teachers have a way of blending direct teaching with indirect methods from time to time, thus increasing the likelihood of reaching even greater numbers of a diverse student population.

When considering the interaction styles and instructional methods of effective teachers, there is a final point worth considering.

Flexibility Stands Out As a Personal Characteristic

By far the most repeated adjective used in the research literature to describe the best teachers is flexibility. It is a characteristic that emerges repeatedly when good teaching practices and outcomes are discussed. Flanders (1960) noted, for example, that superior teachers were inclined to be flexible, in the sense of being able to be more direct or indirect as the occasion demanded, and that *students in all subjects learned more when working with flexible teachers.*

Ongoing studies of teacher effectiveness continue to indicate that there are endless ways for students and teachers to interact with each other; that all students will not respond in the same way to any given teaching style (Berliner & Rosenshine, 1987; Davis & Thomas, 1989; Good & Brophy, 1994; Reynolds, 1992; Skinner & Belmont, 1993; Sparks & Lipka, 1992). Effective teachers have a readiness to take this fact of classroom life into account. Effective teachers are, in a sense, "total" teachers. They seem able to adjust to the shifting tides of classroom life and students' needs, and to do what has to be done to reach, and thereby teach, different students in a variety of circumstances. Sparks and Lipka (1992) have observed that teachers of this sort are master teachers, craftsmen capable of organizing learning experiences so as to enhance the possibilities of making classroom life meaningful for all students.

SUMMARY OF BEHAVIORS ASSOCIATED
WITH EFFECTIVE TEACHERS

A simple truism about teaching is that "effective" teaching is not done in one, specific way with one, specific type of methodology.

Whether we are talking about good teachers or poor teachers, certain observable "patterns," or clusters of behavior, are characteristic of those who fall into one group or the other. Research does not allow us to say that ineffective teachers are always unsuccessful with all students at all times, nor does it allow us to say that effective teachers are always successful with all students at all times. However, current research findings do indicate that particular patterns of greater frequency are more likely to be associated with teachers who are effective or ineffective, as the case might be, than with teachers who fall somewhere in between.

In terms of personality characteristics, intellectual functioning, instructional procedures, and interaction styles, good or effective teachers rank high on more of the following behavioral descriptions than poor or ineffective teachers:

1. They are inclined to combine a warm and friendly attitude with firm, but reasonable, expectations.
2. They project an enthusiasm for their work that lends excitement to their teaching.
3. They are by no means perfect, in the sense of doing and saying just the right thing at all times. (This has less to do with something that teachers consciously do, and more to do, perhaps, with the wide latitude of teacher imperfections that students can live with as long as the core person is basically fair and decent.)
4. Intellectually, they are thoroughly grounded in their subject area, which, by virtue of a broad base of interests, they are able to connect to related areas of knowledge.
5. They are ready to assume responsibility for student outcomes, which they reflect in their efforts to make sure that all students have a chance to learn.
6. They make it a point to know their students as individuals and to respond to them as individuals; they go beyond simply seeing them as "students."
7. They provide definite study guidelines; they are as interested in getting their students prepared to know as they are in evaluating what they know.
8. They are able to challenge without being offensive and to encourage without being condescending; more importantly, they challenge when that is appropriate and they encourage when that is needed. Neither behavior is indiscriminately practiced.
9. They give feedback that is personalized, an effect that makes the feedback more believable and powerful.

10. They take time to reflect about their work, their students, and themselves as teachers; they are, in a word, thoughtful.
11. They work on developing a positive rapport that serves as the interpersonal medium within which high, but reasonable, expectations, and constructive, critical feedback can be transmitted.
12. They are able to be flexibly adaptive in terms of using direct or indirect methods of teaching to meet various student abilities and needs.

Good teachers are good in many ways, each with his or her own style of relating to students and transmitting knowledge. There is no one, best way for doing this, probably because there is no one type of student. Good teachers are good for many reasons, and one of those reasons might be that they are basically good people to begin with. I think it is reasonable to infer from the research that good teachers like life; are reasonably at peace with themselves; are firm but fair; expect a lot from themselves and their students; have a sense of humor; and generally enjoy their work.

WHERE DOES THE IDEA OF A TEACHER'S SELF FIT HERE?

Teachers teach not only a curriculum of study, they also become part of it. The subject matter they teach is mixed with the content of their personalities. We remember our teachers, not so much for what they taught, but for who they were and are. We remember their substance as persons, their style and manner as individuals. Students may be attracted to a teacher's mind, but it is the essence of a teacher's selfhood that is remembered.

Curriculum content of two kinds infuse the lifeblood of every classroom. One is the curriculum prescribed by teachers. It is reflected in the books students read, the units they study, and the exams they take. It is the chief reason students go to school. It shapes what they know. The other type of curriculum is inscribed in teachers. It is reflected in their body language, tone of voice, and in their attitudes toward themselves and others. These two "curriculums" play a significant part in shaping—for better or worse—how students feel about themselves and school.

It is safe to say that the more teachers know about the subject they teach, the better their instructional decisions are likely to be about how to teach what they know. The more they know about their subject matter, the more choices they have for presenting it in a way that is learnable.

Somewhat analogously, it can be said that the more that teachers know about themselves—the private curriculum within—the better their personal decisions are apt to be about how to pave the way for better teaching. This is not merely wishful, wistful dreaming about the way things should be in the best of all worlds. Research has shown that effective teachers tend to be thoughtful and reflective about their practice (Bean & Zulich, 1989; Bolin, 1988; Sternberg & Horvath, 1995). They take time not only to monitor their instruction, to make sure that worthwhile content is being taught to their students, but also for reflection and self-evaluation.

One's Selfhood Is Reflected in One's Personhood

In all of this, perhaps, there is an implicit bottom line that might be stated in the following way: The kind of teacher one is depends on the kind of person one is. This may seem apparent on the surface, but sometimes in our quest for better teaching methods, more efficient instructional strategies, specifically defined behavioral objectives, and more effective methods of inquiry, we lose sight of the fact that the success of those "better" things depends very much on the emotional makeup and psychological underpinnings of the teacher who uses them.

It is evident that the urgency for understanding oneself is probably not as important for some as it is for others. In the case of, for example, the construction worker, the accountant, the engineer, the chemist, or the plumber, where the relationship is between an individual and buildings, numbers, bridges, test tubes, or pipes, we would probably agree that knowledge about one's personal dynamics is not so critical. However, where the relationship is between persons, in this case, between teacher and student, then the matter of self-understanding becomes more important. Here, processes and outcomes are more personal, involving as they do emotional states, subjective views, and personal preferences.

Being aware of who we are as individuals and how we are perceived by others is an important step in the process of becoming a good teacher. In the absence of functional self-knowledge about our emotional deficits and personal shortcomings, we are in no position either to overhaul or to fine-tune those aspects of ourselves that might be blocking our teaching effectiveness. *Consciously, we teach what we know; unconsciously, we teach who we are.* The "who we are" facet of our teaching personality contributes significantly to the positive or negative tone of a classroom and, certainly, to students' receptivity to learning. Which leads us to ask an important question.

WHAT DOES IT MEAN TO HAVE SELF-UNDERSTANDING?

The term "self-understanding" is practically self-explanatory. It means what it implies, namely, that a person has a certain degree of understanding about him or herself. It suggests that a person has developed a level of self-awareness that enables one to more clearly differentiate him or herself from the rest of the world. Self-awareness implies that one has a certain cognizance of oneself. Self-understanding overlaps with this idea and suggests a certain degree of informed knowledge about oneself.

For example, I am aware of a fourth-grade teacher who is the absolute prototype of one who values neatness, orderliness, and punctuality in her life. Everything in her personal demeanor and lifestyle reflects those values. Her life is carefully planned, she is always on time, and everything about her is neat and in its proper place. She does not, however, impose her lifestyle and values on either her students or others in her life. She realizes that her somewhat compulsive need for an orderly, predictable, daily life is a way of managing the anxiety she has about the possibility of losing control in her personal life, a fear that she realizes has roots deep in an orphaned childhood when she felt powerless to control her own destiny. This awareness of herself and her understanding of it is what makes it possible for her to nonjudgmentally accept others, including her students, whose values and behavior may be diametrically different from her own. Thus, she does not get particularly rattled when students are sometimes late, nor is she unnecessarily punitive and overreactive toward those whose work and academic efforts are not as neat and orderly as she might exact for herself. A teacher with similar intrapersonal dynamics, but who had neither awareness nor insight into how she might be imposing her own needs and values on her students, would likely be far less tolerant of students whose behaviors and self-expectations differed from her own.

Self-understanding is the personal knowledge one has about his or her own psychology. It enables an individual to conclude: "I am this kind of person. I have these kinds of values. I am guided by these beliefs. I have these shortcomings, but I own these strengths. You may be far different than me and that is allright." It is a compendium of core insights into the nature of one's being.

How Can Self-Understanding Help
to Make One a Better Teacher?

Just as knowing about our subject area helps us to present its content in ways that make it more possible to learn, so, too, can "knowing" about ourselves as persons help us present *ourselves* in ways that enhance learning. As teachers, self-understanding can help us put the interpersonal dynamics of a classroom into proper perspective. Self-understanding enhances self-awareness, which is the type of self-knowledge that helps protect us from unconsciously motivated whims, selfish desires, or unnecessarily defensive behaviors. There are at least four ways that self-understanding can work in behalf of helping teachers to be more effective.

Transference Possibilities Are Reduced

Transference is the descriptive label given to the process whereby a person unconsciously responds to an individual or experience in a way that is similar to the way that that person felt about, or responded to, some other individual or experience in his or her life. For example, sometimes a client in therapy will behave toward the therapist as if that person were the parent figure. Or a second grader will behave toward his teacher as if she were his mother. In other words, the client and the second grader "transfer" feelings for one person in their lives to another. This can be a conscious process; that is, we can say, "I like this person (or dislike him, as the case may be) because he reminds me of so and so." When the transference phenomenon is conscious, one is more able to control its effect and expression.

Countertransference Behaviors Can Be Controlled

Countertransference has all of the attributes of transference and is the term given to what happens when individual A *responds in kind* to individual B's original transference behavior. If, let us say, a therapist responds to a female client as if she were his daughter, this would be what is called *countertransference*. In varying degrees, both transference and countertransference are processes that occur all of the time with all persons. They surely go on between students and teachers.

There are many examples of how these phenomena work detrimentally in teacher-student interactions. A high school teacher, for instance, finds herself constantly "picking on" girls in her class who are popular and attractive. "My sister was the glamorous one, I wasn't," said in a sneering sort of way, shed some light on her motives when it slipped out one day. In another instance, an elementary teacher, who was the eldest of six children, and who had spent much of her growing years caring for younger siblings, continually complained that, "the children in my class seem like such a burden at times." As she grew to understand herself better, she began to see that she was unconsciously resurrecting old feelings and reliving her youth in her relationships with her students. When she became fully aware of what she had been doing, her attitude changed dramatically. When her attitude changed, so, too, did her perceptions. She no longer saw her students as burdens, as children to be taken care of, but as young persons to be enjoyed and taught. In her words, "I'm their teacher, not their older sister. They have parents who can take care of them." By understanding more about her psychological history, she was able to put the past aside and be more fully in the here and now of her life.

Unnecessary Personalization Can Be Guarded Against

An example of how one very aware and self-understanding teacher behaved in the face of a class's transference behavior is cited by Solomon (1960) in the following illustration of how a teacher made constructive use of his knowledge of himself and his students' behavior:

> In a (high school] history class . . . the subject of freedom was being discussed. There were muttered swear words, throwing of erasers, sly passing of notes, general disorder. These the teacher recognized, to quote his own words, "not as an affront to me, as I might have formerly thought. But I knew they were mad." And I thought "Better get it out legitimately." So I said, "You seem bothered and mad at me or at somebody in connection with this business of freedom. Suppose you write anything you feel. Anything goes in writing. But no more swearing, et cetera. Here is a way to get out your anger." To give just a sample of the transference evidence, I quote in part from one boy's paper. "There is supposed to be freedom in the U.S. but teachers tell me what to do. The principal tells me what to do. We can't talk. We can't be late. We can't chew gum. We can't do anything but our own school work which is terrible. It's the same at home. The old lady tells me to mow the lawn, sweep the patio, do this, do that. The old man comes home. 'You forgot to do this. You forgot to do that. Leave your car in the garage and walk to school.' And there it starts all over." (p. 88)

This was a wise teacher. He recognized that the students were not angry at him, but at the adults in their lives, whom they saw depriving them of their freedom. A less insightful teacher might have personalized the incident by erroneously concluding that the students were mad at him or the assignment. He could have then gotten angry at them by assuming a defensive and reactive posture (e.g., "How dare you act that way? I'll teach you for acting up like that"), and the entire happening might have been blown out of proportion.

The transference-countertransference idea comes from sound clinical observations, and is supported by empirical research. For example, research shows that just as students react to the ways in which teachers behave, teachers behave in a manner that is basically consistent with how they perceive their students behaving toward them. A case in point is Klein's (1971) research related to student influence on teacher behavior, her general conclusion being that "when students behaved positively, the teachers were positive, and when the students behaved negatively, the teachers were negative." You can see how teacher behaviors of that type are self-defeating inasmuch as they encourage in students the very behavior that triggers a teacher's reactive behavior in the first place. When teachers are aware of what is happening psychodynamically, they are in a much better position to control their own behavior, to be proactive rather than merely reactive.

Relationships between Self-Perceptions and Perceptions of Others Are Clearer

Ralph Waldo Emerson insightfully observed that "what we are, that only can we see." This simple aphorism stands as the cornerstone on which are built our most important principles of how we see others.

What we are inclined to see "out there" in the behavior of others is quite frequently a projection of our own drives, needs, and fears. Those who tell us that persons are basically untrustworthy and cruel—ignoring the fact that they are also dependable and kind—might be saying more about themselves than about the world. There is solid research evidence to support the idea that when persons think well of themselves, they are more likely to approve of others (Epstein & Feist, 1988; Hamachek, 1992; Markus, Moreland, & Smith, 1985). What we find "out there" is what we put there with our unconscious projections. When we think we are looking out a window, it might be, more often than we realize, that we are really gazing into a mirror.

Barron (1968) offers some tantalizing evidence to support this looking-glass idea. While doing research related to the nature and meaning of psychological health, he and his colleagues first had to develop some operational conceptions about what a healthy person would probably be like. They then studied subjects chosen for their general effectiveness as persons. Following this, each staff member described each subject on a checklist of adjectives. The intention was to derive from these checklists a composite staff description of each subject's so-called "soundness as a person." The results were surprising. Individual staff members used quite different adjectives to describe the same person. The most revealing aspect of this was the great consistency with which staff members described highly effective persons, checking off the same adjectives that in private moments of good will they would use to characterize themselves. Barron (1968) went on to add:

> Moreover, they tended to describe clearly ineffective persons as possessing traits which in themselves they most strongly denied. . . . Thus, one staff member noted for his simple and clear thought processes most frequently described an ineffective person as *confused*; another staff member who is exceptionally well-behaved in matters of duty checked adjectives *conscientious* and *responsible* most frequently in describing highly rated subjects . . . another staff member who has subsequently been interested professionally in independence of judgment saw effective subjects as *independent* and *fair-minded. Each of us, in brief, saw his own image in what he judged to be good.* (p. 12)

It is generally true that our view of ourselves and our particular life circumstances serve as a filter through which the world is viewed. The angry person sees aggressive motives; the friendly person see pleasant encounters; the critical person finds things to correct; the accepting person finds things to appreciate; the suspicious individual suspects ulterior motives; the trusting individual sees honest intentions; and so it goes. The way we interpret the world seems to have a great deal to do with our attempts to make it more that way for ourselves. It might indeed be that our perception of what is reality becomes—for better or worse—a self-fulfilling prophecy. Perceptions of reality start, it seems, with one's own self-picture, which is another good reason for expanding self-understanding—to know what that self-picture is in the first place.

A Teacher's Self-Understanding Can Make a Positive Difference

It is important to keep in mind that it is not the teacher's understanding of self, per se, but rather the way it is reflected in behavior toward students, that makes a difference. Thus, teachers who are aware of their personal issues are in a position to be more sympathetic and sensitive to the problems of their students, and more capable of controlling their own behavior. We should also remember that there are many other inputs in the lives of students, and that it is not fair to point a finger at teachers for all the problems of students. Still, the fact is that there are some teachers so busy trying to hold their emotional lives together that they have hardly any energy left over to work effectively in guiding their students' growth.

We might conclude from everything said so far that only "normal" well-adjusted persons should be teachers. To a great extent this is true. The evidence does suggest that healthy, balanced teachers who are warm, flexible, and interested in students, seem better able to affect the attitudes and learning of students positively than do teachers in whom these personal characteristics are less evident. The point can be argued, however, that some teachers are successful precisely because of their neuroticism. For example, the compulsive teacher who places a high premium on order, accuracy, and precision, might teach students the value of order in their lives. We might find another teacher with strong needs for power and domination who vigorously carries students along with his or her own high standards of achievement.

This does not mean, however, that we should recruit more neurotic teachers, or that we should feel more comfortable about our own unresolved personal hang-ups. Absence of self-understanding and flexibility make it difficult for neurotic or emotionally unbalanced teachers to be successful with any group, except that narrow band of students who meet his or her strong, personal needs.

Self-understanding is no panacea, no magic potion that automatically turns a person into a good teacher. It is, however, a door that may lead to useful insights about oneself and others that positively affect teaching practices. Which leads us to an important point.

TEACHER PERSONALITY: THE NEGLECTED VARIABLE IN TEACHER EFFECTIVENESS RESEARCH

Being a good teacher, an effective one, means that one not only has to know his or her material, but one has to be able to communicate what is known, a task done through the medium of this intrapersonal quality known as one's personality. Researchers (Costin, Greenough, & Menges, 1971; Sherman & Blackburn, 1975) have long since pointed to data suggesting a reasonably strong relationship between personality and teaching effectiveness, at least insofar as student judgments are concerned.

We have to be careful here. Research on teacher effectiveness does not allow us to conclude that it is only those teachers with the warm, outgoing, enthusiastic personalities who are likely to be successful. Personality, the kind of presentation of "self" a teacher makes, is only part of the story, not all of it. There are many other factors that must be weighed, not the least of which are the personalities and ages of the students, their differential needs for affiliation versus achievement, student expectations, teacher competency and command of subject matter, and so on. Still, the fact remains that it is the teacher who is in charge, who is the one chiefly responsible for affecting the emotional and intellectual climate of a classroom. This is where teacher personality and self-concept come into play. Along this line, Sherman and Blackburn (1975) have observed, "It is the personal qualities which the instructor *as an individual* brings to the educational setting that spell the difference between success and failure as a teacher" (p.124).

Because of where the research emphasis has been in recent years, teachers have honed their skills when it comes to motivating students, using praise appropriately, asking questions or presenting tasks that require different levels of thinking, and they have expanded their knowledge about how to maintain relevance between teacher behavior and learning objectives, and how to use innovative curricula and teaching methods. However, in the process of emphasizing and teaching these skills, we have not only moved away from exploring further the part that teacher personality and self-concept play in effective instruction, but there appears to be a serious deemphasis of those qualities in current discussions and research related to teacher effectiveness. As one example of this, it is interesting (and revealing) to note that Reynolds' (1992) massive review of literature related to exploring the question of what is a competent beginning teacher, containing 180 references, has only two that are directly related to the personality characteristics of teachers. The influential Berliner and Rosenshine (1987) volume, *Talks to Teachers*, does not mention teacher personality as a factor in teacher effectiveness at any point among its fifteen fine chapters. It is also instructive to note that neither of the two current best-selling educational psychology textbooks targeted for the undergraduate future teachers market (Good & Brophy, 1995; Woolfolk, 1995) contain a single indexed reference to teacher personality or teacher self-concept. I do not intend these observations to be criticisms of the authors just cited. Their publications are excellent, ones I have used with my own students. The fact remains, however, that contemporary research has been less concerned with exploring personality dimensions that contribute to teacher effectiveness and more concerned with instructional techniques and methods that teachers can use. For example, even when there are discussions about some of the more personal characteristics of teachers, such as being proactive or reactive (Good & Brophy, 1994) or inviting or disinviting (Purkey & Novak, 1996), you will note that these behaviors are more directly related to what teachers *do* as instructors than to who they *are* as persons.

Toward Preparing Intra- and Interpersonally Skilled Teachers

The task of this chapter has been to overview and identify some of the important behaviors and characteristics that research has shown to be the earmarks of good teachers, those who are especially effective at what they do. We have explored their personal and intellectual characteristics, along with examining their interaction styles and instructional methods. Great advances have been and continue to be made related to approaches to learning and instructional strategies most likely to facilitate student achievement. There is little question but that we have deepened our knowledge of how to do these things.

In our rush to encourage teachers to be forever on the lookout for more effective instructional methods and more efficient classroom management techniques, I wonder if, more often than not, we may be pushing them to look only "out there" rather than "in here" for answers that could enhance classroom learning. To the extent that "looking out there" is done routinely and exclusively, teachers may be either overlooking or underestimating the impact and effect that their personal manner, individual style, or personality could be having on the interpersonal and instructional dynamics of a classroom.

Sparks and Lipka (1992) have wisely observed that "it is impossible to separate the person from the professional" (p. 310). Embedded in this simple observation is the basic truism mentioned earlier: The kind of teacher one is depends on the kind of person one is. This idea, of course, triggers important questions: How does one go about finding out about the kind of person he or she is? What can those responsible for the preparation of teachers do to encourage this kind of self-exploration?

It would take first of all, I believe, people who value the idea that, to prepare good teachers, effective in all phases of their work, we must offer them opportunity, time, and guidance to grow in the direction of becoming mentally healthy, self-aware persons. I do not think there is only one way for doing this. There are probably as many avenues open to accomplishing those goals as there are faculty committed to the idea of helping prospective teachers deepen their self-awareness.

However it is done, I think it is important that teacher candidates have opportunities for exposure to the idea that intelligence is more than just verbal skills or mathematical ability, or capacity for abstract thinking. They need to see that intelligence also includes, as Gardner (1983) has suggested, an *inter*personal component (the ability to deal effectively with others), and an *intra*personal component (the ability to know one's own feelings and understand one's own behavior). Intelligence has been very narrowly defined for a great many years. Students will need some time and guidance in their efforts to understand the deeper implications of this expanded view of intellectual ability. Once they see the scientific validity behind these "intelligences," which are among the seven that Gardner (1983) identified, they may begin to appreciate in a deeper way the value of, and need for, developing the interpersonal and intrapersonal dimensions of their intellectual skills. They may also see that interpersonal and intrapersonal abilities, like other forms of intelligence, can be expanded and deepened through learning and practice, reason enough to feel optimistic about getting "smarter" in those areas.

The name for this kind of intelligence is what Goleman (1995), expanding on a concept suggested first by Salovey and Mayer (1990), refers to as "emotional intelligence" (EQ as opposed to IQ). As elaborated by Goleman, one's EQ is comprised of five basic components:

1. *Self-Awareness* (The ability to recognize one's feelings as they occur, an ability that enables a person to have more control over his or her life.)
2. *Mood Management* (The ability to exercise control over the duration and expression of one's moods.)
3. *Self-Motivation* (The ability to "get oneself up," to delay gratification and to put the breaks on impulsiveness in order to achieve longer-term goals.)
4. *Empathic Skills* (The ability to perceive the emotional needs of others, to recognize the subtle social uses that indicate what others want or need.)
5. *Relationship Skills* (The ability to manage personal relations, to have productive and satisfying interpersonal connections, and to be able to give and take in relationships.)

Teachers seldom fail or are less effective at what they do because of lack of knowledge or because, in an academic sense, they are not smart enough. Rather, it is more likely to be a combination of factors related to their interpersonal style or intrapersonal makeup that contributes to the failure. Relevant to this possibility, Goleman (1995) observes:

> Academic intelligence has little to do with emotional life. The brightest among us can founder on the shoals of unbridled passions and unruly impulses; people with high IQs can be stunningly poor pilots of their private lives. . . . [A]t best, IQ contributes about 20 percent to the factors that determine life success, which leaves 80 percent to other forces. (pp. 33–34)

I am not suggesting that one's IQ does not contribute significantly to one's ability to be an effective teacher; it contributes significantly. I am suggesting that, perhaps, more than is realized, our curriculums and course content emphasize the "doing" part of a teacher's work (the IQ part) to the relative exclusion of the "being" part (the EQ portion).

At the moment, the development of the self-knowledge component is left largely to chance rather than afforded opportunities for growth through systematic and guided study. It is time, perhaps, to begin committing more of our course time and research efforts to learning more about the development and growth of the kind of inter- and intrapersonal skills and knowledge (one's EQ potential) that can deepen our understanding of what it takes to be an excellent teacher.

REFERENCES

Abrami, P. C., Leventhal, L., & Perry, R. P. (1982). Educational seduction. *Review of Educational Research, 52,* 446–464.

Anderson, L., & Prawat, R. (1983). Responsibility in the classroom: A synthesis of research on teaching and self-control. *Educational Leadership, 40,* 62–66.

Arends, R. I. (1994). *Learning to teach* (3rd ed.). New York: McGraw-Hill.

Barron, F. (1968). *Creativity and personal freedom.* New York: Van Nostrand Reinhold.

Bean, T. W., & Zulich, J. (1989). Using dialogue journals to foster reflective practice with pre-service, content-area teachers. *Teacher Education Quarterly, 16,* 33–40.

Berliner, D. (1987a). But do they understand? In V. Richardson-Koehler (Ed.), *Educator's handbook: A research perspective* (pp. 259–293). New York: Longman.

Berliner, D. (1987b). Simple views of effective teaching and a simple theory of classroom instruction. In D. C. Berliner & B. V. Rosenshine (Eds.), *Talks to teachers*. New York: Random House.

Berliner, D. C., & Rosenshine, B. V. (Eds.). (1987). *Talks to teachers*. New York: Random House.

Bereiter, C., Washington, E., Engetman, S., & Osborn, J. (1969). *Research and development programs on preschool disadvantaged children*. Final Report, OE Contract 6-10-235, Project No. 5-1181. Washington, DC: U.S. Department of Health, Education, and Welfare, Office of Education, Bureau of Research.

Bishop, W. E. (1976). Characteristics of teachers judged successful by intellectually gifted, high-achieving high school students. In W. Dennis & M. W. Dennis (Eds.), *The intellectually gifted: An overview*. New York: Grune and Stratton.

Bolin, F. S. (1988). Helping student teachers think about teaching. *Journal of Teacher Education, 39*, 48–54.

Borko, H., & Livingston, C. (1989). Cognition and improvisation: Differences in mathematics instruction by expert and novice teachers. *American Educational Research Journal, 26*, 473, 498.

Brophy, J. (1983). Research on the self-fulfilling prophecy and teacher expectations. *Journal of Educational Psychology, 76*, 236–247.

Brophy, J. (1992). Probing the subtleties of subject-matter teaching. *Educational Leadership, 49*, 4–8.

Brophy, J., & Rohrkemper, M. (1988). *The classroom strategy study: Summary of general findings*. Research Series Report, No. 187. E. Lansing: The Institute for Research on Teaching, Michigan State University.

Chase, W. G., & Simon, H. A. (1973). The mind's eye in chess. In W. C. Chase (Ed.), *Visual information processing* (pp. 215–281). New York: Academic Press.

Chi, M. T. H., Feltovich, P. J., & Glaser, R. (1981). Categorization and representation of physics problems by experts and novices. *Cognitive Science, 5*, 121–125.

Costin, F., Greenough, W. T., & Menges, R. J. (1971). Student ratings of college teaching: Reliability, validity, and usefulness. *Review of Educational Research, 41*, 511–535.

Davis, G. A., & Thomas, M. A. (1989). *Effective schools and effective teachers.* Boston: Allyn & Bacon.

Duffy, G., Roehler, L. R., Meloth, M. S., & Vavrus, L. G. (1986). Conceptualizing instructional explanation. *Teaching and Teacher Education, 2,* 197–214.

Dunkin, M. J., & Biddle, B. J. (1974). *The study of teaching.* New York: Holt, Rinehart and Winston.

Epstein, S., & Feist, G. J. (1988). Relation between self- and other-acceptance and its moderation by identification. *Journal of Personality and Social Psychology, 54,* 309–315.

Evertson, C., Anderson, L., & Brophy, J. (1978). *Texas junior high school study: Final report of process-outcome relationships,* Vol. 1, Report No. 4061, Research and Development Center for Teacher Education, University of Texas, Austin.

Flanders, N. A. (1960). *Teacher influence, pupil attitudes, and achievement.* U.S. Department of Health, Education, and Welfare, Office of Education, Cooperative Research Project No. 397, Minneapolis, University of Minnesota.

Gardner, H. (1983). *Frames of mind: The theory of multiple intelligences.* New York: Basic Books.

Gillet, M., & Gall, M. (1982, March). *The effects of teacher enthusiasm on the at-task behavior of students in the elementary grades.* Paper presented at the annual meeting of the American Educational Research Association, New York.

Goldsmid, C. A., Gruber, J. E., & Wilson, E. K. (1977). Perceived attributes of supervisor teachers (PAST): An inquiry into the giving of teacher awards. *American Educational Research Journal, 14,* 423–440.

Goleman, D. (1995). *Emotional intelligence.* New York: Bantam Books.

Good, T. L., & Brophy, J.E. (1995). *Educational Psychology* (5th ed.). White Plains, NY: Longman.

Good, T. L., & Brophy, J. E. (1994). *Looking in classrooms* (6th ed.). New York: HarperCollins.

Good, T. L., & Grouws, D. (1975). Teacher rapport: Some stability data. *Journal of Educational Psychology, 17,* 83–93.

Hamachek, D. (1992). *Encounters with the self* (4th ed.). Fort Worth, TX: Harcourt Brace Jovanovich.

Hines, C. V., & Cruickshank, D. R., Kennedy, J. J. (1985). Teacher clarity and its relation to student achievement and satisfaction. *American Educational Research Journal, 22,* 87–89.

Jackson, P. (1968). *Life in classrooms.* New York: Holt, Rinehart and Winston.

Johnson, D. W., Skon, L., & Johnson, R. (1980). Effects of cooperative, competitive, and individualistic conditions on children's problem-solving performance. *American Educational Research Journal, 17,* 83–93.

Klein, S. S. (1971). Student influence on teacher behavior. *American Educational Research Journal, 8,* 403–421.

Land, M. L. (1987). Vagueness and clarity. In M. Dunkin (Ed.), *The international encyclopedia of teaching and teacher education* (pp. 392–397). New York: Pergamon.

Lee, O., & Gallagher, J. J. (1986, March). *Differential treatment of individual students and whole classes by middle school teachers: Causes and consequences.* Paper presented at the National Association for Research in Science Teaching. San Francisco.

Leinhardt, G. (1986). Expertise in mathematics teaching. *Educational Leadership, 43,* 28–33.

Leinhardt, G. (1992). What research on learning is telling us about teaching. *Educational Leadership, 49,* 20–25.

Leinhardt, G., & Greeno, J. G. (1986). The cognitive skill of teaching. *Journal of Educational Psychology, 78,* 75–95.

Markus, H., Moreland, R. L., & Smith, J. (1985). Role of the self-concept in the perception of others. *Journal of Personality and Social Psychology, 49,* 1494–1512.

Mastin, V. E. (1963). Teacher enthusiasm. *Journal of Educational Research, 56,* 385–386.

Mayer, R. E. (1984). Twenty-five years of research on advance organizers. *Instructional Science, 8,* 133–169.

Milgram, R. M. (1979). Perception and teacher behavior in gifted and nongifted children. *Journal of Educational Psychology, 71,* 125–128.

McDonald, F. (1987). *Research on teaching and its implications for public policy: Report on phase II of the beginning teacher evaluation study.* Princeton, NJ: Education Testing Service.

Morse, W. C., Bloom, R., & Dunn, J. (1961). *A study of classroom behavior from diverse evaluative frameworks: Developmental, mental health, substantive learning, group process.* USOE, ESAE-8144, Ann Arbor, MI, University of Michigan.

Murray, H. G. (1983). Low interference classroom teaching behavior and student ratings of college teaching effectiveness. *Journal of Educational Psychology, 75,* 138–149.

Page, E. P. (1958). Teacher comments and student performance. *Journal of Educational Psychology, 49*, 173–181.

Pedersen, E., Faucher, T., & Eaton, W. W. (1978). A new perspective on the effects of first-grade teachers on children's subsequent adult status. *Harvard Educational Review, 48*, 1–31.

Porter, A. C., & Brophy, J. (1987). *Good teaching: Insights from the work of the Institute for Research and Teaching* (Occasional paper No. 14). E. Lansing: The Institute for Research on Teaching, College of Education, Michigan State University.

Purkey, W. W., & Novak, J. M. (1996). *Inviting school success*. Belmont, CA: Wadsworth.

Reynolds, A. (1992). What is competent beginning teaching? A review of the literature. *Review of Educational Research, 62*, 1–35.

Rosenshine, B. V., & Furst, N. (1973). The use of direct observation to study teaching. In R. Travers (Ed.), *Second handbook of research on teaching*. Chicago: Rand McNally.

Rosenshine, B. V. (1979). Content, time, and direct instruction. In P. Peterson & M. Walberg (Eds.), *Research on teaching: Concepts, findings, and implications*. Berkeley, CA: McCutchan.

Rosenshine, B. V. (1987). Explicit teaching. In D. C. Berliner & B. V. Rosenshine (Eds.), *Talks to teachers* (p. 75–92). New York: Random House.

Rutter, M., Maughan, B., Mortimore, P., Ousten, J., & Smith, A. (1979). *Fifteen thousand hours: Secondary schools and their effects on children*. Cambridge, MA: Harvard University Press.

Sabers, D. S., Cushing, K. S., & Berliner, D. C. (1981). Differences among teachers in a task characterized by simultaneity, multidimensionality, and immediacy. *American Educational Research Journal, 28*, 63–88.

Salovey, P., & Mayer, J. D. (1990). Emotional intelligence. *Imagination, Cognition, and Personality, 9*, 185–211.

Schmidt, W., & Buchmann, M. (1983). Six teachers' beliefs and attitudes and their curriculum time allocations. *Elementary School Journal, 84*, 162–172.

Sears, P. S. (1940). The effect of classroom conditions on strength of achievement motive and work output of elementary school children. *Journal of Abnormal Social Psychology, 35*, 498–536.

Sherman, B. R., & Blackburn, R. T. (1975). Personal characteristics and teaching effectiveness of college faculty. *Journal of Educational Psychology, 67*, 124–131.

Shulman, L. S. (1987). Knowledge and teaching: Foundations of the new reform. *Harvard Educational Review, 19*, 4–14.

Skinner, E. A., & Belmont, M. J. (1993). Motivation in the classroom: Reciprocal effects of teacher behavior and student engagement across the school year. *Journal of Educational Psychology, 85,* 571–581.

Slavin, R. E. (1987). *Cooperative learning: Student teams,* 2nd ed. Washington, DC: National Education Association.

Slavin, R. E. (1990). *Cooperative learning: Theory, research, and practice.* Englewood Cliffs, NJ: Prentice Hall.

Soar, R., & Soar, R. (1978). *Setting variables, classroom interaction, and multiple outcomes.* Final report for the National Institute of Education, Propet No. 6-0432. Gainesville, University of Florida.

Soar, R., & Soar, R. (1979). Emotional climate and management. In P. Peterson & H. Walberg (Eds.), *Research on teaching: Concepts, findings, and implications.* Berkeley, CA: McCutchen.

Solomon, J. C. (1960). Neuroses of schoolteachers. *Mental Hygiene, 44,* 87–90.

Sparks, R., & Lipka, R. P. (1992). Characteristics of master teachers: Personality factors, self-concept, locus of control, and pupil ideology. *Journal of Personnel and Evaluation in Education, 5,* 303–311.

Spiro, R. J., & Meyers, A. (1984). Individual differences and underlying cognitive processes. In P. Pearson, R. Barr, M. L. Kamil, & P. Mosenthal (Eds.), *Handbook of reading research.* New York: Longman.

Stallings, J., & Hentzell, S. (1978). *Effective teaching and learning in urban schools.* Paper presented at the National Conference on Urban Schools, St. Louis, MO.

Sternberg, R. J., & Horvath, J. A. (1995). A prototype view of expert teaching. *Educational Researcher, 24*(6), 9–17.

Tikunoff, W., Berliner, D., & Rist, R. (1975). *An ethnographic study of forty classrooms of the beginning teacher evaluation study.* Technical Report No. 75-10-5. Far West Laboratory, San Francisco.

Wilson, S. M., Shulman, L. S., & Richert, A. R. (1987). 150 ways of knowing: Representations of knowledge in teaching. In J. Calderhead (Ed.), *Exploring Teacher Thinking* (pp. 104–124). London: Cassell.

Witty, P. (1967). An analysis of the personality traits of the effective teacher. *Journal of Educational Research,* vol. 60 May, 662–671.

Woolfolk, A. E. (1995). *Educational Psychology* (6th ed.). Boston: Allyn & Bacon.

Wright, C. J., & Nuthall, G. (1970). Relationships between teacher behaviors and student achievement in three experimental elementary science lessons. *American Educational Research Journal, 7,* 477–491.

HOW CAN THE BALANCE BETWEEN THE PERSONAL AND THE PROFESSIONAL BE ACHIEVED?

Richard P. Lipka and Thomas M. Brinthaupt

As with most endeavors in our profession, the questions we addressed in this book have yielded still more questions and challenges. While not a novel idea, it seems clear to us that it is time to step back and examine what teaching really is as a vocation. Until we do this, teacher education programs will continue to be incomplete and ineffective.

There are many who believe that teachers are content technicians whose job it is to gather the "truths" and knowledge of humankind and transmit these in an effective manner to their students. Teacher education programs of this ilk are characterized by lists of technical competencies that, once completed, signal the successful completion of the program. To our colleagues in this venue we would indicate that you are almost half right in your thinking.

Allow us the simile of teacher being like an orchestra conductor. It is our expectation that orchestra conductors be technically proficient with the instruments in the orchestra, but we do not expect Ives' *The Housatonic of Stockbridge* to sound like Tchaikovsky's *1812 Overture*. Each composer had different intentions and it is up to the conductor to capture those intentions with the personnel that are available in the orchestra. Thus, the technical proficiencies are put together as a function of the intended outcomes and strengths in the orchestra. And so it is with teachers where intentions must come together with the strengths of the students in the classroom. But, unlike orchestra conductors, we expect the teachers and their students to become composers and arrangers as well as performers of the "music" in a classroom. Such an undertaking in a classroom requires a sense of equity that is all too lacking in most classrooms.

Is the teaching profession really any different from other professions? This is a vital question, given the possible responses of critics to the contents and contributors of this book. After all, there seem to be few other professions where "getting to know oneself," "showing self-knowledge and self-understanding," and "feeling good about who you are" are important job requirements. Why should such factors be stressed for teachers but not for other professions? We would point out to such critics that there are indeed other related professions where self-knowledge, self-insight, self-reflection, self-analysis, and self-stability are important professional attributes. These include the professions in which one works with others who have problems or who need help acquiring new beliefs or skills such as the ministry, therapy, and counseling of various kinds. As with these occupations (and unlike many other occupations), in teaching the person cannot easily be separated from the craft (as McLean points out).

Are we advocating that teachers must now take on yet another "hat" as part of their job description? No. We are simply pointing out that demonstrating effectiveness and mastery in teaching requires a unique blend of professional, interpersonal, and intrapersonal skills. We believe that our contributors have provided more than enough evidence that addressing (and redressing) the balance of these skills is critical to the "professionalization" of teaching. In teaching, what you think of yourself and how you feel about yourself is indeed crucial to "doing a good job."

We agree with Professor McLean that an equity between teacher and student must begin in the teacher education programs. Teacher educators and their students (beginning teachers) may have very different knowledge bases about teaching, but to conceptualize these differences as deficits in the beginning teacher only inhibits the process of their own professional development. Teacher education should be characterized by the very highest levels of teacher-student planning, with the realization that for any given task the student may become the teacher and the teacher may become the student. It seems to us, for instance, that a White middle-class teacher educator could learn much from a Native American beginning teacher about how to approach Native American parents to establish a time and place for a parent-teacher conference. Or a teacher educator with facility and comfort in mathematics could gain insight from a beginning teacher for whom math has been a life-long struggle. To maximize the diversity and potential of these teacher-student planning opportunities will require recruitment and incentive systems that will encourage persons of all colors, backgrounds, and interests to enter the applicant pool for teacher education.

The other major problem with the "deficit" mindset, more central to this book, is what being labeled "deficient" does to ones' sense of self. As Professors Zehm and Tickle noted, for teachers to undertake the risks necessary for teaching students, they must have a healthy sense of self. The challenge for teacher educators will be to balance the preoccupation with the technical competencies of the prescribed knowledge base against the importance of personal knowledge of self-understanding and self-esteem processes. Clearly, this requires teacher educators who are skillful in steering beginning teachers toward questioning their own beliefs and knowledge bases without shattering the beginning teacher's fragile confidence in self as a knower and learner.

In our way of thinking, this deficit model would best be eliminated by taking out the final "high stakes" student teaching experience/practicum and replacing it with more integrated, longer-term blends of on-campus and field-experience work. Each of the experiences from the fieldwork would be brought back onto campus into an environment that encourages growth of the beginning teacher as knower and learner. Such a teacher education program would educate beginning teachers to be reasonably at peace with themselves, be firm but fair, and expect a lot from themselves and their students within a belief system that recognizes that people are perfectly imperfect. Further, beginning teachers must have a sense of humor toward self and others, and generally enjoy the work involved in becoming a teacher. If these are the characteristics of a teacher education program, then what are the entrance and exit requirements for such an endeavor? Simple cataloging of grade point averages is obviously not sufficient. A major challenge thus exists to develop a comprehensive evaluation system for selecting potential teachers, evaluating them throughout the course of their studies, and making summative judgments to place their names forward for teaching credentials.

Paralleling the very important issues pertaining to the teacher in training or the beginning teacher, a self-perspective on teaching clearly has important things to say to those who are experienced "conductors." If the real-world experiences of the "oldtimers" are actually more important and relevant to learning the ropes of teaching, then how can those experiences be conveyed to or obtained by the "newcomers"? Regardless of how one answers this question, it seems to us that an understanding of the "selves" of both oldtimer and newcomer is crucial.

We do not think, in addition, that an unabashed embrace of the "self" is the cure-all for the woes of teachers and their students. None of our contributors assumes that this is the case. In fact, as several of our contributors have noted, we must also be sensitive to the downsides of an increased emphasis on self-related professional issues. These include the facts that some teachers are perilously lacking in self-reflection and self-understanding, that addressing the self can be a very threatening and challenging enterprise, and that an excessive focus on "self" at the expense of "other" will be counterproductive. We are all self-protective and self-defensive to some extent and in some circumstances. Increasing the protectiveness and defensiveness of teachers will only make things worse. We are convinced (as our contributors are) that a greater balance of the personal with the professional is an important step in the growth and efforts of teachers and teacher educators.

Our final challenge is our reaffirmation to the research community that classrooms are contexts of interaction effects in addition to main effects. What methodologies will be necessary to explore the interactional and transitional induction process of new teachers? After all, new teachers change as they affiliate with a school and the school changes as its new members usher in different ideas about the act of teaching. Teacher educators and researchers alike must gain the perspective that both teacher and student are whole persons jointly engaged in the interactive reciprocal process of teaching and learning. There is a bidirectional and reciprocal influence of teacher-student relations in shaping the self-concept of students and teachers alike. And, as our contributors have persuasively demonstrated, healthy self-concepts and positive self-esteem in teachers and students are prerequisites for effective teaching and learning in our classrooms.

AUTHOR INDEX

Subject Index